Adrian Wicks

FOOTBALL
ADDICT

# DIARY OF A SEASON

## G2 Rights Ltd

**Football Addict**
**Copyright © Adrian Wicks 2014**

First edition published in the UK in May 2014
© G2 Rights Limited 2014

All rights reserved. No part of this work may be reproduced or utilized in any form or by any means, electronic or mechanical, including photocopying, recording or by any information storage and retrieval system, without prior written permission of the publisher.

Print Edition ISBN: **978-1-78281-117-6**

The views in this book are those of the author but they are general views only and readers are urged to consult the relevant and qualified specialist for individual advice in particular situations. G2 Rights Limited hereby exclude all liability to the extent permitted by law of any errors or omissions in this book and for any loss, damage or expense (whether direct or indirect) suffered by a third party relying on any information contained in this book. All our best endeavours have been made to secure copyright clearance but in the event of any copyright owner being overlooked please go to www.g2rights.co.uk where you will find all relevant contact information.

G2 Rights Ltd, 7-8 Whiffens Farm, Clement street, Hextable, Kent BR8 7PQ

Adrian Wicks

FOOTBALL
ADDICT

# DIARY OF A SEASON

ADRIAN WICKS

# Foreword

## by martin dongworth, Secretary of taunton town football club

It was a great honour to be asked by Adrian to write a foreword for his book. One thing you may not know about Adrian is that he is known as "The Hedge". How did he acquire this nickname? Well, Adrian went off to fetch a ball from inside a hedge during a match - the score at the time was 0-0, a score which Adrian is not particularly keen on. Adrian decided to sulk and remain in the hedge but when a goal was eventually scored Adrian leapt triumphantly from the hedge. Other prolific football travellers were present and one of them decided he should be known as Hedge and the nickname was born!!

I know how enthusiastic Adrian is about non league football as we have often travelled together to games – this book represents a personal insight into the world of the non league football scene and also shows the diversity both in terms of the standard of football and the distance travelled by Adrian to fulfil his love of the game.

I could spend all day talking about our various escapades together – I recall a game at Whitchurch when a free kick was awarded to the home side. Hedge was adamant the ball would go over the bar but the shot hit the back of the net to open the scoring. Amazingly lowly Andover New Street went on to win the match 6-2, even more of a surprise as Whitchurch had won 6-2 at Andover New Street earlier in the season!

I am sure all devotees of non league football will find the book fascinating and no doubt some of you will find yourselves recounting Adrian's experiences of games you have attended or grounds you have visited.

Adrian is also a very keen follower of speedway and has visited pretty much every track up and down the country to give himself something to do when football is in its summer recess, something which seems to get shorter every season. Perhaps one day we will see a book on Adrian's speedway experiences hit the shelves – what about it, Hedge?

# Introduction

The beautiful game has been a part of my life for as long as I can remember. When I was seven I began collecting football stickers, and I still have my first album, complete with George Best on the front cover. Indeed, I also possess the albums for the subsequent three seasons, along with the various coin collections that the likes of Esso brought out.

This was the 70s and Leeds United were my team, mainly because my birthday was the same as Peter 'hotshot' Lorimer's. The Elland Road side wore sock tags with their numbers on and I purchased a pair of number 7s, which I still have. As part of a school project I wrote to the club, who sent me an autographed sheet along with some other bits and pieces. It seemed great at the time although, of course, the sheet was a standard printed copy – surprise, surprise, I still have that too!

However, it never really crossed my mind to consider the possibility of actually going to watch my heroes in the flesh, which is just as well because I lived in Exeter and had no means of getting to Leeds. My parents didn't like football and I was too young to travel on my own then, so that would have been that. By the time I got around to watching Leeds play at their Yorkshire home I had moved on and was no longer a supporter. I only went there so that I could complete the 92 football league grounds – it was one of the last ones I did – and they beat Stoke 2-1 under the reins of Billy Bremner.

By the time I'd reached my teens I still hadn't attended a live game. For some strange reason I thought you had to buy a ticket in advance, and I was too lazy to do that. In the end it was a classmate of mine who mentioned the idea of going up to St James Park and watching Exeter City in the old fourth division, which I readily agreed to.

It was Saturday, 26 February 1977 and Halifax Town were the visitors for what would be the first of many games I've seen, although I would never have believed it at the time. City won 1-0 with a second-half goal from Alan Beer that I can still replay in my mind: Beer's angled shot down at the St James' Road end from Lammie Robertson's pass – the first of many goals I've seen, not only there but at many other venues. I also seem to recall that Halifax had two sent off in that game.

Anyway, I attended six more games that season as Exeter clinched promotion as runners-up to Ron Atkinson's Cambridge United, finishing in style with a 3-0 win against Aldershot. Beer and strike partner Tony Kellow's goals were the main reason for their success, and they took this momentum into the 77/78 season, until Beer picked up what would prove to be a career-ending injury at Shrewsbury. Nowadays he is the president of local Peninsula League side Budleigh Salterton, so when I see him I'm tempted to tell him he netted the first goal I ever saw live, but somehow I don't think he would share my enthusiasm!

That friend who allowed me to tag along with him and his dad was Dave Bennett, who continues to watch ECFC on a regular basis – unlike yours truly – and is chairman of the supporters' club. He also, unknowingly, planted a small seed in my mind that grew and grew into what I am doing now. So it's all down to you, Dave!

As 1978 reached its conclusion I had become a habitual spectator at Exeter home games – a ritual that would possibly have carried on if it hadn't been for another friend of mine at school, who asked if I wanted to go with him to watch a first division game at Arsenal. Wow! Not only that, but they were playing Liverpool, so it wasn't too difficult a decision to make. Thus began a new adventure with my first trip to the capital on the train, then my first experience of the Underground system that took me to Arsenal station.

We went in about two hours before kick-off and were virtually the first ones to enter Highbury. Remember, these were the days when you could just show up on the day and pay on the gate, not like today when attending such contests would require you to try to book months in advance and probably not get a ticket anyway! Oh, and the cost of watching this top-notch game was £1.20, with a programme costing 20p.

I remember walking up the concrete steps from the turnstiles at the North Bank end and seeing the vastness of the ground in front of me with those magnificent stands. The scene in the film Fever Pitch when Paul does the same (albeit in the stand) reminds me exactly of how I felt that day, even though the ground was empty. By 3pm, there were 51,902 crammed in to see the hosts win thanks to a David Price goal just before half-time at the Clock End, consigning 'Pool to a rare loss that season. I have been to many big games since that December day but have never since felt that feeling, and I probably never will – at least not in a footballing sense!

Inevitably, after having tasted some of the good stuff I wanted more, and I started going to Arsenal games when Exeter were away. This resulted in me going to away games at West Bromwich Albion and Southampton and an FA Cup semi at Villa Park. From here I started going to other first division games, until I moved to London for work reasons. Suddenly I realised that I could pick off lots of league venues that were within easy reach, thus spending the next couple of seasons doing grounds such as Southend, Watford and Brighton. By the time I returned to the South West in 1986, I had done so many that it was only natural that I should go on and complete the 92.

I accomplished this on 14 March 1987 with my visit to Roker Park for Sunderland's 2-1 win over Plymouth – a great day as I was treated well by the hosts, who gave me a complimentary ticket and a VIP tour. For some strange reason I thought I'd feel different in some way after having done what I had wanted to do, but of course things were just as they had been 24 hours earlier.

The question now, though, was what next? The answer was not forthcoming for a while as I merely revisited league grounds. I had thought of tackling the Scottish League but ended up doing a handful while realising the impracticalities due to the humungous amount of travelling I'd have to do. As a novelty, I did watch some Conference games and looked locally to the Western League before the eureka moment arrived in April 1997.

This was when I read in the local paper about something called the Devon

League groundhop. I didn't know anything about this level of football, but luckily for me the opening game was but a short walk from my home in Alphington. I went along just to see what it was like and enjoyed a 2-1 home win watched by as many as 532. This began a four-game day that I now wish I had attempted, as I have never seen four matches in one day.

I immediately decided that this was for me, and I went to less well-attended matches in this league along with the end-of-season League Cup final at Cullompton – I was hooked! From then onwards I gradually started to attend fewer Football League games and now watch matches at various levels in non-league circles. If you'd told me 20 years ago that that would happen I would never have believed it, as for some bizarre reason I thought non-league was rubbish! Now I only wish I had been converted sooner and been able to visit more grounds than I have so far.

One thing is for sure: I have come one hell of a long way since that first game and have had many ups and downs, but one constant remains – I am a football addict.

# Dedication

I wish to dedicate this to my mother, who passed away due to cancer in 2006.
I miss you now and always, and am grateful for the times we spent together.
Put simply, you are a mum in a million. Thank you.

ADRIAN WICKS

# Preface

At the start of any season, I like to set myself some sort of target, and this story is about a campaign in which I set out to do something I had never done before – not to visit any ground on more than one occasion during the August-to-May period.

Being someone who regularly goes to well over 100 games each year, I realised it would not be easy, but what you are about to read is how I managed to accomplish the task despite having made sacrifices to achieve it – an example being my missing Buckland's Devon Bowl final win at Tiverton (I had been there already and was really gutted to miss that one). I have done it in a diary form that includes personal anecdotes from past visits where appropriate, and ground details that should give you some sort of idea what kind of venues I visit these days.

I regret to say there will be no hilarious tales involving wine, women and song, as virtually all my travels are done by car with me as the driver or passenger. I did my fair share of socialising in that respect when I was younger but, nearing 50, I think I am getting a little too old for that.

You will note the distinctive lack of Football League entries and, I hope, see the variety of matches that I tend to go to. If you do not already attend non-league games, I hope this will encourage you to do so. I can thoroughly recommend it, so why not give it a try? It's the best footballing decision I ever made.

My entries will also offer opinions on certain aspects of the game. While you may not agree with them, I hope you will find these viewpoints and the rest of what I comment upon interesting. Here goes then ...

# Saturday, August 7

I start my season on a positive note with a new ground. Tadley Calleva is the only Wessex League club on the mainland that I've yet to visit, and today provides me with an opportunity to see them play Amesbury in a first division encounter.

Now that I have almost completed the Wessex grounds, it seems funny when I recall my first-ever game in this league. Along with a mate of mine, I travelled up from Exeter intending to watch Bashley, but it was called off when we got there. By chance, a local person told us that Brockenhurst was on, so we followed him to the ground to watch a game that the hosts lost 3-0 to Wimborne. I don't remember much about the contest, but I do recall my indifference to it all. This was probably because I wasn't seeing what I had gone to watch when setting off that morning.

Looking back now, it seems daft, and if you had told me that I would do more than 40 grounds in this league I would never have believed it. So that was an unexpected beginning to my saga of Wessex football that continues this afternoon.

I allow plenty of time to get here due to holiday traffic on the A303, even though that means taking a couple of shortcuts to avoid congested areas; perhaps an unnecessary tactic, because I find myself within 10 miles of my destination with two hours to spare. To kill time, I park in a side street not far from the main shopping precinct in Basingstoke's town centre – a free facility sadly lacking in my home town.

Now, I am one of those blokes who regard wandering around shops as an onerous chore to be avoided as much as is humanly possible, especially on a Saturday. With this in mind, I keep my perusing to a minimum, stopping in a couple of bookstores and a collectables shop from which I have previously made purchases in the form of Cherished Teddies, which my mother used to collect.

I say 'used to' because, sadly, she passed away three and a half years ago after losing her second battle with cancer. By then she'd amassed over 500 Teddies thanks, in part, to the countrywide travels that saw me call in at a hell of a lot of shops. These bears are made out of a solid substance and are hand-painted pieces that have their own specific number, name and ... an adoption certificate! They are usually issued in sets, such as the 18 that formed the overseas collection. I recall this well because, having found 17 of them with ease, the last one was proving to be somewhat elusive – Franz the German bear.

Goodness knows how many shops I visited before, at last, I found him in his Bavarian costume waiting to be picked up from a little shop in Melksham. To say I was chuffed would be an understatement, as a long quest had been fulfilled. When I handed it over to my mum she was tickled pink, and her delight made all that trekking around worthwhile.

In some ways I sort of miss not doing it any more, which may explain why I am about to buy an old Teddy – Mayor Wilson T Beary, a 1995 issue that I never thought I would find. Old habits die hard, I guess.

Enough of this. It's time to make the short drive north for what I am principally here for, and I arrive with still about an hour to spare. The ground is located on a minor road to the north-east of the village and isn't too difficult to find. Upon approaching I make the mistake of turning in beside the ground, which turns out to be an error as you have to drive well past before turning in and effectively doubling back to the car park. Next to this is a newly built changing room complex, located behind a goal, and you enter the ground on the other side of this.

Upon entering you are met by a railed-off pitch with open hardstanding all around. Floodlight pylons are sited in each corner and the dugouts are either side of the halfway line on the far side. I am informed that a stand is to be erected opposite this and, in fairness, the foundations are in place, so at least an effort is being made to upgrade facilities here. With the exception of the lack of cover, this is your standard Wessex One ground.

The visitors make the better start of what, to be frank, is a poor opening and really should have scored, but wasteful finishing in front of goal will ultimately prove costly. Near the end of the half the home side put the ball in the net with their first real chance, but it is ruled out for what I think is a dubious offside call, and at the break it is goalless.

Just 36 seconds into the second period, though, Tadley take the lead when right-back Andy Johnson's centre from the right touchline is over-hit and ends up going in off the angle of the far post and bar – I am directly in line with it and stand disbelievingly as it goes in.

The game as a whole improves after this, and it could easily have yielded more than the one more strike that we are to eventually see. That goal sees substitute Alex Frankling net with an angled shot after being put in on the right, sealing a two-goal opening success for the home team.

Amesbury should never have lost, but there we are. Not the greatest start to my campaign on the pitch, but I am made to feel welcome, and having a social chit-chat with a couple of supporters makes for an enjoyable visit. However, it is unlikely that I will return.

# Wednesday, August 11

Having been to more than 160 games in each of the last two seasons, I feel I should cut down on the number of matches I see. To that extent, my quest only to visit grounds once this time round will help. Another way, of course, is to stay at home on certain days, and last night was one of those times.

It is unusual for me as I would normally take watching footy on Tuesdays as a given, but I have come to realise that I am watching too much and must cut down. I guess I'm getting old and must face up to the fact that I can no longer traipse around like I seem to have done for years and years. I didn't feel that I missed out last night, though. Honest!

Being the hopper that I am, though, I couldn't possibly miss Tuesday AND Wednesday, so when the opportunity comes up to go somewhere I have not been for a while, I can't resist. Slimbridge is the destination and one which I will not be driving to – at least most of it, anyway. I have a good friend called Martin who lives in Taunton and I will meet him at his place, leaving my car there and making the journey north on the M5 in his. He owns a Rover that is so old, the registration number is written in Latin!

It gets him from A to B, though, and as he is a fairly fast driver we get there in ample time for a Hellenic League game that sees the Swans entertain Highworth Town. This is my third visit to Wisloe Road but my first league game, the previous ones both being in the FA Vase.

The second of those contests was on a wet Saturday against eventual winners Truro, when my view of the visitors' second goal was marred by the line of umbrellas blocking my line of sight! The hosts' showing that day was a bit of a let-down, but doesn't compare with the end of the season when, after securing the title, they declined promotion at the last minute. As a result they were demoted to the Gloucestershire League. However, they have fought their way back through the system and are back to where they were.

One thing that hasn't changed much is the ground, which is just as impressive as I remember. As you enter behind the goal, the changing room and clubhouse building are directly to your right and a significant alteration since my last visit is a small covered standing area at this end. I am a little puzzled as to how high the roof is, and given its size I cannot imagine it being that handy on a wet and windy day, but it's dry and bright so this will not matter this evening.

There is hardstanding all round with a tidy seated stand on one side, and the opposite side is open with the dugouts either side of halfway. A line of tall fir trees sits behind, while the far end is open and uncovered, and three floodlit poles on each side provide the lighting.

Having won the Hellenic West title on the final day of last season, the hosts are hoping to get their Premier campaign off to a flying start, and after just four minutes they open the scoring when Mike Bryant sweeps the ball into the bottom left corner from 10 yards. Both sides create good chances before Joe Tustain doubles the lead with a predatory strike 10 minutes before half-time.

The visitors pull a goal back on 65 thanks to Ritchie Saunders' close-range finish to a cross from the right. Highworth now have the momentum and are only denied a share of the spoils by a couple of fine saves by Dave Evans, but in my opinion Slimbridge shade a match that has lived up to its pre-match promise.

Overall, I have to say this is a venue well worth visiting if you have not done so already. It can be seen from the motorway and is easy to reach, especially from the north. No doubt I shall return here myself some time in the future, as I really like it.

# Thursday, August 12

Not normally a night for watching football, especially this early in a season. Andover New Street, however, have for some reason decided that their midweek night is a Thursday, and who am I to argue?

This also gives me the chance to revisit a ground for the sole purpose of getting a programme this time! One was not issued on my previous visit, and the absence of a gateman, meaning free admission, hardly boosted the club's coffers either. Maybe it was just as well we didn't have to pay, because it was an awful game, with a solitary visiting goal against a lacklustre home side, but in all seriousness it was something that should never happen at this level.

I am returning a favour from last night and picking Martin up from Ilminster, and it's nice to have his company once more. It is a straightforward drive up the A303, then towards a village to the north-west of the town. As we arrive at Foxcotte things look promising as there is someone taking money and, upon entry, we find there is a programme as well – hurrah!

Unsurprisingly, the ground hasn't altered and is respectable enough with hardstanding all around and three sides open to the elements. The exception is the near side, which has some covered standing to your right as you enter, sitting in front of the clubhouse and refreshment facility. To your left is a rectangular, box-shaped wooden stand with bench seating, accessed by a wooden stairway. Floodlighting is provided by four pylons on each side. Perspex dugouts are located on the far side in their orthodox positions either side of halfway.

Fleet Spurs are the visiting side for this, my second Wessex One game already. I'm not really sure what to expect from this one, but hope for better than what I saw at Tadley. For me it is always great when someone grabs an early goal, which duly arrives when Luke Walsh taps in a left-sided cross from close range to put Fleet one up.

Around the half-hour mark they score two quick-fire goals to take control of the contest, with the first a comical own-goal; Ant Waters slicing into his own net at the far post from a right-sided cross. Before you can blink, Fleet are breaking down the left and crossing low for Adam Crittenden to sweep home. On 36 Ben Clisby's speculative shot from the right creeps under the keeper and in off the near post, making it 4-0 at the break.

Any thoughts of a comeback are ended a mere seven minutes into the second period when Crittenden finds space in the box to fire home his second of the night. It's all too much for Mr Stockwell of Andover, who gets himself sent off in the aftermath. The 10 men do get one back as Danny Sullivan breaks through, rounds the keeper and slots home, but he then gets red-carded for a second bookable that just about sums up New Street's evening.

The away side add two more to their tally in the final minutes, with Sam Knowles coming on and notching both strikes with a header and a deflected shot, completing an emphatic away win. This is the same scoreline as Norwich's first home game last year, but here there is no season-ticket throwing and I'm sure the manager will not be sacked after a poor display by his side tonight.

To be fired after just one game is plainly ridiculous, although in the Canaries' case it proved to be a good decision as the new man guided them to promotion. For me that was lucky on their part, but is something that is par for the course in this modern age of wanting instant success, and is one of the reasons I have stopped going to Football League games. As a rule, non-league clubs are more tolerant, and I am sure this will apply to New Street after tonight's performance. Shame it was so one-sided, but it was a good night out and I'm glad I did this one.

# Saturday, August 14

After much deliberation, I decide to stay local and do Willand Rovers' FA Cup tie versus Merthyr Town. The away club have reformed during the summer after the demise of Tydfil and are starting their new life in the Western League first division.

It's strange having a Wales-based club in this league, and I am sure some clubs in this division will not be looking forwards to the trip across the second Severn crossing, especially as it costs so much to do so! On the up side, there will be the boost in gate and refreshment takings from the large contingent of fans that go to their away games, so it's swings and roundabouts.

One thing our Welsh visitors will not have to contend with is a difficult route to this ground, as it's not far off the motorway and is sited beside what used to be the A38. Today, though, they have other issues to tackle as the usual holiday traffic delays them, and kick-off is three-quarters of an hour late. That's the trouble with the South West, as I have found to my cost – hence my short journey today.

A few years ago, I set out to watch Almondsbury's first Western League game and just made it, although as it turned out I might as well not have bothered as it was a dull, goalless draw. The following year I left earlier to do a similar thing with Portishead, but the M5 was even worse and I missed 10 minutes. A goal was scored seconds before my arrival, and Sod's Law ensured it was the only goal of the game – the only time I have achieved this somewhat dubious feat.

Of course, it would be perfect if you could ring a club and ask them to put the start back because you are running late, wouldn't it? Although I have never tried this tactic, I think it might be somewhat unsuccessful!

The one thing I hate about coming here is the lack of car parking, with a small area available beside the entrance. Otherwise, you park on the side of the main road and risk getting your wing mirror knocked off. You enter and walk down the near side and around to the clubhouse behind the goal. This now has a covered area in front of it. Official parking is next to this building, accessed via a tarmac road down that open near side that has housing beyond a wire fence to the rear.

The opposite side has a small seated stand flanked by the dugouts and with open hardstanding, like the near end. There are four floodlight pylons on each side. Despite the parking problem, this is a tidy set-up.

The visitors may not be called Merthyr Tydfil any more, but it is apparent looking at their line-up that they have managed to keep some of their Southern League players. This poses the question as to who exactly the underdogs are today: is it the lower league side or the Premier Division hosts? Well there aren't many clues in the opening half hour or so, but the breakthrough arrives moments later when Dean Stamp puts Willand in front with a low strike from the edge of the area.

Moving into the second period, it is the home side who are in the ascendancy, with a second goal duly arriving thanks to a clever move down the left that results in a low cross towards the far post, where Ben Mammola taps in. His side see out the remainder of the game to seal a place in the next round, with the Martyrs clearly not having enough on the day to trouble the hosts. They have certainly shown enough for me to believe they will join Willand in the Premier Division next year although, from a neutral point of view, it isn't a game I will remember for long.

Annoyingly, I later find that my alternative choice of game today finished 4-4 and I hope that's not a portent of things to come. We'll see.

# Tuesday, August 17

Back in February, I attended my first-ever game in the Somerset County League. It was at Winscombe, and was such an enjoyable experience that it left me wondering why I had left it so long to try it. Still, it's better late than never, and I followed it up by travelling up to do a few more Premier Division venues at the back end of the campaign.

Tonight, I am continuing the quest to do the remaining grounds at this level and am driving up to watch Stockwood Green play Castle Cary. It will be the first time I have seen the home side in action and the second for Cary – I saw them at home against Cutters Friday in April.

Stockwood play at Hursley Lane, and it's one of those venues that is not in the place itself. It is a fairly easy place to find, but getting there varies in degrees of difficulty. For me it involves avoiding the rush-hour traffic on the southern outskirts of Bristol and cutting across from the airport to the A37, although I have to pass the right-sided turn and double back as I am forbidden to cross the carriageway. No problem, though, as I turn into the small parking area and ahead see what I was expecting, as this is a typical scenario for this league.

In short it's an open, railed-off pitch with no hardstanding and a clubhouse/changing room building set back from the pitch. It's a 6.30 kick-off as they naturally have no lights here, but the thing I cannot comprehend is that, like quite a few clubs in this competition, they allow you to watch for free. This is great for yours truly but somewhat baffling as I, and I'm sure everyone else, would not quibble at handing over two or three pounds. While there is no programme, I still feel a little sheepish at not paying, even though I am not doing anything wrong. I do wonder if someone might come around with a moneybox or something, but there we are.

The home side have just been promoted from the first division and look the better outfit as the game gets under way. They are rewarded midway through the half when a low cross from the right byline is turned into his own net by Matt Robinson. Cary respond well and are level within 10 minutes as Rees Heyhoe's angled shot hits the right post, rolls along the line and goes in off the left one. One-all at the break.

On resumption, both sides continue to make a positive impact on the contest, and the only surprise is that we have to wait until the 70th minute before Stockwood retake the lead through Chris Saunders' low shot. Five minutes later he gets his second with a close-range finish after an initial effort is blocked, and despite hitting the woodwork and having a couple of goal-bound attempts well saved, it is enough to seal the win.

Overall, this has been a fine match in which both sides have played their part, and I have enjoyed my visit here.

# Wednesday, August 18

For the second night running I'm off up the motorway to watch a Somerset County fixture, this time for Langford's home game with Cutters Friday. As with last night, I will be seeing the host club for the first time, while I've seen Cutters twice before, at the back end of last season. I have already mentioned their win at Castle Cary and the other was a home draw against Taunton Blackbrook, so by rights they should lose tonight!

Langford play their home games on what is basically a field that is railed off on three sides. The changing rooms are located a distance away, through a gap in the trees and next to the neighbouring Conference home of Weston-super-Mare. Indeed, you have to use the latter's car-parking facilities, although this is not the first time I have parked next to one ground to attend another.

The strangest example was my last visit to Anfield, when I parked bang in front of Goodison Park's main entrance. You probably cannot do that now – this was in 1992 – because of the parking restrictions that dog the motorist these days, but there we are.

The facilities here are understandably on the scanty side, but although I am sure there is a reason for it I cannot comprehend why they are playing home games in a location that's five or six miles away from Langford village. Then again, you have Stockwood not playing in Stockwood while Cutters Friday do, and nearby Western League outfit Hengrove are the same, and for sure there are many others.

Of course, I have no problem with this but it can be frustrating, especially if, like me, you do not have satnav! In my defence, I don't recall any instance of me going to the wrong place, unless you count the time I went to Rochdale and from the rail station made my way to the rugby league ground by mistake! Of course, Spotland was on the other side of town, necessitating a dash to make kick-off, which I did, thank goodness.

I tend to rely on the old-fashioned method of looking at the club address then at a map, although in tonight's case I have had to check with a friend to make sure I was heading to the right place, and when he told me it was next to Woodspring Stadium I knew it was easy to find.

Despite their club having started the season well, it is evident as we get under way that for whatever reason, be it the six-mile trip or not, the village populace are not avid footy fans: there is barely a double-figure crowd. It's certainly not the weather as it is fine again tonight. After 20 minutes or so I am beginning to think they have the right idea by staying away, but as usual my pessimistic outlook is confounded when Ross Neads fires the hosts in front from the edge of the box, and things improve from there.

A controversial moment arrives six minutes into the second half when a right-wing cross is headed in by Ryan Bending at the far post, only for it to be harshly ruled out by the linesman's flag. In some ways this is a crucial moment, because Cutters are visibly affected by what they see as an injustice. Langford then strike twice in a minute to rub salt into their wounds: first Joe Popperwell heads in a corner on the left, then Ryan Havard breaks free on the right and expertly slots under the onrushing keeper. Grant Giles comes on and promptly bags the home side's fourth with a low drive into the left corner, before the visitors get an injury-time consolation through a penalty converted by Bending.

On the whole. this has been a decent game that the home side have won deservedly with a strong performance. However, if that goal had been allowed to stand things might have been different. We'll never know.

# Saturday, August 21

I made the relatively short drive to a village near Bridgwater yesterday, to stay with friends for the weekend and also enable me to have a longer day out today. This is because I have a pet basset hound who needs looking after when I'm away on trips, so my friends will look after him on this occasion.

At least it makes it easier to leave early enough to dodge the holiday traffic and reach my destination on time. That was originally to be Fleetwood but a phone call has resulted in a change of plan, as their game against Luton is all-ticket. Instead, I'm heading north-east and ticking off Chesterfield's new ground earlier than planned.

That describes my arrival there as well, with a nice and easy drive resulting in my occupation of a handy parking space in a nearby side street with two hours to spare. Nothing to do, then, but take a stroll into town and have a look around. I reacquaint myself with the crooked spire that most people link to this place, then spend some time wandering around the open market.

This, I am glad to say, is something that has managed to survive the modern-day trend of shopping in out-of-town malls, and long may it continue. There is something like an old-fashioned atmosphere at these places; the sellers expressing aloud how you will regret not taking up their generous offer of a pound of apples at a giveaway price. Being outdoors gives it that extra quality you don't see at those that are within, although with our weather the latter form is more practical!

There are bargains to be had if you are prepared to look – which is what I do, without spending any money, of course. Frankly, I hate shopping and I head eagerly back to the car, grab a bite to eat then make the short walk to the ground.

It's actually a fair distance out of town unlike the old Saltergate venue, which I visited on a couple of occasions without too much to show from them. There are similarities in that you can park nearby and not have to pay a king's ransom to do so.

That's the trouble with some of these new league grounds. It's all very well building these out-of-town stadiums, but clubs then seem to go out of their way to make it as hard as possible if you go there by car. This gives me another excuse not to bother with the Football League, and I am only here this afternoon to recomplete the 92 (technically, this is 91 with Morecambe's new ground to come).

To gain access to the B2Net stadium, one must first queue to buy a ticket, which takes a while as there is only one window operating. I get a ticket labelled for the stand behind the goal where the away fans congregate, but am informed that, once inside, I can walk around and sit in the stands on either side – a rather odd arrangement. I sit on halfway after managing to acquire a team sheet to go with my matchday programme. This has now become a fixation of mine, although it's always a bonus to get one at Football League level.

I am sitting opposite the main stand and it, like mine, has shallow, curved roofing while the stands behind the goals are of a more orthodox, cantilevered style. There are gaps between the stands of this all-seater stadium, and here we have the floodlight pylons. Most new stadiums are fairly bland, but this one is not too bad – certainly better than the old one!

The game starts and the good news is that both sides want to play a passing game that is pleasing on the eye. In the eighth minute, home striker Jack Lester is needlessly fouled in the area and Danny Whittaker's spot kick is expertly placed into the top left with the keeper having no chance. Stuart Fleetwood squanders a good chance for the visitors, Hereford, before Whittaker doubles the Spireites' lead with a shot that takes a deflection before nestling in the right corner.

Four minutes after the break, Hereford are given a lifeline when they are awarded a penalty of their own, but Ryan Valentine's strike from 12 yards is superbly tipped around the post by Tommy Lee. On the hour Mattis' run takes him inside, and his low shot is parried out, only for Whittaker to follow up and complete his hat-trick. Within minutes, a fourth goal is scored by the hosts when a corner from the right is met by Simon Ford's header.

Despite the best efforts of both teams there is no further addition to the score, so the result is a comfortable win score-wise but a touch harsh on the away side, who have been made to pay for missing their chances.

It has certainly been an entertaining contest and I am well satisfied with what I have seen. What with a quick getaway after the final whistle and a good run back down the motorways, I reckon things have turned out really well – I'll still be glad to get back to non-league, though.

# Tuesday, August 24

Clevedon United have dropped out of the Western League and returned not only to the Somerset County Premier Division but also to their Coleridge Vale ground. Prior to this, they ground-shared at the Hand Stadium – home of neighbours Clevedon Town – and I saw United play there on a couple of occasions.

One of those was a Christmas Eve league game against Shepton Mallet – the only game I've seen the day before Christmas. I do recall that there were poor attendances on both visits, made more obvious by the size of the ground. It must be disheartening playing your home matches at stadiums that are sparsely populated every time, and the higher the level, the worse it must be.

Take Darlington as a prime example. Here is a club that, to my knowledge, has never played in their 20,000-plus capacity arena in front of anything like a full house. I went there in their first season after leaving their quaint Feethams home, and it was weird watching a game in front of a crowd that was scattered on all four sides, resulting in a poor atmosphere that must have affected performances.

It's not looking good at Darlington now. Unfortunately, this is an instance where the chairman's ego has got in the way, and as a consequence the club has suffered in the long run. Of course, it's the fans that feel it most and it's they who will aim to see Darlo through their crisis. For their sakes, I hope their efforts prove to be worthwhile.

This evening's Premier Division fare sees Easton-in-Gordano in town for what I guess you could say is a local derby. The ground is centrally located and is one of those places that is easy to get to, just as long as you know where to go. By that I mean that, being tucked away in a housing estate, it would not be straightforward to find without prior knowledge of its approximate siting.

Anyway, when I arrive I find what could only be called a basic venue. The pitch is located at one end of a recreation area and is railed off on three sides. Down at the far end is a clubhouse/changing room complex with parking to the fore, reached down the side by a road that is part of the housing estate. The near end has a tree line that divides the pitch from another road, while the far side is open. They won't win many ground awards here but, to be fair, it serves its purpose.

There is a slight delay in kick-off due to the late arrival of some of the visiting players. I know this is a game between two clubs that are quite near each other, but this doesn't make it any easier for them to get here for a 6.30 midweek game as, of course, they have daytime jobs after which they have to tackle rush-hour traffic to play a game for which they get paid peanuts or, in some cases, nothing.

Maybe that is one of my many reasons for liking non-league stuff like this. There is no doubt in my mind that, because of the tiny amount of money these lads get for playing, they are on a more equal footing to the people watching them. As a result, there is more interaction and a togetherness you won't see in the Premier League – a league that, in my opinion, is just about money.

I'm not saying, of course, that the top players should play for measly wages, but it's all got out of control now and put some clubs into severe financial meltdown in their attempts to keep up. Wouldn't it be nice if they said enough is enough and paid some of those guys less, allowing for lower ticket prices? Yeah. Methinks there is more chance of spotting the Loch Ness monster on holiday in the nearby Severn Estuary!

Back in the real world, the match finally starts and there's a goal inside two minutes when the hosts' full-back, Billy Astle, slots in from close range, and 10 minutes later he is fouled in the area. Sadly for him, his strike colleague Tony Cook misses the resultant spot kick with a scuffed effort that goes well wide of the left-hand post. Clevedon control the remainder of the half but fail to add to their tally.

In the second half, Easton gradually come more into it but, thanks to some woeful finishing, it appears they will come away pointless. Rob Dumphy is particularly guilty in this respect, but as we go into stoppage time he makes amends by getting in on the left, rounding the keeper and finding the net from an acute angle. Result: a share of the spoils, and that's just about fair as neither side has done enough to warrant the win in a disappointing match.

I would say that this was possibly the second sub-standard game I have seen in my limited number seen in this division and, bizarrely, both have involved Easton. Perhaps I should avoid seeing them in future! I cannot say the same for a possible second visit to this venue, but in all likelihood I will not be back. It was good to get this one done, but I predict this will be my first and last visit here.

# Wednesday, August 25

For the second week running I am doing Somerset County games on consecutive nights, and this one is at one of the few grounds with floodlights. Unlike for the other three, though, I am not travelling alone as I make my way up to Taunton, where I will leave my car at Martin's place and get a lift to watch Cheddar play Taunton Blackbrook (or Taunton Reserves, as I keep telling him. They aren't really, of course, but it's a bit of banter).

The weather has been poor but apparently there isn't a danger of the match being called off, although this doesn't stop me worrying, gloom and doom merchant that I am. At least the rain has stopped by the time we arrive, which is a relief in more ways than one: Martin's Rover undoubtedly has the noisiest windscreen wipers in the world!

Cheddar play at Bowdens Park, which is located to the south of the town on the main road to Wells. You drive straight into the car park sited behind the goal, with a decent clubhouse to your right. Follow this around and along to halfway, where the changing rooms are, and the roof provides an overhang at the front, providing cover from the elements. Hardstanding is provided along here, but the remaining sides are grassy and uncovered. The lighting comes from poles down each side and the pitch looks very good.

All in all, this is a decent venue, although there is talk that Cheddar may be moving to another site and building a superstore here, which would be a pity. The home club want to gain promotion to the Western League and may see a move as a step towards fulfilling that aim, but I would have thought that what they have here should be adequate for them to accomplish their ambition. If it were up to me, I would let them in for sure.

At least they play on their own ground unlike the visitors who, of course (!), play at Taunton Town's Wordsworth Drive headquarters. I suggest that Blackbrook's players face a similar scenario to the one faced by the Clevedon United lads when playing on such a ground. Having not seen them at home, I cannot say for sure, but I'm willing to bet that's the case.

We begin on time and from the off the hosts demonstrate why they are one of the better sides in this league with some crisp passing that inevitably sees them take an early lead; Callum McManus, the recipient of a squared ball from the left, strikes low into the right corner. The same player then hits the post and is denied by a fine save before Blackbrook almost level out of the blue just past the half-hour mark, Ross Macnab wasting a one-on-one chance. Naturally, the ball quickly finds its way down the other end, where McManus is presented with a similar opportunity that he takes to put Cheddar two up at the interval.

Any hopes the visiting side have of taking anything from this game are extinguished on the hour when Paul Marquiss gets in on the right and takes it round the keeper before calmly slotting in from a tight angle. Five minutes from time the scoring is completed when Rob Edwards skips through to fire in from 15 yards and complete what frankly has been an impressive showing from the Cheesemen. Then again, I suppose they should be well capable of handling the bread and butter of league football!

# Saturday, August 28

A no-go as far as travelling is concerned as it's a bank holiday. I guess most people hardly look forward to endless queues on the motorway or trunk roads, but I have come up with a cunning plan for my proposed destination today. I am off to watch Tavistock play Taunton Town (the first team!) in an FA Cup encounter, and my astuteness lies in the route I plan to take. It's hardly rocket science, but it involves me avoiding the standard route I normally take and going across Dartmoor via Moretonhampstead.

It turns out to be a stress-free journey on a fine, sunny day, and the only regret I have is that I did not leave sooner so that I could have stopped for a bit on the moors and taken in some of the wonderful scenery. I was able to take it in to a certain degree, but it's not the same, for obvious reasons such as keeping your eye on the road ahead. I certainly didn't want to run down a stray sheep as it wouldn't do my car much good – I can't imagine the sheep would have come out of it in great shape either!

Anyhow, I arrive at the ground at that annoying time that bridges the gap between too early and too late, so sit in my car for a bit before going in. I'm not of those people who go into grounds early; I try to leave it as late as possible, which can backfire sometimes.

An instance of this occurred at Oxford United, where I left it fairly late to enter the Kassam Stadium despite having parked up with an hour to spare. I didn't realise you had to queue to purchase a matchday ticket and, with only one booth open, there was a long wait. In the end I just made kick-off, thank goodness, because if I had missed it I would have had to revisit (I have a rule that says I must see a full game to count it). At least I learned my lesson from that and, touch wood, it has not happened since.

Tavistock play in the Peninsula Premier Division, two levels below their visitors, this afternoon. As their secretary, Martin is here, as he goes to all their games every season including friendlies. I am sure I could have got a lift with him, but as he is on official duty I feel it wouldn't have been the right thing to do. I see him inside and he gives me a team sheet, which I didn't expect.

Now I wish I hadn't purchased the programme, mainly because Tavistock issue a standard one for every game with an insert giving details of that day's game. I understand why they do this but am glad I don't attend every home game, thus effectively obtaining several of what would be the same thing every time. I'm pretty sure they have been doing this for quite a while, so it's not unexpected. It's just one of those things that suit the club in question, and you cannot criticise them for that.

You certainly can't fault this club's efforts to upgrade their ground as it has improved greatly in recent times. Gone is the dilapidated stand on halfway, which has been replaced by two small stands either side of the players' entrance from a large, white-painted building that holds the changing rooms and hospitality areas. This is flanked by open hardstanding that goes around most of the perimeter. There are four floodlight pylons on each side and a small standing enclosure opposite the seated areas.

The ground now has a wooden fence perimeter where once it was open. Now you enter behind the goal next to the car parking, whereas before the pay booth was located at the turn off the road. The old clubhouse still exists, albeit in a smaller form, mainly because of a fire that destroyed part of it plus the old changing rooms beside it. This is a tidy venue on the whole, and one worth visiting.

Maybe today is not the afternoon to be visiting Langsford Park, though. At the break that thought is on my mind after witnessing a half in which the only point of note has been one we could have done without. Taunton's James Clough would certainly agree if he was not in such agony after having his leg broken from what can be mildly described as an X-rated challenge.

The Southern League visitors are in control, though, and break the deadlock on the hour, a cross from the right being met by Macnab's angled shot (yes, the same Macnab who played for Blackbrook on Wednesday – told you it was Taunton Reserves!) Moments later, a lapse of concentration from a corner sees Jamie Ahearn bullet in a header to equalise. Taunton win it, though, thanks to Rodney Marsh's sublime chip from just outside the box that his illustrious namesake would have been proud of.

Not a bad cup tie overall, just a shame about that so-called tackle (and he wasn't even red-carded for it!) and the result is just about right.

# Wednesday, September 1

Bank holiday Monday has come and gone without me seeing a game, which doesn't normally happen. There were certainly options open to me but I declined to take them up as, indeed, would be applied to last night.

I had it in mind in pre-season to cut down on my football watching compared to recent campaigns, and so far I have succeeded, being 10 games down on this time last year. Part of this can be attributed to my one-time-only visit to a ground policy but, on the whole, I don't feel I have missed out in any way as yet.

Most groundhoppers will tell you there will be times when you pick the wrong game or miss a game that, with hindsight, you wish you had gone to. On the other hand, you can feel relief at missing a poor encounter, or pleasure when you pick one that is a classic. These are the ups and downs of doing what we do – I guess you just hope that the highs outweigh the lows. I know it is going well so far, although it's still early.

I couldn't possibly go a whole week without a game, though, could I? Well no, because this evening I am picking Martin up on my way to Sherborne for their FA Cup replay against Hamworthy United. My astute navigational skills get us there in plenty of time, unlike our last visit here when we seemed to run into every traffic jam in the county before reaching the turnstile as the game kicked off. No such worries this time.

That game against Dawlish was one of my two previous visits to Raleigh Grove, and both games finished 2-1, so no prizes for guessing what I think the scoreline will be tonight – just for who will come out on top. Hamworthy play in the Wessex Premier and the hosts are Western Premier – both step five – making for an even contest on paper.

If it were to be decided on the standard of their respective grounds, I am in no doubt that Sherborne would triumph. There is a decent grandstand on halfway, at a slightly raised level from the pitch, that provides good viewing, while there is open hardstanding elsewhere. Four corner pylons provide good lighting and the clubhouse is situated behind the goal to your right as you enter from a large parking area.

In comparison, the away club's ground is not as good, particularly as it resides at Dorset FA HQ although, in fairness, I haven't been there for a while and it may have improved since then.

As I expected, there isn't much between these two teams in an end-to-end cup tie that one feels will be decided on who can take their chances. As it turns out, it's home marksman Phil Ormrod, who gobbles up his best opportunity with a well-struck shot to splits the sides at the break.

To all intents and purposes, Sherborne win a place in the next round with a quick-fire double early in the second period. In fact it is the goalscorer who makes the initial impacts, first having his effort cleared off the line in the opening minute, then winning a penalty which is duly converted.

The visitors are clearly rattled by this surge and before they know it they are three down thanks to Danny Thompson's thunderous strike. Ormrod, through on goal, is brought down from behind, resulting in a straight red for the offender, and after the free kick goes close, the game peters out to its inevitable conclusion. Well, I did say there would be three goals!

It has been an acceptable cup tie from a neutral standpoint, although I think I would have felt disappointed if I was an away fan – their team can concentrate on the league now, and I can do the same for my next match …

# Friday, September 3

… which provides me with a dilemma: do I go to Crediton or Newton Spurs? That question of choice I have already mentioned rears its ugly head again. I got it wrong in August by opting for Willand instead of Buckland, so my theory of swings and roundabouts may be put to the test here tonight.

In the end I opt for Newton Spurs, simply because Martin's going and I can get a lift with him and enjoy his company once more. I do go to a lot of matches on my own, mainly because I don't know many others who live nearby who are as daft as me and choose to attend local games, so it's always nice to go with someone.

I remember the first time I went to a game on my own, as it was the 1979 FA Cup semi-final at Villa Park between Arsenal and Wolves. Somehow I managed to get a ticket, so I travelled on the train to Birmingham feeling apprehensive, which seems rather silly now. I stood in the Holte End to see the Gunners win, and it must have gone well because I repeated the experience two weeks later, this time going to the Hawthorns to see WBA. I still have the programme with its picture of Brendon Batson, Cyrille Regis and Lawrie Cunningham, aka the Three Degrees.

These were the first times I'd been anywhere without friends or family, but having got over my unease it was all systems go and my solo trips increased in number with time, to the point where I sit currently.

Tonight's selection is a South West Peninsula League Division One East game in which where Spurs' opposition is Galmpton, one of the better sides on paper at this level. Unfortunately, their ground does not match up to the quality of the Recreation Ground, which has undergone change in recent times.

The principal of these has been the installation of floodlights down each side, although when the first game was played under them there was a delay in kick-off because of a dispute between the club and the company that put them up. As a result, there were no fuses and the club resorted to breaking into the box to fit new ones so we could get on with playing the game. This evening we'd have little use for them as, indeed, would be the case for the covered areas, as the weather is fine.

As you enter there is a seated area to the right that was initially a place for standing, and that now sits at the far end. On both sides it is open hardstanding with the dugouts on the near side, behind which lies a cricket outfield. The far side is lined by some trees and a wall that divides the ground from some retirement flats, although no one living there seems to want to take advantage of the free view!

The far end has a tall fir tree line, while the near end has a wall and netting separating the pitch from the car park. Clubhouse and changing room facilities are to the left as you go in, with a small paved area to the fore.

When you bear in mind this is the same level as the Somerset County Premier divisional matches I have been seeing recently, you'll see just how good a standard the grounds in this league are as a comparison.

As we pass the 30-minute mark, the same could not be said for the quality of this encounter which, frankly, is dire. Out of nowhere, though, Kevin Wiltshire hits a speculative effort towards goal from the right that arcs over the keeper's outstretched hand and into the net. On the stroke of half-time, Jon Glasser mistimes a tackle badly and is sent off, so at the break the visitors are one up on the scoresheet but one-down on the field of play.

Newton Spurs push forward in search of a leveller, and midway through the half find it when Ashley Webber receives the ball from a pull-back on the left and scores with a low strike into the bottom corner. For some reason the hosts do not really build on this and, what with Galmpton settling for what they have, a draw is inevitable. And so it proves in a contest I can't really get into with any gusto.

Looking back, I think my pre-match indecisiveness hasn't helped, and with hindsight I should have stayed at home. It has hardly been disastrous, though, even if I did pick the wrong game – the Crediton one finished 3-3. I'm sure that on another day I will make the right selection. Pity it wasn't tonight.

# Saturday, September 4

No doubting my choice of match today as I get back on the new-ground trail with yet another Somerset County encounter, this time Watchet's league game versus Winscombe.

From Exeter it's not exactly the easiest of drives, taking in a windy route via Tiverton, and it is not helped by part of my proposed route being closed due to roadworks. I am supposed to drive up to Minehead and then east, but I decide to be clever and take a route that cuts across. In theory this should be shorter but probably isn't really. Anyway, despite my little detour I get there with an hour to spare, which is just as well because there is not exactly ample parking space.

At least I get there eventually, unlike a few months ago when a scheduled trip to Witton Albion went decidedly awry. I set out giving myself enough time to get there in case of traffic delays and, having passed through the notorious M5/M6 interchange unscathed, I was so far ahead that I slowed to about 50mph to avoid getting there too early. Approaching the first Stoke turn-off, a road sign warned of an accident beyond that junction, which made me consider exiting there and rejoining further on.

It would not have been a problem of course, as I had time in hand to do so.

However, the next sign indicated a mere 10-minute delay, so I drove on – big mistake! Two or three miles past Keele services, we slowed and slowed and ... stopped. The time was 1.15 and initially I was fine. An hour later, though, there was no movement, despite the signage telling us we could do 40mph – fat chance!

As three o'clock passed I had obviously resigned myself. Meanwhile, the vacant southbound carriageway at least gave some lads the chance to kill some time with a kickabout, and I couldn't resist joining in – after all, it's not very often you get to kick a football around on the M6, is it? In the end it was just after 5pm before we moved, and I had no option but to return whence I had come.

Later, I found out that the problem was a fatal crash, which certainly put things into perspective. At least I was able to return home, unlike those people. It was obvious something really bad had happened so, after first being hacked off at being stuck with nowhere to go, I just calmly accepted it. I just wish I'd ignored that damn sign and turned off!

With time to kill today, I go for a stroll and there's a chance to see a local steam train passing nearby, followed shortly by another coming the other way. I'm not exactly an avid train buff, but it's nice to see these trains which, unlike modern ones, have some character. The line passes to the far side of the ground, so during the game puffs of smoke reveal the passing of another locomotive.

The venue is called the War Memorial Ground and it's worth the visit as it is in a nice location with the Bristol Channel not too far away. There is what appears to be an old cricket pavilion on halfway, holding the changing rooms and a refreshment area. Built into the front is a stepped standing enclosure with the technical areas either side. Behind the goal at the sea end is a small, white-painted shelter that passes for covered standing and the other sides are grassy, open spaces that are roped off from the pitch.

I think anyone who knew the name of this ground and came here for the first time would feel let down at what they'd find, but I quite like it. Given my low expectations of ground standards in this division, I suppose that should not be altogether surprising.

Winscombe are certainly caught unawares because they fall behind inside the first minute when a long throw from the right is flicked on to Jamie Milton, who nods in. The hosts dominate the rest of the half, but have to wait until the 42nd minute before Aaron Deeks dispatches a one-on-one, although he should have had a hat-trick by then.

As if to prove the first goal was no fluke, Watchet proceed to net in the opening minute of the second period as well, thanks to John Harris's near-post header from a corner on the left – 35 seconds in compared to 56 in the first. Three down, the visitors finally wake up and create chances, eventually grabbing a consolation goal with Evan Day tapping in after a terrific solo run and set-up by Damien Hill. Five minutes later, the home side restore their three-goal advantage when Louis Allen is on hand at the far post to convert Deek's centre and complete the scoring.

If Winscombe had got going sooner they might have gained some reward from this match. I think it has been a good game but one thing is for sure – with free admission again, these Somerset League encounters are good value for your money!

There is a slightly annoying occurrence on my drive back as I am able to travel back along the road that was supposed to be closed, so my pre-match detour turns out to have been a waste of time. Thankfully, the same cannot be said for my day as a whole.

# Wednesday, September 8

As a rule, I do not like to attend games involving a reserve side, although there are times when its definition can be somewhat obscure. A case in point is when you get pre-season friendlies involving sides that, while they are not officially labelled 2nd XIs, quite clearly are – especially when you look at the fixtures for that day and see that club is playing in two matches at the same time!

In the past, I have been to similar types of matches in the form of 'turning on the floodlight' games, which have featured clubs like Ottery taking on top-flight opposition who clearly are not going to be at full strength.

At least you are aware of it, though, unlike at a game I attended at Exeter City, who played Glasgow Rangers as part of an agreement to sign Chris Vinnicombe. I didn't expect the Ibrox club to field a full first team but I expected a stronger line-up than the one that played. It left one thinking it was a bit of a swindle. Nowadays, I simply solve the problem by not watching any friendlies, and I haven't seen one for quite some time.

My outlook on this subject is the main reason I am travelling up to see my choice of game tonight, as the only visit I've made to Bitton was for a league match against Yeovil's second team. It still counts, of course, but I feel I must see a visiting first team play here to dot the i's and cross the t's, so to speak.

I did something similar with Larkhall against the same opposition that very same season, in a game I remember as being the proverbial game of two halves. The first 45 was anonymous but the second period yielded six goals and three sendings-off! The revisit against Keynsham was a total non-event, so I am hoping history will not repeat itself here.

The Recreation Ground has certainly altered since that initial visit, in Bitton's first year in the Western League. They are now a Premier Division outfit, and their ground is enclosed all around and has a good-sized seated stand running along most of one side. There is also a covered standing area opposite, next to where you enter. Elsewhere there is open hardstanding and there are floodlight pylons in each corner. The clubhouse is just outside the ground, next to the car park.

Wells City are in town this evening, fresh from their First Division title success, and playing one of the better teams is going to test their new-found standing. This is emphasised early in the game as they go behind after just six minutes when Luke Clarke's angled drive sneaks past the keeper and flicks the inside of the right post before going in. Despite the fine efforts of both teams, this is the only goal of what has nonetheless been an enjoyable half.

Prolific marksman Mark Salter doubles the lead two minutes after the break with a typical striker's finish, only for Wells to hit back immediately with quick-fire goals that level the scores; Jones' left-footer from the left edge of the box going in off the post and Andy Edwards converting at the far stick after a good run and low cross from the left. Bitton are not put off their stride, though, and forge ahead once more with Salter putting his head on to a swinging left cross. But the visitors aren't done for and clinch a deserved point from a free kick on the right side of the 18-yard area, dispatched via a low sizzler from Ross McErlain.

Both sides go for the win in the closing stages but to no avail as the final whistle concludes an excellent match which has done credit to the league. If I see a better game than this over the next months I will be astonished, because this is as good as it gets.

As a footnote, this has been the fourth time I have seen Wells play and they have all been draws – a sad statistic, I know, but what is worse is that I didn't need to look it up. I can remember it (and who they played) which, I guess, demonstrates the oddities of the human mind – at least mine, anyway!

## Saturday, September 11

The FA Cup resumes today and I am off down the A30 to watch what I think will be an intriguing tie between Peninsula outfit Bodmin Town and Wessex League leaders Poole Town.

In theory, this means a straight run down the dual carriageway and an hour's drive, but this afternoon doesn't prove to be as easy as that. First there is an accident the other side of Launceston, which sees me cunningly turn off down a side road I know to be the old road. This takes me to the other side of the incident. Then there is a hold-up at the end of the dual carriageway, where there is a short run of single road just before Bodmin, and this I circumnavigate by a lane that, as before, takes me past the problem. In the end I turn up about 40 minutes before the start, so my usual plan of allowing extra time pays off.

Mind you, I am at an age where I can remember when this would have taken twice as long to drive, as the A30 back then was undualled. It was a journey undertaken twice a week by my father, who worked for Crown Paints doing deliveries to Cornwall, and I went along with him. I can still recall the long, arduous run, although as a young lad I obviously didn't think that way at the time. It's certainly not a drive I would like to do these days, with so much more traffic on the roads than back then.

As you drive down towards the town Priory Park can be seen on the left, but to reach it you have to turn left at a roundabout, left again at some lights and through a car park to the end, where you pay at the gate. This takes you into the club parking, which looks over the pitch at one end.

# DIARY OF A SEASON

On a rainy day you can park facing the pitch as there is little in the way of cover here, the sole provider being the seated stand that dominates this venue. It has wooden bench-type seating on steep stepping and to the front of this is a tarmacked area giving limited cover and views that are obstructed by the dugouts. The remainder is open and railed off, with some hardstanding in the form of a mix of gravel and wood chippings.

There are four tall, thin floodlight pylons along each side, a couple of them far from perpendicular due to the battering they must take from the elements. The dressing rooms are sited under the stand with a refreshment kiosk to the rear, while the clubhouse is on the top side of the parking area.

You will probably not be shocked to hear that I have seen the home side play a few times, but that's not so in the case of Poole. My two visits to the Tatnam Ground have both been for Vase games, and the second was one that I had to watch from just outside the venue over the low perimeter fence.

This was because I brought my dog along in blissful ignorance of the club's 'no four-legged friend' rule – a stipulation of which I was only made aware after I had been let into the ground. I did not want to leave the dog in the car while it was dark, so my only option was to observe from the outer confines.

Rightly or wrongly, I told the officials what I was doing and they were OK about it, although in hindsight there was not much they could have done as it was a public walkway. In my defence, I did pay something so it wasn't a freebie as such, although it would have necessitated a revisit if I hadn't already been there.

There must be something about that part of the country, as I watched my first game at the Dell from the block of flats that overlooked Southampton's old home. I travelled up not knowing that it was an all-ticket game, which resulted in me knocking on doors pretending to be a home supporter in order to watch the action from up high. It didn't help that the jeans I was wearing had a couple of Arsenal patches on the back pockets but I got away with it, although I had to fake happiness as the home side won 2-0. At least it wasn't a wasted journey and, yes, I did go back there – many times.

As a follower of the Peninsula League, there is not much doubt about whom I want to win. There is also the prospect of a minor cup shock, which is always nice to see. When I acquire the line-ups there is a surprise as regular shot-stopper Kevin Miller is unavailable and Mike Searle – someone I confess I haven't heard of – takes his place. He makes a good start with a fine save in the opening minute, and after withstanding an early onslaught from the visitors, Bodmin open the scoring when Chris Luxton scrambles the ball home after Mark Berry's free kick isn't cleared.

Nearing half-time, things are looking promising, but it all changes in the final moments of the 45 when Poole bag a double to turn the tie on its head. Steve Richardson is left unmarked to score at the near post, then a moment of madness by Searle sees him completely miss a long through ball, allowing Steve Smith to run the ball into the unguarded goal.

Two minutes after the break it gets worse for the home debutant as he hesitates from a right corner kick, allowing Lamim Dibba to head in. Bodmin react well to these setbacks and, with a bit more luck, could so easily have got back into the tie, but Smith makes sure with Poole's fourth when a miscued shot falls for him to tap in from close range.

It was that manic period either side of the interval that did for the home side, but they can console themselves with the fact that they have competed well in a good contest overall.

# Tuesday, September 14

With no cup replays of personal interest to attend, I decide to undertake a long midweek jaunt to Oxfordshire and visit Kidlington's Yarnton Road, as they have a derby fixture against Old Woodstock in the Hellenic Premier Division. It certainly has the makings of a good contest as both sides are in form: the hosts have won six in a row while Woodstock are unbeaten in seven.

Of course, the problem with this kind of trip is that I must negotiate rush-hour traffic, but I plan sufficiently to avoid the worst of it. Thus I arrive in ample time at a place to the north-west of Oxford and a short drive from the A34. There is not a great deal of parking to be had here, but there's more than enough to accommodate tonight's crowd.

Access to the ground is attained the other side of a combination of clubhouse and changing rooms. To your left as you go in is a covered standing enclosure, while down the right-hand side as you look is a plastic-seated stand of similar ilk. The remainder of the pitch perimeter is open hardstanding that is railed off, and there are three floodlight pylons on each side.

The dugouts are placed either side of halfway on the open side and the far end has a line of tall trees that extends down the stand side, separating the ground from the road. It's a nice setting in which to watch football.

Unlike the hosts, Woodstock do not play at their New Road ground as it doesn't meet the Premier ground standards, so they ground-share with North Leigh. This was the reason they were able to gain promotion and, for me, that cannot be right. From what I gather, there is no chance of their own home being upgraded – if that were being done in the future, it would be fine. That's not what is happening here, though. If we were to apply this ruling to everyone, what could stop other clubs doing likewise and us ending up with a ton of ground-sharers, making a nonsense of it all?

I'm all for clubs progressing, but you've got to have your own ground to play on, for goodness sake. I accept there are instances that make sharing all right, but it seems unfair on the clubs that want to go up but cannot do anything about it. Like it or not, I feel you must have the ground in place or have plans set down for you to go up, or else you must stay where you are.

I realise, of course, how easy it is to make these comments as an outsider, but let us make a comparison with a non-football-related subject. If I want to upgrade my car to, say, a Ferrari, I can go one of two ways: first, by buying one and burdening myself with a sizeable debt; second, leasing one – costly in the long run but in theory making me look impressive. Woodstock and others have taken the second option, when what I believe they should be doing is keeping what they have until they are in a position to move up. Nothing personal, I just think that is the way it should be.

Kidlington play in green, but there's nothing sickly about their showing as they play decent football against more direct opponents who are strong at the back. This ultimately leads to them working the home custodian more, and five minutes before the break they go ahead when the ball ricochets to Ryan Brooks on the right and his shot goes in off the far post.

Into the second half, the hosts level out of nowhere, but what a super 30-yard hit it is from Andy Styles, whose shot arcs over the keeper and into the top left corner – Kidlington's first shot on target! Eight minutes later, though, Woodstock get what proves to be the winning goal as Luke Ingram curls in a sublime effort from the left edge of the box. Late pressure from the home side, including a succession of corners, proves to be in vain and, to be honest, an away win is a fair outcome.

It has been a fascinating contest and as a complete package this has been a good visit. I had heard good things about this place and sometimes this can be misleading, but not so here. If you have not been, I recommend you do so.

# Saturday, September 18

Having ground-shared at Windsor for a season or two, Bedfont have returned home, so to speak. They did play at Western Avenue on the A40 before going up into the Southern League, hence their move to Stag Meadow. Presumably they had it in mind to go to Hatton Road, and they have changed the second part of their name from Green to Town.

They were a Combined Counties League side before being promoted into the Southern Midland, now Central, Division. This is one of two feeders for the Premier Division, the other being the South and West. Does anyone know why it is called the Central? I suppose it is better than Midland, but not much. Along with other teams in this division, such as Ashford and Uxbridge, you can hardly say Bedfont are centrally based. For me, a simple solution would be to call it North and East – surely that makes sense – but I guess that would be asking too much.

Most people travelling up to the London area go via the M5 and M4, but I always travel cross-country as it's not a bad run and is shorter. Today, though, I have no realistic alternative as, shortly after departure, I see a warning sign indicating a closure on a section of the M4, which doesn't bode well.

My fears are soon proved correct as every Tom, Dick and Harry is going my way as a result, so congestion is the order of the day. Just as well I've allowed my usual extra time for something like this, but more is to come. An accident on the M3 and queueing means exiting and picking up the A30 to head straight to the ground. More queueing near Egham and lengthy delays put me in a state of panic, as I will miss kick-off for sure now. Nothing else to do but turn back and dive down some side roads and drive around the problem – a tactic that pays off.

The dramas are not yet over, though, as near my destination I check with a passer-by that I am on the right road. In the process I wind down my electric passenger window, only for it to malfunction in my attempt to wind it up again! Parked in the club car park with five minutes to spare, I get the window up to leave a tiny gap as that's the best I can do. All in all, I think I can say this has been anything but an average journey.

You enter the Orchard ground in one corner, with the clubhouse directly to your left and the changing rooms on the far side of this building. On halfway there are small, seated stands on each side, while there is standing cover at both ends. At the far end this is in the form of two structures side by side, whereas the near end version is a narrow strip. The medium-sized lights are located in each corner of what is a perfectly acceptable venue, much better than I thought it would be.

Soham Town Rangers might not have come as far as I have, but it's still quite a journey down from a place sadly more renowned for the brutal murder of two girls a while back than for football. Their club name is unusual – you'd think it would be either Town or Rangers but not both together. I have yet to go to their Julius Martin Lane headquarters and, to be honest, don't relish the long drive to get there – an issue I have with a lot of grounds that I would not mind doing but keep putting off. If I want to complete the Southern League, I'm going to have to go there some time soon. We'll see.

It's the away side who attack from the off and they come oh, so close to netting in the first minute, but with their first real attack it's Bedfont who notch the game's opening goal from the penalty spot. In fact it's double trouble for Soham, as not only does Leon Jarnie score but centre-half Joe Stroud is harshly red-carded for committing the offence. On the stroke of half-time, the debut man bags his second with a cool right-footed finish from 15 yards.

At the interval the visitors make a substitution that changes the game, as Kieran Napier is a major threat with his industry. He is rewarded when he curls a beauty around the keeper into the right corner from the edge of the box.

The last 10 minutes are open, with Soham leaving gaps at the back in an attempt to force a leveller, giving the home side plenty of chances to finish things off, but no more goals are forthcoming. This game has been quite good, especially as these sides were occupying the bottom two spots in an albeit 'too early to tell' table.

Homeward bound, then, and an uneventful drive back – not! Driving down the dual carriageway, I spot a stray dog on the side of the road. I slow, but all of a sudden it leaps out in front of me, barking away, and I can't help but hit him. Being the owner of a dog myself, I have the instant thought that I have killed or maimed him, but a quick glance to my left and there he is, still yapping away before running off behind.

I drive on, thinking I have got off scot-free, but after my petrol stop at Ilminster I return to my vehicle and notice something hanging down behind the bumper – a loose panel – and on closer inspection the bumper is broken. Aaargh! Thankfully, a mechanic pal of mine is able to fix it the following day, so that's a relief. This has been one of my more unforgettable footballing days.

# Friday, September 24

Since its formation in 2007, the Peninsula League's cup competition has been known as the Throgmorton Cup. Cullompton's Speeds Meadow home hosted the final last season, and it is here this evening that the competition starts afresh with a first round encounter between the hosts and Royal Marines. Martin, whom I haven't seen for a while, is attending and I'll see him there – Cully is about halfway between our homes, so that makes sense.

That final – won by Buckland after extra time – was the 11th consecutive one I have seen, going back to 2000 when Exeter Civil Service shocked Stoke Gabriel, winning on penalties after 120 minutes of goalless action.

Before the forming of the Peninsula, the Throgmorton would have been called the Devon League Cup if not for a local businessman called Carl Throgmorton. He and his wife Valerie have been sponsoring this cup for nearly 20 years now, and there is no doubt that their generosity has been a boost to the local league scene. Seen regularly at league games, they never demand special treatment and it's a pity there are not more around like them. Needless to say, they are here tonight.

Cullompton have ambitions of getting into the Western League alongside their neighbours Willand, and it would be nice if these local derbies were to return. They had some interesting clashes in the Devon League, although the one I seem to recall best is one that was played on an extremely wet pitch, and would have been called off but for it being the groundhop game.

If they do get to the Western League it will be just as much down to their long-serving secretary, Marcus Scott, as the players. In my view, Marcus is one of those people who, if you cut him in half, would have Cullompton written through him like a stick of rock. Of course there will be others here who keep the club running, but it would not be the same without him. I do feel, though, that his club's idea of going up, while a good one, is probably an unlikely scenario, but only time will tell.

The construction of a new changing room complex has taken Cullompton in the right direction in terms of promotion, anyway. You enter through a gate from the car-parking area behind the goal, and it is ahead of you to the right, next to the existing building that holds the clubhouse and refreshment facilities. The impressive new building is a light-coloured, wooden structure.

Another change is within the small, covered enclosure at the midway point on the opposite side, which now has plastic seating. Open hardstanding leads around to this, with a similar version running along the clubhouse side. Along here we have the bricked dugouts, which sit either side of the halfway line.

Beyond the seats is a grassy area that extends around the far end, where a small ditch runs along the back, and along the near side to the clubhouse. This has a raised patio-style area in front, with a wheelchair-accessible ramp leading up and a sliding door providing a secondary entrance. A fir tree line runs behind the stand, continuing around to the near end and up to the entry point.

Cullompton have the standard four floodlight poles on each side that can just about be seen from the nearby M5 motorway, with the national rail line between the two. Barring a gap down the far end of the near side, the pitch has a single railed perimeter, while the playing area is susceptible to the weather – the club tend to have a few games called off here, although thankfully that is not an issue tonight.

The game starts well and Dan Boere opens the scoring for Marines with a far-post header, only for opposing skipper Brett Worbey to level matters with a low strike from 20 yards. Just before the break, the away side restore their advantage when a cross from the right breaks to Lloyd Gardner, who rifles the ball into the bottom right corner.

Twelve minutes into the second half, Cully are back on terms when a blatant handball gives Worbey his second goal from the spot, but on 72 the visitors take the lead for the third time when Martin Finneron's right centre is tapped in by Boere. The home side are unable to respond in kind and are ambushed near the end as Shea Saunders scores from a break, clipping the ball over keeper Moore and in. Six goals, then, in a decent match, and one that has proved well worth attending.

# Saturday, September 25

Oh dear, it has been all of three weeks since I went to a Somerset County League game, so I must be having withdrawal symptoms. No better way to counter them than to get in another new ground that involves a small amount of driving.

To be honest, I am still a little wary of my car after what happened last week, and despite being told there is nothing to concern myself about, I am not so sure. Anyway, I am off up to Bishops Lydeard for what will be my sixth new ground for the season in this league already. And I only started doing games in the Somerset County seven months ago.

The logical route for me to take is via Taunton, which is a trouble-free run done in less than an hour. I get there bang on three o'clock. Kick-off time? Not quite; this game doesn't begin for another hour, due to a reserve cup tie that started at two, so I watch the second half of this game and indeed see a few goals as the away side book a place in the next round.

I am at a loss to work out why, at this early stage of the season, there is a need to double up today. After all, there's hardly a fixture backlog, but it is what it is and

I am certainly not concerned. For the record, I *was* aware about this arrangement beforehand and, on a sunny day, I thought I'd get to see a little extra footy for my money, although I will not count it as a game seen: (a) because I only saw the second half, and (b) because of my rule about seeing reserve teams – hence my deliberate non- attendance of the first 45 minutes.

Darby Way is situated to the north of the village and is quite a way out from the centre – much further than I estimated it to be. Parking is behind the goal at a lower level next to the road and there is a tree line in between. The far end, with its foliage and no perimeter railing, is similar. Both sides do have this, though, with one side open and the other having a modern-style clubhouse/changing room building, and it is the area along here that has the only hardstanding. No lights, of course, but this is a good set-up in a nice location with hills in the background.

While I like what I see off the pitch, the same cannot be said of the first half of the game. After having impressed when I saw them not that long ago, today's visitors, Cheddar, are seemingly off colour. The little quality they do show is countered easily by the hosts, who show resilience in a half without goals.

Approaching the hour, Paul Marquiss gets the ball into the box from an acute angle on the right and Ryan Hawkins is on hand at the far post to score with a looping header. Given that, on paper, the away side are the better team, I expect them to build on their lead, but having seen Lydeard's first-half display I should have known better. And so it proves as they find an equaliser with Kirk Poulson's fine strike. Amazingly, they win it in stoppage time when the right winger is tripped in the area, allowing Matt Fowler to thump home the penalty.

An unexpected home win, then, from what has been a competitive game that, once again, I have watched without paying. One and a half times zero is still zero, so game value isn't applicable, and with a good crowd here it's an avenue of revenue that is yet again unexplored.

Still, it makes for a cheaper day out for me and at the end of it, unlike today's visitors, I'm not cheesed off about that whatsoever!

# Tuesday, September 28

Last season I tried my first taste of Midland Alliance footy when I went to Alvechurch, mainly on the grounds that they are an ex-Southern League club who still play at their Lye Meadow home. It has to be said that it was something of an uninspiring contest and certainly didn't make me want to rush back and watch more matches in this league. Reasoning that I could just have been unlucky that day leads me to try once again this evening as I venture up to see Studley play Malvern in the hope that it will be better this time.

The Beehive is sited just off the A435 trunk road between Evesham and Birmingham, and is to the north of the village. I had been past it several times in the past on my way to other sporting events or for work, so guessed it was about time I actually saw a game there. This is one of several examples of football venues that you pass by on main routes – Walsall being a classic example – and I try to make a point of actually seeing a game there if possible although, without meaning to brag, it seems that nowadays this is a rare occurrence.

However, there is one that is really bugging me, and that's Motherwell. Fir Park's lights can be seen from the motorway and the rail line passes nearby, but despite my having passed several times I have not, as yet, done a Scottish Premier League game there. Needless to say, the 900-mile round trip by car is a tad off-putting and that, along with the fact that I no longer get up that way through work, means that it is one that may elude me – who knows?

One thing I can definitely say is that passing a football ground does not mean I absolutely must see a game there, unlike a friend of mine in Plymouth who sees this as a given. I have enough grounds still to visit without bringing in that stipulation, but I can hardly criticise him for what he does – after all, he is a Plymothian, and he can't help that either!

Unlike 10 days ago, it is an uneventful drive up and I arrive half an hour before kick-off. I park up behind an impressive complex that, among other things, holds the clubhouse and changing rooms, with entry to the ground being next to this.

To be frank, I'm a little disappointed with what I find within. There is a box-shaped stand, with a mix of plastic and wooden bench seating, immediately to your left. The rows of seats are on a level, which is rather odd. I later try to watch the game from the rearmost ones, only to find my view obstructed by the people sitting in front, so no surprise that no one is there during the action. The trouble is that this is the only cover available here, so when it rains you either get wet or watch in the dry from a poor position. Luckily, it's fine this evening, so you can stand in the open hardstanding areas behind either goal or in front of the clubhouse.

The opposite side is a thin, grassy strip behind a metal rail that surrounds the pitch, and there is an artificial playing area to the other side. The dugouts are along here as well, while floodlighting is provided by four low-level, old-style pylons on each side.

Early indications are not good as the game progresses, with Malvern edging a scrappy first half that ends without a goal. The visitors have had three really good chances but demonstrate why they have only netted three times so far this season.

Studley have never looked like scoring, but on resumption appear to wake from their slumbers, and break the deadlock on 63. It needs a stroke of luck, though, as Jake Edwards strikes an effort that takes a hefty deflection before nestling in the right corner of the net. Seven minutes later, Jamie Bailey provides a fine finish to a passing move that belies what has preceded it as he curls his shot into the top right corner.

Leon Blake comes perilously close to adding a third for the hosts near the end, but at the final whistle I feel not only relief that this game has not ended goalless but also a tinge of sympathy for Malvern who, while not world-beaters, have been beaten by a bit of luck and the one piece of quality the home side has conjured up all night.

While it has been a competitive encounter, it wasn't exactly awe-inspiring, and

I can only look to the positives and believe that at my next Midland Alliance game it will be third time lucky! It won't be here, though, as this will definitely be my one and only visit.

# Wednesday, September 29

I am getting my car serviced today, and it's being done by the pal who helped to patch it up after that little incident a week and a half ago. He always does a good job and doesn't charge a small fortune, unlike car dealerships. Perhaps not surprisingly, he gets a lot of work and will sometimes have several jobs to do in a day. Today is obviously one of those as, despite him picking my car up early in the morning, I have still not got it back by teatime. It's not looking good for my evening excursion to Budleigh. With the strong possibility of having no means of transport, I ring Martin, who is going, and ask for a lift. Even though this means him going out of his way, he has no gripes, which is typical of the good friend that he is.

Having just avoided the rush-hour traffic, it's a straightforward journey down to the east Devon coast – or at least it should be. About halfway there, one of the tyres on Martin's car develops a puncture, so we have to stop. Martin is going to call the AA out; apparently he can't change the tyre. Cue Mr Coolness-Personified as yours truly steps in, gets the wheel off and puts the spare on. It does seem to take a while as this is something I have not had to do that often, but a man's gotta do what a man's gotta do and we are away once more to our destination.

Apart from running into stray dogs, I like to think that my driving history is quite good given the thousands of miles I have driven over the years. I have been involved in a couple of nasty accidents, the most memorable when I was T-boned by a car in Aylesbury.

As I write this, my mind goes back to that day. It was going badly enough even before this moron smashed into the side of my SEAT, thanks to a series of postponements, although I am relieved to say the impact was on the rear door. Minding my own business, then BANG! – that sickening sound as my car lifted and came down.

Close to the ground and with not long to go to kick-off, I quickly exchanged details, naively thinking it to be a cut and dried case with him at fault. Unfortunately, he was a local and knew there was a small layby next to where our collision occurred (or I assume there was – I've no idea), so he came up with the notion that I had pulled out of this layby. With no witnesses, this resulted in a 50-50 claim and me having to pay out a large insurance excess.

This is the one time I wish I had not been on my own, although I now realise I should have tried to get hold of a passer-by going to the game, or called the police. Having made wasted trips to Marlow, Windsor and Thame beforehand, I did not want to miss out on seeing that game, and my football addiction ultimately cost me dear. Lesson learned, but hopefully it's not one I will ever have to call on.

We arrive at Greenway Lane about 10 minutes late. I, of course, have to go and get washed as I am a bit on the dirty side after my heroic deed! At least we haven't missed any goals, but it's not long before one arrives.

Axminster are the visitors and it's they who score when a corner on the left is not cleared, allowing Jamie Barfoot to bundle the ball in. The home side respond well but are unable to break down a unusually solid back line, and at the interval this Peninsula League game is delicately poised.

I take a stroll around the pitch perimeter. The ground is reasonable enough, with a small seated stand on halfway and open hardstanding leading to it from the car park end, where you enter next to the clubhouse on the left and the changing rooms, with a gabled roof, to the right. This used to be on halfway before the pitch was rotated, enabling floodlights to be erected down the sides. Beside the dressing rooms is a small standing area with a single step, while the remaining parts are open and railed with the exception of the far end, which is tree-lined and has netting in between.

We get under way again and Budleigh level in the 58th minute when Adam Clark's 20-yarder is mishit into the ground but evades the keeper with a wicked bounce. The away side are not long in restoring their advantage, though, Ben Vine breaking free on the left and shooting under the keeper. Back come the home side three minutes later, Khaled Badani rounding Higgs before tapping in. A frantic half sees the game settled in added time thanks to Badani once more, firing in from the edge of the box after the ball breaks out to him from a scramble that sees the first two efforts on goal blocked.

The final whistle comes not long after and you have to feel sorry for Axminster, who have deserved a share of the spoils. Afterwards it's a slow but incident-free run back on a night that has been, shall we say, different!

## Saturday, October 2

Today is FA Vase first round day, so I take the opportunity to get in another ground that I have yet to visit and pick off a Hellenic League venue. I am not doing too badly in the Premier and West divisions but am short in numbers for the East.

This is yet another instance of my taking to this level of football at a late stage and, having missed out on most of the hop games, I have given myself a lot of unnecessary travelling. I did make up some ground in the previous two seasons by doing some of the designated matches on the hop – the most productive day being the Cricklade/Newbury/Ascot treble – but the fact is I still have much to do.

Binfield is my destination for what looks an intriguing encounter with Hillingdon Borough, a South Midlands League side these days. When I went there, not that long ago, they were in the Southern League, although I went for an FA Trophy game. It's a venue that, to be fair, has seen better days but there are a few

# DIARY OF A SEASON

stadiums like that around now. What with the current financial climate, one can hardly ask them to go massively in debt to make changes that you could argue weren't essential anyway. Their Breakspear Road headquarters are far from the worst I have been to, that's for sure.

Finding the village, to the north of Bracknell, is easy enough, but Hill Farm Lane is not a venue that can be spotted from the main road. Not being in the built-up area means you head out north and look out for the right turn indicated by the road name. This is a short, winding trail down to the ground. My research prior to departure means it is simple enough, but I know of at least one person who has not been as successful, and I believe a small sign opposite the turn indicating that the football club is down the lane would be helpful. It's just a thought.

I arrive and park up about an hour before the action begins, and spend some time in the clubhouse that sits behind the goal at this end and holds the changing rooms too. There's a small bunch of away fans here already, so I take time out to have a chat with them. They seem optimistic about their chances this afternoon and agree that a close contest is in store. Both sides have made reasonable starts to their league campaigns, so there is no reason to doubt this.

Soon it is time to pay my entry fee and acquire a programme. These FA-run competitions usually mean a slight increase in admission prices – a ruling I have never quite got my head around. Whether that applies today I do not know, having not been here before.

No matter; I enter next to the clubhouse that sits on top of a grass bank, with hardstanding to the fore running alongside to the left and behind the far goal. That side has an open expanse beyond the railing with a hedgerow down the end. The right side has a 100-seater stand near midway and the dugouts either side of this. There are three floodlight poles on each side.

Binfield get off to a flying start when Tim Walsh runs down the left and squares the ball to James Suarez, who sweeps it in off the right post, and the same player goes close minutes later with an angled drive. Approaching the half-hour mark, Danny Wing puts Ian Davies in on the left and he slips the ball under the onrushing keeper to double his side's lead – and that's how it remains at the midway point.

Early in the second period, Walsh is through on goal only to be hauled down unceremoniously by Peter Lyall, who is rightly red-carded. Although the free kick goes wide, respite is brief as Davies slots home his second, finding space at the far post to meet a cross from the left. It looks all over, but on 81 the visitors get one back when Ethan Hughes manages to find room behind the back four and score with a shot on the turn that zips into the net.

As the game is about to go into injury time he gets another as he blasts in from close range after a cross from the right is knocked into his path. Suddenly, from being in command the hosts are a shade flustered, almost conceding again but holding on for the win.

A match, then, that has lived up to its billing (not that it had one as such) and played in a nice setting. Well worth a visit here, as long as you can find it!

# Tuesday, October 5

Sometimes I get days when attending a game just feels right, even though I am not really sure why. That certainly can be said for my choice of match this evening as I make the short journey down to sunny Dawlish for their Western League game against Barnstaple.

Of course, the sun is not out tonight, although it has been a fine day, but rain or shine I admit this is not a drive I relish much, as the latter part of the run is tied down by speed limits that, while understandable in parts, are puzzling in others. Things aren't helped when I get stuck for a bit behind the slowest bus driver in the county, but it's no problem as my policy of giving myself extra time gets me there without any need for panic.

As this is a midweek game I am able to park in the car park next to the clubhouse, across the road from the ground. A word of warning though: if you go there on a Saturday, you have to pay. Having made many visits before last year with no payment required, I parked there for a Vase game only to return to find a ticket on my windscreen as a result of not paying the required fee. I was in the part used for the club's parking, so it was a little odd. With assistance from the secretary, I appealed against the fine and won – which was a relief as I would never have parked illegally. Another lesson learned.

Sandy Lane is one of those venues I visited for the first time for a turn-on-of-floodlight game, and while most of it has stayed the same, it is a lot better now they have made improvements. Hardstanding now runs along the far side, where the dugouts are, and at the sea end, meaning it is like that all around. These, plus the far end, are uncovered with a grass banking on the dugout side and a wire fence at the top. With a playing field beyond it was simple to watch for free from here, but the club have done something to stop this by filling it in with sheeting.

You enter on the near side, with the dressing rooms the other side of a small hospitality area to your left, while there is some cover to your right in front of the refreshment kiosk. Further down there is now a seated stand which, overall, provides a lot more cover than there used to be – that being virtually none.

I recall coming here on a wet and windy night and huddling under a brolly for a Vase game that was abandoned with 20 minutes to go and the home side 5-0 up. You can imagine how annoyed Dawlish were about that decision, but at least they won the restaging, so justice was done. In fairness, this happened during a period between the stand being built and the loss of the old wooden version that burned down and, due to lack of funding, was not replaced for a little while.

Dawlish were once beaten 18-0 in a Western League game at Clevedon. I recount this as on that day I was watching a goalless draw not that far away at Ashton Gate – not exactly one of my better choices. Just to make the day complete, I then went on to Swindon to watch speedway that evening, only to find it called off as I arrived!

In more recent times it was nice to see Dawlish win two cup finals in a week or so at the back end of a campaign that also saw them finish high in the league.

Having witnessed both of those games, I have to say they were deserved wins.

I've seen some good openings to games recently, but tonight that is far from being so. Stan Paxton provides us with the first shot on goal, but what a cracker it is – a 30-yard curling strike into the top right corner to give Barum the lead. The hosts react by hitting the woodwork twice and missing two other gilt-edged chances before the break.

Ten minutes into the second half they find the net when Dean Stevens runs forward with the ball and, unchallenged, strikes it low into the bottom left corner from 25 yards. Suddenly it's end-to-end stuff and, while there is no further scoring, it turns out to be a decent game with a draw leaving the away side feeling happier than the homesters, I think.

As to the question of whether my instinct to come here was correct, well, I'm not sure, but I feel happy enough with what I have seen.

# Friday, October 8

I hate goalless draws, and it doesn't matter whether they are good games or bad As far as my thinking is concerned, 0-0 is exactly what it is – a game in which no one has scored.

It's something that crept up on me in the 80s and I wish it hadn't, as without doubt it has spoilt my enjoyment of certain matches and ultimately clouded my judgment of how good or bad a game actually is. I'm not so bad these days, but I still have this bugbear when it comes to seeing no-score draws at grounds I am visiting for the first time. This is because I feel that having not seen a goal I must revisit and, as a result, have made return trips I could have done without. After all, in effect that means a wasted day as I could be doing a new ground instead.

The worst instance I have had of this was a visit to the Edinburgh derby. It was a good match but no goals meant going back to fulfil that self-imposed obligation. Then there was my Serie A trip to Lazio in which the only goal came in the 85th minute – phew, that was close! While returning to Rome could be described as not all bad, it would have put my ruling to the test for sure, and it is unlikely that I would have gone back.

In March, Martin and I went to Wantage. Despite both sides hitting the woodwork there were no goals, so we're going back this evening hoping for better luck. My companion doesn't have the same hang-ups as me but still feels the need to return. As it is a Friday with no other realistic alternatives, it makes for a good opportunity to get the ground done once and for all, and we get there in good time.

Alfredian Park is to the south of the town and just off the main road in from the M4. You go down a narrow lane and straight on into a tarmacked car park behind the goal with a large clubhouse to the rear. Parking is available down the near side, which has open hardstanding and dugouts on halfway. This continues around an open far end and down in front of a covered area, a combination of mostly seating and some standing which runs along most of this side. Floodlighting comes from your standard Hellenic side-located pylons.

Oxford City Nomads are in town this evening – a nice name but not as good as the Quarry Nomads they were once called. I guess it gives them a sense of identification, seeing as their home games are played at Oxford City's ground just off the northern section of the bypass. One thing I did check on beforehand was if they were a reserve team; if so I would not have come here. As I have already stated, I do not like watching reserve sides, but at least if my facts are wrong I can fall back on the first game here when it was a first team.

Looking in the programme, the visitors' tendency to let goals in was a good sign that we should avoid the dreaded 0-0, but it wasn't a given – it never is. Midway through the opening half, the away side unveils a unexpected tactic by getting one of their players sent off for a blatant off-the-ball kick at a Wantage player! Four minutes from the break it pays off when Felipe Barcelos is fouled in the area and Ben Moses sends the keeper the wrong way from the spot.

At half time we have a celebration cup of tea at having seen a goal, mixed with the possibility of the home side doing something in the second period, and as soon as the game restarts it is evident that the hosts have been given a stern lecture. They look more purposeful, and inside six minutes they level when a free kick on the right is headed in by Tony Rowe. After hitting the crossbar, prolific marksman Richard Claydon gets on the scoresheet with a penalty after a foul on John McMahon.

In an attempt to get something from the game the Nomads push players forward, but in the final attack, home midfielder Graham Edney goes down the left then ignores shouts to take it to the corner flag, instead going inside and cracking a low right-footer inside the near post. Four goals, then, in what can be described as a game of two halves.

On the way back we reflect on a good night, but it's not over yet. Just past the Burnham turn on the M5, we come to a stop because there has been a bad accident. Early indications are that we'll be there quite some time but, unlike what happened to me on the M6, the police instruct us to turn and drive the mile or so back to the junction before – in the wrong direction! An eventful end to a trip I'm glad I have made.

# Saturday, October 9

Devon Premier Cup time, and the second round sees the first involvement of Peninsula clubs. This gives me the opportunity to get a Devon & Exeter League ground done as I prefer not to watch games at this level. Three years ago I did a game in this league at St Martins, a ground close to where I live, but I didn't enjoy it and have not felt the need to do more.

This cup gives me the chance to circumnavigate that problem, although some might say it's a cheap way of getting in a new ground for my season. Either way, it's Hatherleigh I am visiting this afternoon as they play Axminster. This has the makings of a cup upset given that the Peninsula outfit are struggling in the league, but for once I am not siding with the underdog as I have my Peninsula-supporting hat on for this one. Who cares if the name of the road I live in is that of this market town? I'm sticking to my guns. Come on the Minstermen!

Sited beside the main road southbound towards Okehampton, this ground is one that will not tax my navigational skills. It is accessed by a short, narrow passage through a set of gates into the parking area alongside the pitch.

Down in the corner to your left is a small clubhouse-cum-refreshment facility with the changing rooms at each end of the building. The playing area is railed off, with the dugouts on the other side to the parking that has the only means of firm standing here. There is no cover and, as I expected, no programme. I thought they might issue a team sheet and charge a nominal amount, given that higher-league visitors are in town, but there we are.

In fact it turns into a struggle to get the hosts' line-up, not helped by the home secretary being absent – probably having lunch with the Prime Minister! Hatherleigh's version shows up minutes from the scheduled start, and delays it as she seems to be the only one capable of filling out the sheet they must give to the referee before we can get under way. This is not a requirement for D&E games, so it is understandable to a degree, but surely someone else could have done it.

Extra time and penalties are in prospect if the game cannot be decided in the 90, as is the vogue in cup competitions these days. I get the reasoning behind it as far as early cup rounds are concerned, but I am totally against penalty kicks deciding finals. How, for instance, can you claim to be World Cup winners on the basis of a lottery shoot-out? Then there are the Football League play-offs, where you can slog through 49 and a bit games and lose out the same way.

I think a better solution is out there and, while it's not foolproof, I may have one. Surprisingly, it comes from the States, where I believe they still use it to decide drawn games – not that I want to see that. Instead of one shot from 12 yards, why not ask a player to take the ball from a spot near halfway and try to score past the keeper in a certain amount of time? Surely this is better; there is a skill element involved – not just plonking the ball down and hitting it – and it's still dramatic. Anyway that's what I think, although if I had my way we would go back to the old-fashioned method of replays.

Look at other sports. Can you imagine the golf Open being decided on a putt-off, or Wimbledon men's singles tennis honours going to the winner of a best-of-five-who-hits-the-most-aces contest? I think not.

Under way at last, and at games like this you can pick up what the players are shouting. From this it is evident that our late-arriving secretary has put down the line-up randomly, so I confirm the correct numbers with the home side's physio. At least it gives me something to do, with nothing much going on pitch-wise as the homesters fight to contain their opponents.

Ironically, it is during Hatherleigh's best spell of pressure that they fall behind; Ben Vine finding space on the right and netting with an angled drive. On the stroke of half-time, Jon Hurford chips a second, giving the hosts much to do. Try as they might, they cannot break their duck, and when Joel Seward beats the offside trap and slides home Axminster's third, it's over.

Near the end, Ben Turner also finds himself through on goal and he, too, converts in-off the post to round off a comfortable win for the Peninsula side (actually called the Tigers!), who have shown why they are a division above their opponents.

# Wednesday, October 13

Having watched the newly-formed Merthyr Town two months ago, it is time to see them in a home game and recomplete my set of Western League grounds.

In fact you could say that I have already done this, as the Martyrs are not playing their home matches at Pennydarren Park for now. They plan to go back some time in the future, but in the meantime they are ground-sharing at the home of Welsh League Taffs Well, which lies between Cardiff and Merthyr. I have been to the ground that they will soon be returning to but not their temporary residence, so a midweek game is a chance to tick off another new ground.

Martin has been here before to see the landlords in action, but the good news is that not only does he want to go tonight but he has volunteered to drive, which is handy as he will know the way to this venue from off the A470. We get there about an hour beforehand, and with limited parking at the ground we find a spot nearby.

The quaintly named Rhiw Dair ground is, like Cullompton, one of those places sat next to the main carriageway, only for it to be accessed by a route that takes you the long way round before arriving on the doorstep. Having ascended from the road, you enter and find the clubhouse behind the goal and to your right. Down the left side is a seated stand, set well back from the pitch giving poor views. Elsewhere is open hardstanding with the dugouts directly opposite the stand either side of halfway. Four floodlight pylons are on each side.

We spend time in the clubhouse and encounter someone I know from times we've met in the past but cannot put a name to. The conversation gets on to the thorny subject of whether Welsh clubs should be allowed to play in the English pyramid – a topic about which I try to be as diplomatic as possible, even though he isn't Welsh.

I seem to recall that not that long ago the Welsh FA tried to force the Cardiffs and Swanseas to leave the Football League, something I could understand even if it was unworkable. In the case of the two clubs mentioned, it would have been calamitous, especially now that they have both moved into brand-new stadiums. Imagine the Bluebirds trying to sell tickets for a game against Aberystwyth – I cannot see them being inundated with enquiries about that one, somehow! The idea seems to have died a death now, and I think that is best all round.

Back in the present day, we kick off and to no one's surprise the home side make the early running. Almondsbury are the away team trying to thwart them while offering little up front. They have a game plan that, while not pretty to watch, is proving effective. It helps, of course, when the forwards fail to capitalise on the clear-cut chances that come their way. Four minutes from the break, however, resistance is broken when Craig Stiens turns and fires into the left corner from 10 yards out, giving Merthyr a lead that they hold on to without difficulty until the interval.

Time to grab a snack from the refreshment kiosk conveniently placed in the narrow entrance to the clubhouse! A mix of queueing amid others coming in and out results in utter chaos, which is not helped by the service being so slow. As a consequence, we just about make it back out for the resumption of the game – and I mean just.

Having finally broken through, I expect the hosts to build on their lead, but for some reason they are content to sit on a one-goal lead, giving us a lacklustre half only enlivened in the closing stages as Almondsbury find the confidence to go for an equaliser. They almost get it, but a couple of fine saves from the home custodian enable his side to complete a scrappy win.

If the key to success is triumphing in games in which you do not play well, then Merthyr seem to have found it, and I confidently predict this league fixture will not be replicated next season.

# Saturday, October 16

While the other night I went to a ground that is a temporary Western League venue, I look upon today's choice of game as a chance to go to a venue that used to host football at that level but no longer does.

The fact that I am a latecomer to the non-league scene means that I missed out on grounds like Clandown, for instance. My biggest *faux pas*, though, has undoubtedly been not going to Yeovil's old Huish ground – that defies belief, really. Still, not much I can do about it now. But I can mop up one or two that I missed out on, and with Ilminster at home to Minehead in a Somerset County League Cup tie, this is the perfect time to go.

This contest bears similarities to my cup game last week in that the hosts play a division below their Premier opposition, although they have another common link in that they are both ex-Western. In terms of travel from my place, there's a vast difference in that my journey here is a lot easier, and upon arrival I have no difficulty in locating it – unlike my first visit to Irnham Road, which is tucked away off the main road.

The Recreation Ground is to the south of town and has the whiff of a ground that has seen better days. There is a good-sized, wooden grandstand down one side, painted blue and with bench-type seating within. The dressing rooms are underneath and the players come out on the halfway line, while the clubhouse is beside this at the road end. A small covered enclosure, a more recent addition, is on the far side of the stand.

There is railing behind both goals with the far end and side being open, grassy areas that form the remainder of what is a public park. The near end has a tree line separating it from the road behind and a pathway with benches to sit on if you wish to watch the action from afar – not that there's any need to do this as the game can be viewed from close up without payment.

There's an earlier start time as the club have no lights and, with extra time and penalties a possibility, it's a no-brainer. At the half-time break I am thinking we'll need that as it's hardly an extravaganza! At least Ilminster look like they might score, and it is only thanks to the away keeper that they have failed to do so.

This pattern continues into the second half, this time the hosts hitting the woodwork and having a header cleared off the line. Minehead finally register a shot on goal with 15 minutes left, but an extra 30 seems inevitable. Thankfully, we are spared that when Chris Luke races on to a long ball that is misjudged by a centre-half, and applies the coup de grâce with a fine finish. Minehead do apply some pressure at the end but, quite frankly, they suffer the cup exit their efforts deserve.

To think this is the club that once finished second behind Wimbledon in the Southern League, the equivalent of what is now the Conference Premier. Those days are long gone, and if today is anything to go by they are a million miles from recreating those heady times.

I feel for the handful of their fans who have come down and encouraged their team with vocal support; it's these hardy souls that for me depict the real face of the game. Despite the disappointment of this mild cup shock, they will be back watching their beloved team next time even though they could so easily give up.

I must confess that I applaud such people as I can never see myself applying such devotion, especially now as I view every match I see through neutral eyes, even when my local team is involved. That is what groundhopping can do to you. Next game, please.

# Friday, October 22

Thanks to the league secretary, I'm able to get an extra game in tonight with a handful of Throgmorton Cup second round ties being brought forward from tomorrow. Of these I have chosen Saltash against Launceston, a match-up between two Premier outfits.

Another reason for going to Saltash is Martin, who has similar thoughts to mine, so I will give him a lift from my place. It's a straight run down the Devon expressway and just inside Cornwall on the other side of the Tamar bridge.

Saltash is one of those venues at which my first visit was a goalless one against Liskeard in the club's Western League days. They won that league before transferring to the South-Western, remaining there until becoming one of the founder members of the newly-formed Peninsula along with tonight's visitors.

I have been here a few times and seen a sizeable number of goals, although strangely one of the best games was an FA Cup tie last year against Gillingham (the non-league one) that finished 1-1 but was entertaining. Days later I went to the replay at Hardings Lane and both teams carried on from where they had left off, with the hosts nicking a late clincher in an 11-goal thriller that broke the Ashes' hearts.

Since joining the Peninsula, they have always been there or thereabouts in league and cup, but always end up falling just short. The same cannot be said of their goalscoring prowess; although I don't expect them to knock in many against a useful opponent this evening, they are more than capable of doing so on their day.

Kimberley Stadium hasn't changed that much over time. The main feature of this ground is a cantilevered seated stand on halfway and directly to your left as you go in. On the other side of the entrance is a clubhouse that is split into two levels, the second being the hospitality area. A door at that end leads out to an open patioed area located in the corner of the pitch and at this end there is a grass banking with hardstanding at the front.

The banking gradually shallows out along the far side past the dugouts and is uncovered; likewise the other end, which is a mix of stone and concrete standing running around to the stand. At the back of this seated area in the middle is the refreshment kiosk, with the changing rooms on the ends. This means that the players come out on to the field of play via some steps at different points – something you do not see that often. With the obligatory floodlight poles down each side, this is a reasonable enough ground.

Behind the goal at the grass bank end is a prefab perimeter that divides the ground from the area where I have parked tonight, but on my initial visit I made what I now see as a daft decision to park on the Devon side of the bridge, walking across and up the hill to the ground. This I did to save myself paying the toll on the return journey. I don't do that any more, despite it saving me a whole pound! Even if I did, I cannot imagine Martin would have been enthusiastic about what is a fair hike by foot. We will never know because, for once, common sense rules.

The referee is certainly keen to get this encounter under way, as he begins a tad earlier than 7.30. It makes me wonder if this is to become habitual as my last visit here saw the game start a couple of minutes early too.

The home side make the running in the first 15 minutes and score when Carlton Farnham's effort is blocked on the goal line only for Sam Hughes to turn in the loose ball. A superb save denies him another and the post is struck before Chris Wright exchanges passes with Hughes and fires a low shot into the right corner.

Being two down going into the second period, I expect Launceston to come out with the aim of getting themselves back into the match, but they do not look like getting one let alone two, and in the end it is only a brace of fine stops by keeper Scarry that keeps the scoreline respectable.

Indeed, the conclusion of this encounter feels so anti-climactic that it is a relief when the final whistle sounds. It brings to an end a low-key tie that sees Saltash ease into the next round without any trouble. I have seen some good cup matches in my time – it is safe to say this was not one of them.

# Saturday, October 23

In April I made the journey to a non-floodlit Hellenic game only to be held up, arriving 10 minutes late. I didn't miss anything relevant, but what I should have done was go to another match that started later, which would have least ensured that I see a game from start to finish. That alternative was a Premier game between Ardley and Fairford, and today presents me with the opportunity to watch this season's version of that encounter.

My drive up the motorway to Gloucester and across from there is somewhat less eventful than back then, even presenting me with an half-hour browse in Chipping Norton. Upon arrival in the village, I turn off the main road and head down into Fritwell Road, which according to my Hellenic guide is the address of the ground. It's not long before I am out in the countryside with no visible evidence of a football venue, so I double back and pop into a hostelry to ask where it is. Turns out it was just off the main highway on the right, through a wooden gate and on a different named road – all a bit annoying, but no matter.

I park up in the gravelled parking area. This is the first time I have seen Ardley, but I have seen the visitors at their Cinder Lane HQ, and what a match that was. It was an FA Vase game against Cullompton that saw the away side storm into a shock three-goal lead before the hosts forced extra time with a last gasp goal. Cully then struck 20 seconds into the extra period before Fairford restored parity and won on penalties, as neither club wanted to tackle a midweek replay. As I make the 200-yard walk up to this ground, I think of how great it would be if today's game were to replicate those levels of excitement.

Some venues have names that could not be more appropriate and, when you come across this ground for the first time, you will find it to be in this category. The Playing Field has a railed-off pitch and floodlight poles sited in each corner. It is open down the far end and especially on the near side, whereas the far side has hardstanding with a covered area that is three-quarters plastic seating and the rest standing.

Approaching the pitch at this end, you pass through a gate and down a path to a gable-roofed brick building – one that holds the dressing rooms and refreshment kiosk on the ground floor of a two-storey structure, with the top floor being the clubhouse with two dormer windows looking out over the playing area and beyond. This is without doubt the stand-out feature of this venue, which I think is overall quite pleasant.

The table-topping hosts are favourites to win and emphasise that by opening the scoring from a corner that is headed in off the underside of the bar by Danny Bone. Troy Bryan turns in number two from close range as the visitors fail to clear the ball in a goalmouth scramble. Only keeper Clatworthy is preventing the home side from running riot, but out of the blue Fairford break down the left and, thanks to a silly foul, win a penalty that James Skinner converts. From being in control the home side briefly panic, enabling Dan Bailey to score, only for his effort to be disallowed. At the break it is game on.

Time to sample the delights of the first-floor facilities. On a rainy day this is a good spot from which to watch the action below, especially with a pint in your hand. A cup of tea will have to do for me today as a passing shower clears in time for the restart.

Ten minutes into the second half, a slice of luck gives Ardley a two-goal lead once more, with Ian Concannon's 20-yard drive taking a big deflection off the centre-half – one that gives Clatworthy no chance – and on 71 the keeper is unlucky again as his excellent stop from Richmond's strike falls to Concannon, who taps in.

Fairford don't give up and bag a late consolation through Bailey, and the upright is also struck in the final throes of an entertaining Hellenic game – one that has turned out to be much closer than most reckoned on. Even the handful of visiting fans are happy enough with their team's performance, so it's smiles all round.

From my viewpoint, the visit has worked out well because that match back in April finished 1-1, meaning I picked the right one of the two. What with the welcome I have got here and the 90 minutes of fare, it is safe to say that my pre-match hopes have been fulfilled – once I got there that is – and I return home a happy hopper.

# Wednesday, October 27

With nothing on of any note locally, I resign myself to a week off. That is until Martin rides to the rescue with his offer of a lift to Tipton for their FA Cup replay against Northern Premier Division One side Sheffield FC – one that is gleefully accepted as it gives me the chance to do another Midland Alliance ground.

This is another instance of a first-time visit for me, while it's a return for Martin, so finding the ground, upon completing an incident-free drive up the M5, isn't a problem. There is a decent-sized car-parking area here, which is needed this evening as a large crowd turns up for what is a big game for the hosts. They have never reached the fourth qualifying round before, and it's an achievement that has certainly grabbed the locals' attention to such an extent that nearly 1,500 of them end up watching the game.

Isn't it amazing how these people appear from nowhere when this kind of match appears on the horizon? What do they do the rest of the time? No doubt some will be like the two of us and come as neutral observers, along with those who don't actually support Tipton but become fans on the night because they want them to win as representatives of the area, in this case the West Midlands.

That's fair enough, but the ones who annoy me are those who turn up at these games acting as if they are lifelong fans and have no qualms about slating the players or the club, even though they are hardly in a position to do so. Still, the positive aspect about games like this one tonight is the valuable revenue that will be generated, and I'm sure that will be most welcome.

Despite our relatively early arrival, we snatch one of the last parking spaces available and join the long queue entering about half an hour before the start. We look around for a programme seller but cannot find one, which could be something to do with the fact that they've sold out – aargh! Enquiries lead to the taking of names and addresses, a thoughtful gesture that means I will get one at a later date. Martin, though, must have conjured up a cunning plan, because he comes back with two programmes in his hand, along with the bonus of a team sheet. I knew he had his uses!

Now we have to find somewhere to stand, which isn't going to be easy tonight. If there's one type of ground I cannot stand, it is those where there is a running track between pitch and spectator areas. Sadly, this is one of those places, with metal fencing running around the edge of the track. There is a seated stand on the near side which, unsurprisingly, is full, while on the opposite side is a steep grass bank, from which we end up watching the game.

You are wasting your time behind either goal as the view is distant and, in the case of one end, next to impossible due to the metal cage that is used for the hammer event when they stage athletics meetings here. The floodlight poles are down the side and slightly obstruct views from where we are, but there is a panoramic vista from up top.

Games like this, with much at stake, can be cagey to begin but here it is end-to-end stuff that yields half-chances in what is becoming an absorbing contest. Twenty-four minutes in, Tipton open the goals account when Eric Bowen tries his luck from 25 yards and his shot deflects off Callum Harrison, looping over the keeper and in. The visitors finish the half in a flurry, with winger Matt Outram a constant thorn, but fail to take their chances.

After the break Ash Burbeary hits the bar but the hosts hold firm and seal it six minutes from time. Sergeant's incisive ball sends Danny Campbell away before he calmly draws keeper Whatsize and slots home. There is still time for Tipton to add to their tally, with Bowen dithering when through on goal and Ricky Baker rattling the bar in injury time, but at the final whistle there are celebrations all round after a fine win on a night I'm sure will be remembered by the locals for a while.

Pity they are away rather than at home to Carlisle next, but I'm sure they will have a great day out and certainly, given the distance, a long day! That's what the FA Cup is all about and what makes it the greatest cup competition in the world despite certain elements who seem determined to devalue it. What do they know? They should have been here this evening – I'm glad I was.

# Saturday, October 30

Just as groundhoppers have differing views on what constitutes a visit to a new ground, so the same must apply for the question of which venues you choose to go to.

Some do new visits off the cuff, randomly picking off grounds with no set plan. Personally, I regard a ground ticked off if I see a full game with a programme (if there is one) in my pocket and at least one goal seen. As for the other, well I do have a system by which I keep to certain leagues in the quest to do all the grounds in them. My main reason for this is that I do not have enough time to do all grounds from step seven upwards so, for the time being anyway, I focus on completing what leagues I have seen games in.

Today, then, will be a mini red letter day as I am scheduled to finish the Hellenic West Division grounds with a trip to Bicester to see them play league leaders Headington Amateurs. Martin has a free day as Taunton are without a game, so I pick him up on the way.

We encounter some delays in the Bristol area but still pull into the car park an hour before start time. Nothing for it, then, but to spend time in the clubhouse, where we grab a bite to eat and watch sport on the TV. Quite an old-fashioned establishment, it's sited behind the goal. Come entry time this building is to your left while the changing rooms are in a separate part to your right.

As part of his contribution to the petrol costs, Martin pays for me to get in and ends up paying senior citizen rates for the both of us. I know I'm getting on in years but I didn't think it I looked *that* old!

Looking around, I see a covered stand down one side and open hardstanding at our end and along the other side. That side really is open, with a rugby pitch running parallel, and from what I can see, you can get through here without paying – senior citizen or not. A stroll down to the far end finds the one side with no firm standing, and three floodlight poles are on each side.

This venue isn't as good as I thought it would be, seeing as Bicester were a Premier side last year, but at least they have lights, unlike most in this division. Headington is one of those non-floodlit venues but, as I found on my visit there, it has a pitch that guarantees you will see a game there on a rainy day.

When I went it was absolutely chucking it down and nearby Oxford City's was among many games called off, much to the chagrin of my companion on the day as he had come up to see the match that was due to be played there. I turned up at the Recreation Ground expecting it to be postponed but was amazed to find it was fine. In fact, I enquired about whether there were any doubts and in return got a quizzical look – as if there were any! No wasted trip, then, and nine goals to boot.

The people there were a friendly bunch, but the facilities are basic and that seems to typify grounds in this division and its eastern equivalent. The Peninsula Premier Division is supposed to be the same level, but in ground terms these are poles apart thanks to the fantastic progress being made by clubs in the South-West.

Shame they cannot do the same up here, but with things the way they are it's understandably unfeasible. Talk has been rife about the Hellenic in this respect, but where does the money come from to do it all? In an ideal world, all Hellenic grounds would have cover and lights, but this is the real world, so let's just get on with it.

That is what the visitors do from the off, and their positive start brings dividends in the 11th minute when a cross from the left is met by a diving header by Luke Cuff at the far post. They continue to impress but fail to add to the score despite hitting the post through Jay Hill's strike just after the break.

Just past the midway point of the second half, a trip in the box enables Neil Lockhart to send the keeper the wrong way from the spot and double the lead. The hosts' James Kyberd is booked after conceding that penalty, with another yellow and thus a red following shortly afterwards – a passage that sums up Bicester's day. They rally a little near the end but there is never any danger of Headington losing their 100 per cent record in this game, which, nonetheless, has been quite competitive and good to watch. It would have been nice if we had seen more goals, but there we are. For me it's ground ticked, division complete, job done.

# Wednesday, November 3

It's raining again. Oh no, my world's at an end. OK, so the second line of that Supertramp song is rather over the top, but yesterday's downpours put an end to my prospects of seeing a game last night.

Today, however, is a bit better on the weather front, so the prospects of a fun-filled, action-packed night out are looking good. I might go to a game instead, though!

Pondering my options, I get a text from Martin and decide to liaise with him in Taunton for tonight's bill of fare. Of course, first I have to get the car out of the garage and go through the routine I've done many times before; engine on, reverse gear, release clutch and … don't go backwards! The front wheel on my side refuses to turn and scrapes along as I strain to reverse.

Not being an expert on cars, I take a punt and press the brake pedal in and out to see if it might be something related to the disc, and it solves the problem. Away I go and everything is all right, although I will get it checked tomorrow.

From Martin's place we head north for Cadbury Heath, a suburb on the eastern outskirts of Bristol. Passing through the centre is the shorter option, but it is quicker and easier to leave the motorway and head east via the ring road, turning off just after the main Bristol-to-Chippenham road. It's not the simplest of places to find, with a small, unsigned turn into a narrow lane taking you to the car park that is just down from the venue.

This seems to be a common theme in this area as nearby Oldland and Longwell Green share this hard-to-find situation and Roman Glass St George is even worse – not even satnav will save you from the rigours of locating that one! At least, having visited Cadbury already, I'm aware of how easy it is to miss the turn and spot it before Martin drives past.

As we walk up and around to the entrance, I note that there are no significant changes to when I came here before, that being about 10 years ago in Cadbury's first season in the Western League. The big difference is that back then they could not play games midweek at this time of year as they had no lights. Now they have four down each side.

The roof on the covered standing on halfway, next to the entrance, looks new and the concrete hardstanding along that side isn't showing much signs of wear either. This extends behind one goal, while the remaining sides are grassy and uncovered with the dugouts on the far side opposite the stand. Planning permission has been granted to complete the hardstanding all round and plans are afoot to replace that covered area with a seated stand and new changing rooms to the back of the existing structure.

There is a high wire perimeter fence of a ground surrounded on three sides by housing. For me this is, for some reason, one of those places that looks good under lights as well.

Tonight's Western League First Division game against Bradford Town kicks off a tad late for some unknown reason. I see that Cadbury play in red and white when really, of course, they should be wearing chocolate! It is the first time I have seen the visitors away from home, having been to their place twice and seen them lose both games. The last time saw them winning at half-time only for them to lose 7-1, so on that basis any away supporters might as well have gone home before the start!

Maybe not, though, because it is they who look the better side and when they open the scoring it is hardly against the run of play; Jerad O'Pray volleying in from 15 yards from a Sam Jordan assist. Five minutes later the hosts win a corner on the right and from it Toby Colbourne heads Cadbury level. Sixty seconds after this he sets up strike partner Sasha Tong, who strikes low into the left corner.

So a complete turnaround, and that is confirmed in the opening minute of the second half when an excellent run down the right by the winger sets up Colbourne for an easy, side-footed finish. Bradford's woes continue as their keeper fumbles a corner, allowing Dwayne James to prod in the loose ball, and on the hour it's five as he gets a second goal with a low shot through a crowded goalmouth that nestles in the right corner. The rout is completed eight minutes from time from yet another corner – this time finding the head of Simon Brown – and by the end the few that have travelled across from Trowbridge Road probably wish they had stayed at home.

I certainly don't, that's for sure, although to be fair the winning margin does not reflect the game as a whole. I have enjoyed it and, who knows, I may even make a third visit here some day – not this season, though.

# Saturday, November 6

Well, it has taken me about 10 months, but today will see me complete the Somerset County Premier Division grounds – even if I have cheated a little.

I say this because of the reserve teams that play in it that I have not seen at home or, of course, away. Having seen the first teams in action at these venues, I see no reason why I should really, although there will be some out there who will see it differently. As I have said before, groundhopping has no set of guidelines for all, with each of us having our own rules as to what counts or not.

The ground that is getting the honour of being the final Premier venue for me is Penpole Lane, home of Shirehampton. Fans of Western League football 30 or so years ago will recognise this as being the then home of Portway-Bristol, which would have given me the incentive to do this one even if I had not done any other first-team grounds in this league.

The ground is not too difficult to locate and is not that far from the motorway. There is no parking within the facility, so I have to park in the lane, which at least ensures a quick getaway afterwards. Not that there is any reason to concern myself in this matter as, unsurprisingly, a massive crowd is not predicted!

One thing is for sure: while Western League football may have been staged here in the past, there is not much chance of seeing it here in the near future. There is hardstanding along most of the far side with some standing cover that, in all honesty, serves little purpose. You can just about get around behind both goals, where it is overgrown with shrubbery, and the near side is completely open.

The first-floor clubhouse is set well back from the playing area on this side in the corner, next to the entry from Penpole Lane, while a small refreshment area and the changing rooms are on the ground floor.

Watchet are the visiting side for what promises to be a good match-up between two of the better teams in this division. This is ably demonstrated in the opening exchanges and leads to the first goal with six minutes played. Nick Alexander receives the ball from the left and instinctively hooks the ball over the keeper from 15 yards to put the hosts ahead. Moments later he is denied by a fine save from which Watchet counter and, as a result, equalise with Luke Taylor smashing into the roof of the net from Aaron Deeks' pull-back from the left byline. In a flash the two combine again, this time on the right with the scorer setting up Taylor for a far-post tap-in.

It's all too much for a pair of old-timers who, from being happy, are now facing up to the fact that their side are behind. Thus begins what seems initially like a bit of banter between themselves and the visiting club linesman that quickly gets nastier when the home side are losing. Every offside call is deemed wrong, and it isn't nice.

At the break, when he returns to the dressing room, I feel strongly enough about it to have a word with the official, telling him to ignore the critics. He thanks me, saying he isn't that bothered, but I feel the level of criticism is uncalled for. While I look upon club officials as a necessary evil at this level, I can see that he is only trying to do his job to the best of his ability. If he does make any mistakes – and I don't think he has – then they are not intentional; let's face it, we are only human, aren't we?

Ten minutes into the second half, the officials have on-field issues to deal with as a scrap breaks out between a player from each side that sees both red-carded and a continuation of their disagreement off the field. They are pulled apart and things calm down, although the incident seems to affect the contest, which becomes scrappy, the away side seeming content to hold on to what they have.

Just when it looks as if they will succeed, a rash challenge in the box sees the ref blow for a penalty even though in the aftermath Beecham nets with a low shot. Jack Barnes ensures justice is done by converting the spot kick, thus saving the ref some embarrassment.

Both sides have opportunities to take all three points in the 10 minutes of added time, but to be honest a draw is the right result. Given the level they play at, this game has been of a good standard; what with all the goings-on this afternoon it has definitely not been your ordinary football day out, but I have loved it.

# Wednesday, November 10

I don't know why, but there are some grounds I do not particularly like visiting, and tonight sees me in that situation. I am crossing the border into Somerset to see Wellington play neighbouring Taunton Town in a Somerset Premier Cup tie.

This is one of those times when my one-visit rule for this campaign bears no relevance, as there is absolutely no way I could come here more than once in a season. Anyway, I have come tonight in the hope of seeing Martin's side earn a spot in the next round, making this one of those rare instances when I leave my neutral hat at home.

Sited close to the town centre, this place – like Dawlish – has public car parking that is only free for midweek games. When I arrive here, though, I see the lights are not on – surely it can't be off? No, it's a floodlight failure. Thankfully, power is restored and the game starts on time. Wellington have four poles down each side and the lamps do not exactly provide the best of lighting, but it's obviously better than none at all.

Things work out all right in the end here, but there have been a few instances I can recall when this has not been the case. Ironically, one that comes to mind was when the lights failed just before a game at Holsworthy was due to get under way, with a bad choice of two being confirmed later via Martin's text informing me of an 11-goal thriller at … Wellington!

Another concerns a game at Lydney on one of the groundhop days, which was abandoned due to waterlogging. I went to the restaging at the end of that season, which saw the lights go out just before the break! In the end they played the second half with the middle one of three lights on the far side switched off – which was a relief as I was exasperated when the lights failed and was beginning to think the contest was jinxed! Still, it worked out well in the end.

This ground is open on the far side, but upon entering I see the club have put a fence along there. For some strange reason, they have left so little room that you cannot watch from that position or even walk along there. The remaining sides are railed off, with the town end backed by large trees and the far end mostly open except for the fairly recent addition of a seated stand in the near corner. I presume this is the only place it could be put as it seems a strange location, but at least the obligatory seat allocation has been met now.

Along the near side is the clubhouse building, with the dressing rooms at one end and a small, raised covered standing area at the other. The wooden dugouts are also on this side and, positioned as they are, provide obstructed views of the action in places – especially in that raised section.

A good-sized crowd see Taunton make the livelier start but without reward, and it is the home side who open the scoring when Craig Herrod sets up Alex Pounde, who nets from the left with an angled drive. Ex-Taunton boss Gary Domone has certainly got his troops fired up for this one, but if anything his side relax a little, enabling Alexis Piper to curl a free kick into the top right corner and restore parity.

Once again, it's the away side who come out of the blocks sharper on resumption, and in no time they score when Jon Vance fires across the keeper into the far corner of the net after finding space on the right.

The Southern League side have control now, and they finish in style with two goals in the last eight minutes. First a mishit clearance from the keeper falls to substitute Corey Lewis, who slots into an empty net with his first touch of the game, then an attempted back pass falls way short, enabling Lewis to nip in and slip his shot over the onrushing goalie.

So ultimately no cup shock, as the higher-division outfit has shown precisely why they are that.

# Saturday, November 13

Whoever said there are lies, damn lies and statistics was correct in some ways, but not all. I have kept stats of all the games I have been to since that day way back in the 70s, although I didn't actually start doing them for a year or two and merely updated. Three thousand-plus games later, I am still at it, although it can cause problems.

I keep seasonal records and come the final reckoning I like if possible to have a good one to look back on. Part of this entails me attaining a good goal average which, while being out of my hands to a degree, can be manipulated at times. I call it goal hunting.

Today I am admitting to a shift in this direction as I head off to watch Pegasus Juniors play Ardley in a Hellenic League fixture. The home club's name does conjure up images of a team of kids playing in the big boys' league which, judging by their defensive record, might have been true. Of course they are not, but with the visitors being a goalscoring side there is not a cat in hell's chance of this game being goalless.

If it is as stress-free as my journey up, I will be quids in, because I am parked up with about an hour to spare. Located on the northern outskirts of Hereford, the Old School Lane venue is a fairly typical ground in this league. Early indications are not good as you enter the car park, which is positioned at a lower level behind the goal, as some of the wooden-fenced perimeter has been blown down and not fixed.

The clubhouse and changing rooms are at the far end of the parking, and access to the ground is attained by ascending a concreted path to one corner, next to where the spectator entrance is. On this side is a seated stand, while directly opposite is a small, wooden covered area for standing. Elsewhere is open hardstanding except for the car park end, from where you are not allowed to watch the game. There are four floodlight poles with twin lights on each side.

I passed Hereford United's ground on the way and they are at home, which may or may not explain the minuscule attendance. There is only a handful of away followers, although given the small number who witnessed the game I saw there last month, I'm not altogether surprised. I am, though, when a familiar face pops up on my stroll around – it's Kerry Miller.

Many will know Kerry as a respected writer and expert when it comes to football stadiums. His total makes my tally of grounds visited seem pathetic, not that you will hear him bragging about it. He is in the area visiting a friend, so spending a couple of hours in his company is a pleasant bonus with the added extra of having someone to natter to if things get a tad boring.

As expected, the visitors make all the early running, but maybe they are taking things too lightly, spurning the chances they create. The half-hour mark passes and still they have not broken through. That's the down side with goal hunting: when the so-called poor side show defiance and their opponents fail to unlock the door. It can be frustrating, but on 37 minutes a goal finally arrives when a corner is flicked on to Gary Wickens, who taps in. Two minutes later, Danny Bone finds space on the left and fires into the roof of the net to give Ardley a two-goal half-time lead.

Any thoughts of a goal avalanche are dispelled as the hosts have failed to read the script, so it's not until the 70th minute that a third goal arrives. Ian Concannon has only been on the field a matter of minutes but when he's put through the middle he shows why he is such a prolific marksman with a cool finish. This lad knows where the net is, although if rumours about how much he is being paid are correct then one can only hope that his club get full value for their money.

Stuart Bridges bags Ardley's fourth with a rasping 30-yarder and the game finishes with Pegasus providing us with a brace of near misses which, at least, mean they don't go the whole game without an attempt on goal. No goal glut, then, although on reflection I am quite glad as common sense has finally taken over.

I take a shorter route back via Chepstow and the old Severn bridge. This proves to not be as short as I would have liked, as I try to be clever at Monmouth and take a so-called shortcut. I get stuck in a one-way system and head south on the wrong road, which takes me to Chepstow but by a longer route – serves me right for trying to be a clever dick.

It doesn't mar a good day out, and it was good to see Kerry. The funny thing is that his football work sees him take in games in the Andover area, but on the night I was at that New Street game he was away – yet he turns up here. It is indeed a small world we live in.

DIARY OF A SEASON

# Saturday, November 20

The term masochism can be defined as the endurance of mental pain, so after a whole week without a game I must be feeling that way as I tackle the journey to watch Finchampstead play Penn and Tylers Green in a Hellenic East encounter. Given that they are two of the bottom three sides in a poor league, and have rotten goalscoring records, it hardly has the makings of a classic! At times like this I wonder what on earth goes through that brain of mine.

Watching two struggling sides in a game like this one is asking for trouble, but it can also apply at the top, as I have found to my cost. Leamington were playing Evesham in a top-of-the-table encounter. A glance at their respective defensive records should have set the alarm bells ringing, but I went anyway. Lo and behold! a match that, in polite terms, I'd define as a stalemate and a blasted revisit for yours truly. Oh, how annoyed I was on the drive back home, but I had only myself to blame. It was not one of my better decisions.

Another one is my departure time today. It's not like me to misjudge this, although it doesn't help that I somehow miss the turn-off at Sandhurst, thus arriving in the ground's car park a mere 10 minutes from kick-off.

This is a village somewhere to the south of Bracknell and it's your typical leafy suburb with the ground just off the main road. It's called the Memorial Ground, but there's not a great deal to remember about the place. Put simply, it is a pitch surrounded by a grey metal railing, with the clubhouse and dressing room facilities located well away from a pitch that is shared with cricket. The setting is a nice one but the ground can only be described as basic.

Given the ground's open status, there is no specific entry to this ground and you can watch for free if you so desire. As it is, I pay by means of purchasing a match programme, so presumably if you do not want one then it becomes a matter of conscience when deciding whether you contribute to club funds or not.

Mind you, they're not exactly rushing from all parts to witness this match, and my estimated crowd count doesn't take long. The same can be said about the opening quarter of this game in terms of goalmouth action. as both sides seem intent on seeing how far out of play they can kick the ball.

After almost 40 minutes have passed, one of the Penn players decides to ease the boredom by having a shot, and the goalkeeper actually has to make a save from another on the stroke of half-time! Despite this, an air of resignation hangs over me as I stroll back to the clubhouse for refreshments. On this showing, I simply cannot envisage a goal being scored.

The game gets under way again and I wonder whether the same teams have reappeared. Perhaps aliens have taken the first lot away and replaced them, because an immediate improvement is clearly evident. In fact, having done nothing whatsoever in the first period, it's the home side who look like getting a goal – if only they can get a shot on target. On 62 minutes the goal comes – but it's Penn who get it. A corner on the left is touched on at the near post for Dan Arnett to convert from close range. What a relief!

The visitors are now on top and hit the woodwork twice, while James Louison is denied on two occasions from well-struck free kicks that are saved, one magnificently tipped over the bar. Seven minutes from time he shows he's as much a provider of goals as a dead-ball specialist by swinging in a cross from the left that is met by the head of Jack Dean. Finchampstead squander a clear-cut chance of a consolation in the dying embers of the game, but are beaten by the better side on the day.

In the end my fears prove unfounded and I really enjoy the second half – oh, ye of little faith. Given my low expectations and how I felt at the midway point, I am well pleased with the way things have turned out.

I was hoping for a quick getaway but on the final whistle I get chatting to a man. This turns into an interesting conversation, as he is telling me about how he used to work with famous bands, and it really is fascinating. I must admit that when he began I was a tad wary, thinking they were the rantings of an old man with elaborate, made-up tales, but clearly this is not the case.

When I finally bid my farewells I feel it has put the icing on the cake of a good day. My apprehension beforehand was misplaced – or was I just lucky? Who cares?

# Tuesday, November 23

There have been times when my choice of game has been an erroneous one, but it's not often I can say I've been to the wrong ground. This happened once on a Good Friday in the days before the internet when, having perused the local newspapers, I decided to go to Welton Rovers for their game against Glastonbury.

I made my way up by car for the morning kick-off and arrived at an empty stadium. My initial thought was that it was a later-than-advertised start, but someone appeared and informed me that the game was taking place at what I'd presumed to be the away side's venue. I headed south and arrived on half-time to watch a goalless second period, having missed the goals from the first. Damage was limited slightly in that I did a game in that area with a 3pm start and no, I did not count the 45 as a game seen.

At least I got something from that trip, unlike my only other slip-up in this respect. This was back in my Football League days and on the day of the football centenary festival at Wembley. With no league games on, I was 'forced' to watch something else. As a result of reading about Northwich leaving their Drill Field home to ground-share with Crewe for a short period, I decided to go there by rail.

Of course, when I arrived at Gresty Road there was no game, and I pathetically tried to hitch a lift, with no luck. A wasted trip, then, thanks to something I had read that never happened – what a fool! Still, I'm wiser now but it was yet another lesson learned.

I did get to Welton eventually, for a Western League Cup game. A glance through my stats, though, has told me that this is the only Western League ground at which I have not seen a league match, so this evening I am putting that to rights by attending their Premier clash with Bristol Manor Farm. Although I have not been there for quite some time, it is not a hard venue to locate and I encounter nothing more than the usual traffic at this time of day.

West Clewes is the oldest ground in this league, dating as far back as the 19th century. This is visibly so in the shape of the wooden, green-painted stand that is set back from the pitch with a tarmacked area in between. Next to this is the clubhouse, which you pass on your left as you enter through the car parking behind the goal. The changing rooms are accessed down a tunnel in the middle of the stand, while beyond this structure is some old uncovered, stepped terracing.

Hardstanding runs along the far end and the narrow side opposite. There are four floodlight pylons on each side and the overall impression of this ground is one that has inklings of the past before modern-style updates were introduced. There is a bit of character about this place that is likeable.

A couple of local hopper pals of mine have had like-minded thoughts about this game, and they arrive just after me. When the game gets under way, the early indications are that a good match is in prospect. Manor Farm play a good passing game, even if at times they over-elaborate, while the hosts play a more direct style. The away side look more likely to score and should go ahead when Jamie Jordan misses a sitter. In stoppage time, though, their efforts reap dividends when Ben Hiscox fires in a low shot that is half-stopped and falls to Phil Vice, who makes no mistake.

The second half starts in similar vein, but on 64 Welton catch the visitors napping when a run and cross from the left finds Jordan, who volleys in to level the scores. This doesn't deter Manor Farm, and they forge ahead again as Kyle Mountford is able to turn and place his shot into the bottom left corner from the edge of the area. Ten minutes later, another penetrating run down the right flank sees Chris Bribble's attempt to clear the cross loop over his own keeper and into the far corner of the net – an unfortunate incident that proves to be the final noteworthy chance despite the best efforts of the homesters.

My friends and I agree that the better side has won as we go our separate ways at the end, knowing that we'll meet up somewhere else before the season's done – that's for sure. It's always nice to bump into people you know when you don't expect it, especially as it's a reminder that I am among many who share my hobby – my addiction.

# Saturday, November 27

Boy, it was cold on Tuesday night, and that theme has continued since into a cold spell. As a consequence, phone calls have to be made this morning as a wasted trip is definitely not on my agenda – the upshot being the opportunity to get a new ground done. It really is a brand new one too, as Totton & Eling have recently moved from their old Sports Ground home, so with the chance presenting itself to re-complete my Wessex mainland grounds, it is too good to refuse.

The trouble with travelling by car to grounds in the South from my place is the road I have to go along. To be fair, a lot of it is good, but certain bits are really annoying. The part that irritates the most is through a village called Chideock, near Bridport on the A35. This is at the bottom of a steep hill from both directions with speed cameras positioned just beyond where the 30mph limit begins, thus requiring a lot of braking – and I mean a lot, especially when heading eastwards. I pity anyone who has to commute along this passage every week: they must wear their brake pads out in no time.

So, after negotiating that and the rest, I arrive at a ground that is simpler to reach than the old one, which was more centrally sited in Totton. Here it is but a short drive from the M27 and has two new stadiums back to back. The other will house Southern League outfit AFC Totton, but due to delays it's not ready yet. Parking is shared, or will be in future, and while it's good enough for Wessex games I can't help but wonder why they could not have made it bigger for AFC. It will be interesting to find out when I come back to see a game there.

Unsurprisingly, the venue at which I am watching this game is the smaller of the two. It is called Little Testwood Farm and is a functional ground – so common these days with newly-built arenas. On one side you have two buildings at each end, the nearside one being the changing rooms and the other for refreshments and a hospitality area. In the middle of this is a covered stand which has broad bench-type seating within. The idea behind its extreme width is that one person can sit on the front bit while the rear part is used for the feet of spectators perched on the higher level, but it has an unsteady feel about it.

There is a small covered standing enclosure behind the far goal that used to be part of the old Southern Gardens ground, which is a nice touch but realistically a practical one. Elsewhere is open hardstanding that has that green coating you see on artificial playing surfaces.

The green theme continues with the roof of the stand and the pitch surround, which is a metal rail with wire mesh filling in the gaps. Given that the home club play in red and black, this is a little strange. Maybe whoever painted it was colour-blind! Perspex dugouts sit either side of halfway on the open side, with floodlighting provided by poles sited in each corner of the ground.

I did go to the old place, which was pretty average really, although at least there was a clubhouse there. There is one on this site, although whether it is AFC's or shared I do not know. It could be that they still use the facilities at their old home, but to be honest I did not feel the need to ask. I saw an emphatic home win – T&E went on to win the First Division – but having acquired the teams I am not expecting this encounter today to go the same way.

Mind you, I was also not anticipating the expensive price of the programme, £2 being a tad too much, I think. There is a glossy front cover but the content does not warrant such a price. Out of principle I would not have bought one if it hadn't been on a new ground for me, which makes it necessity for my collection.

There are four Wessex clubs who play on the Isle of Wight, of which I have done only one: Newport. One of the remaining trio is Brading, who come a-calling this afternoon for a Premier Division clash.

The visitors are high up in the table, but it is the mid-table hosts who make a better start to this game, alas without creating a clear-cut chance of note. Brading go close when Kyle Levrier strikes the underside of the bar and the hosts gain possession, transferring it down the other end. Jo Tessem, on the right, hits an angled shot that comes back off the inside of the far post for Chris Marwood to put it in off his shin.

One-nil at the break, then, and a bonus as the hosts' secretary invites me in to the hospitality for tea and biscuits. I have had a chat with him beforehand, but I am surprised when he makes this offer as I walk around during the half. It's a fine gesture. I have a nice chat with the officials and feel in good spirits as the game begins again.

Not much more than a minute in there is drama as Jamie Feasby hauls down a visiting player and is red-carded. The resultant spot kick is tucked away by Alex Przespolenski, but the 10 men reply by retaking the lead when Marwood comes in from the left and strikes a low shot past the unsighted Gareth True and into the corner.

Things appear to settle down, but going into the final 15 minutes it starts to go badly wrong for the home side. Scott Jones equalises with a superb volley, then another cross from the left falls to Josh Appell, who half-volleys in at the far post. Totton then go down to nine as Nick Jenkin receives a second yellow, and from the awarded kick Brading bag a fourth, Jamie O'Rourke's final touch on a Dean Stuber strike completing the scoring.

His side play out what is left of the game to complete a bit of a smash-and-grab win. A thoroughly enjoyable contest from a neutral point of view, and a great day out for me.

# Saturday, December 4

Any thoughts I had of getting a midweek game in have been wiped out by the cold snap that looks set to continue. Even though the temperatures in the South-West tend to be milder than other parts during times like this, it is still chilly enough for matches to be called off today. Luckily, the game I have earmarked has beaten the cold conditions, and a short drive along the East coast will take me to Beer Albion for their Devon Premier Cup tie against Peninsula club Plymstock United.

I am in Stovar Long Lane with plenty of time to spare as my up-and-down journey is not as bad as I had feared. Furzebrake does not have much parking and what there is runs alongside the pitch, so it is as well I get here when I do. I head for the clubhouse – located in the corner next to where you come in – and have a bite to eat. Getting the teams is going to be difficult, especially with there being no programme, but I scribble them down on a piece of paper that I've brought in anticipation of this happening, à la Hatherleigh.

The guy I rang to confirm this game is on is here, and he has the information I need, saving me the bother of scrambling around in the quest to attain such details. That man is Dave Baskwill, who happens to be the Plymstock secretary and has been for God knows how long.

Here is someone who, like Marcus at Cullompton, lives and breathes his beloved club, even if he is a hotbed of pessimism when it comes to their prospects pre-season. For me, Dave is the epitome of what football at this level is all about, and his enthusiasm is never-ending. He knows and accepts that his club are never going to rise above its current level.

Of course, this makes winning trophies even sweeter, none more so than their triumph against the odds over Upton in the Devon Premier cup final at Plainmoor – one that I had the pleasure of witnessing. Another feather in the cap was when they overcame Ottery in the final of the Throgmorton Cup, from which I think Dave derived more pleasure as it was harder to win. There are probably only a handful of clubs for which I have a soft spot, and the Dean Cross outfit is one of them, even though they are a bit too close to enemy territory!

Dave will be the first to admit that his club's ground is not the best in the Peninsula, but it's safe to say this venue must be one of the better ones in the Devon & Exeter Premier. There's a stand on halfway on the far side with a little bench seating and the dugouts flanking it. Hardstanding leads to it from the front of the clubhouse, to which the changing rooms are attached. Surrounding the playing area is a single rail held by wooden posts, while the pitch slopes slightly at each end. If you walk down the car park side to the end, you can look right and see an excellent view of the Jurassic coastline, albeit slightly obstructed by trees. It is well out of town but set in a good location.

From the off, this is a competitive contest, with the lower-division hosts feeling they have a point to prove. Plymstock stand firm, though, and as the half progresses they are retaining possession more. With five minutes to go until the break they go in front when Dan Murdoch receives the ball from the right. His goal-bound effort is saved, only for it to come out to Chris Stofell, whose shot arrows into the right corner of the net and comes back out.

At least the referee gives the goal this time, unlike in a Devon League game at Buckland, where Plymstock's Glen Palmer did the same thing but was baffled like the rest of us when the game carried on. You don't see that too often, and thankfully not here as the visitors go in at the break a goal to the good.

For the second Saturday running I see a penalty given about a minute into the second period, this time to the home side as Matt Rowson is fouled by the keeper. James Gill could have been sent off but stays on, only for John Cooper to beat him from the spot. On 53 Aaron Hulme is in acres of space to fire Plymstock back in front before being put through on goal minutes later, this time rounding the keeper and sliding the ball in.

Beer come right back into it on the hour when Luke Bartlett's shot cannons off the top of the crossbar and drops straight back down for James Melville to tap in, whereupon the hosts apply pressure on the visitors' goal. Rowson goes so close to scoring his second but it's not to be as Stofell turns in a fourth on the counter.

Hulme completes his hat-trick in stoppage time – the Plymstock striker forcing home the rebound after James Yates had rounded keeper Rooke only to see his effort cleared off the line – and that is that. It is a flattering final scoreline really, with Beer's players doing their club proud in a good cup tie.

# Saturday, December 11

The cold snap shows no signs of abating, so seven days go by without me seeing a game. To be frank, I am at an age where going out on a freezing cold night is a bit much for my aching limbs. I have serious ligament problems in both of my ankles – the left being the worse – and these chilly conditions don't help. Call me a wimp if you like, but the notion of standing around in an all-out attempt to catch double pneumonia is no longer my idea of a good night out.

One thing this weather has thrown up is in my favour today, as Perranwell's Cornwall Senior Cup tie with Penryn is on after being postponed last Saturday. A slight thaw has ensured the game goes ahead, so I'm Cornwall-bound for a game that has the makings of an upset.

This is a village club located a couple of miles off the main Truro-to-Falmouth road, and they play in the Cornwall Combination, a league below their Peninsula visitors. The address leads one to think it is near the railway station, but on arrival this information proves to be bogus. For some unfathomable reason, my instincts tell me this as I descend into the village and turn into the road leading me to the ground, although I do stop to ask a local and make sure.

One thing is certain: the ground may have a grandiose name but it doesn't live up to that title. The King George V is anything but a palace, which to be fair I was forewarned about. Turning into the car park, the clubhouse/changing room building is at the far end, while the pitch is away to your left. This has no perimeter and the sole feature is a covered standing area with a small refreshment kiosk in the corner. There is no hardstanding, with two open sides and a tree line behind the goal at the far end.

Coming down with low expectations of what I'd find have made it all easier to swallow, otherwise this venue would have been a let-down. I guess most leagues have a good mix of clubs whose facilities differ in quality, with the Cornwall Combination having good ones such as Illogan and St Day to go along with those at the other end of the scale. Variety is indeed the spice of life – and grounds.

One good thing about this place is the issuing of a programme. At this level you normally only see one for a senior cup game like today, but here they do one for all home games – except this one! Apparently the guy who does it has been unable to oblige. Oh dear!

Time for plan B, and that means getting an issue from the last game played here and turning it into what will look like one for this game. At least it will give me something that resembles a record of my attendance and, perhaps, as it's the sole one I could make millions by selling it to a collector at a later date! Also, unlike in the Devon Premier, they write out team sheets with correct player numberings, so there's no wandering around this afternoon trying to ascertain who is playing number nine or whatever.

We kick off early as there are no lights and there is extra time to consider. Not that that seems to bother the officials; at the due start time they are still in their little cubbyhole. Eventually they honour us with their appearance as the match starts 10 minutes late.

Pretty soon the pitch starts to cut up, making it very tricky for the players, and skilful play is out of the question. The opening goal on eight minutes amply demonstrates the silliness of it when Dan Richardson loses his footing in the act of shooting. His half-hit shot is parried out to Marvin Brooks, who fires Penryn in front.

The home side level 15 minutes later when Barry Leete's cross from the left is missed by Dominic Pullen, who stumbles in the boggy area. The ball comes to Shane Richards, who takes a touch and fires into the net. Sean Johnston rattles the bar with a 25-yarder and Kevin Lawrence shaves the post as both sides attempt to master the conditions, which are bordering on farcical at times.

With the light fading, extra time comes to pass. In that extra 30 Penryn are the stronger side and squander two golden opportunities to put the tie to bed, making a replay look inevitable. Dale Band has other ideas, though, and gives his side a dramatic winner, latching on to a half-blocked shot and blasting into the roof of the net with the home defenders appealing in vain for an offside flag. Frazer Cadman takes his pleas a bit far and is sent from the field of play amid moans and groans from the home supporters.

With no time for the 10 to respond, it gives Penryn a deserved victory from a match that concludes in almost total darkness on a pitch that looks like a ploughed field. Still, they got it played and that's the main thing, although I suspect the prospects of any football being played here in the near future are bleak. I do know that Harry Hopper'ere will not be in attendance on that day – whenever it is – and it is highly unlikely that I will ever come back to this place.

# Saturday, December 18

Let it snow, let it snow, let it snow! Oh, the weather outside is indeed frightful if, like me, you wish to attend a game this afternoon. All non-league games are off, although that's not relevant in my case as my car is snowed in. In fact I am cut off from the main road nearby, which to my knowledge has not occurred since the 70s.

We get snow here in Exeter, but normally not enough to cause this level of chaos. At least it looks nice on the ground I suppose, which cannot be said for rain or indeed frost to a certain extent, but it means resigning myself to a rare Saturday off.

Hang on a minute, though. Exeter City are at home and they have pulled out all the stops to get their game with Sheffield Wednesday on. Unbelievably, their efforts have paid off, so it means dusting off my Football League hat and setting off to St James Park.

Ah, but there's the small matter of getting there. I live on the other side of the city, and walking up in these slippery conditions is probably not a good idea, especially for this accident-prone person. A pair of skis would be handy but somewhat impracticable – and impossible too as I do not actually possess such a thing. To be honest, I don't regard the notion of hurtling down a steep slope at high speed without brakes as anything but an act of insanity. I could do what the Eskimos do – being pulled along in a sled by huskies – but there's a slight snag in that. For one thing I don't think a single basset hound would suffice and two, I do not have a sled!

No, my brain comes up with a more realistic option that sees me ring an old neighbour of mine. He is a season ticket holder and is only too willing to give me a lift. Thanks to our car-hating council it means a bit of a walk as there are so many resident-only parking restrictions, but it only takes about five minutes. This is hardly taxing, even in my condition, and my walking stick gets put to good use.

There is quite a decent crowd for what is the only game being played in the Football League's two lower divisions. We stand on what was the big bank behind the goal, now called the Cliff Bastin stand. This is the end where I watched my first ever game in the days when this end was uncovered. After a while I made Cowshed covered terracing alongside the pitch my regular haunt, developing a camaraderie among those standing around me.

The Cowshed sat on top of a steep but short grass bank, which has now been replaced by a seated stand with hospitality boxes at the back. The St James Road end, used by the away support, is an open, narrow side, while the old stand sits at the top of steep banking that overlooks the railway line. These two sides have remained pretty much the same since my first visit.

The floodlighting is on top of both stands, with poles either side of the old one. There used to be two telegraph poles at each end with lamps – probably a unique layout. Not many grounds could claim to have lighting on all four sides, although Hull City's old Boothferry Park stadium had four corner pylons plus two facing each other on halfway. It certainly was different, but now it is just like your average venue in this respect.

I suspect it will not shock when I say that this is the ground I have been to most often, and by quite some distance too. Of course, I have seen a lot of ups and downs here – mostly downs, it must be said. Beginner's luck saw the Grecians win promotion right away, but success has been thin on the ground since. A Fourth Division title win under Terry Cooper in 89/90 is pretty much as good as it has got although, to be fair, the club's trophy cabinet wasn't exactly overflowing prior to all of this.

Highlights have mainly been confined to fleeting moments of glory, which I am sure I will always remember. The FA Cup run to the sixth round with that long trip back from Newcastle on a train without heating on a freezing night; queueing all night for a Spurs ticket; that stonewall penalty that wasn't given at White Hart Lane; flying back from the States overnight so I could watch ECFC in a cup game; discharging myself from hospital so I could see the vital last League game versus Southend that saw City relegated – oh and of course every win over that lot down the A38! I'm sure there are others, but those are the ones that come to mind right away.

The lowest point in the club's history actually became a positive, with the club now being run by the supporters' trust. Everybody knows, though, that if it were not for the Manchester United cup ties there would be no Exeter City around now. I did attend both games and even now cannot believe I saw my local side draw at Old Trafford, even if it was a weakened home team.

Although I recall it as being a great day, I have to admit that by then I had become more cynical about the club as a whole, and that has remained to this day. Why? Well, it all stems back to their first year as a non-league club.

Virtually from the off, it was decreed that City were too good for the Conference and would go back up right away – wrong! This attitude came mainly from fans, but as League status remained unfulfilled the same vibes gradually came from the club itself. As I have said, my cynicism started to blossom to the extent that I did NOT want them to go up and admit to not being downhearted when they deservedly lost to Morecambe in the first of the Wembley play-off finals. Twelve months later a league place was restored via the same route, and I have to say I had mellowed a bit and was delighted to see City win at the national stadium.

On the whole, I think my conversion to non-league has brought around my way of thinking as, from what I could see, Exeter did not treat the Conference with respect. This was made to look even sillier when it took them so long to get out of it. Anyway, they are back now and, despite any misgivings I may have, they are still my hometown club, and I want them to do well.

Whether it is because they are playing a big-name club or not I do not know, but what I do know is that the hosts are straight into a pleasing brand of passing the ball around with Wednesday responding in kind, meaning this is hardly going to be dull. Twenty-nine minutes in, Ryan Harley pulls the ball back from the right byline for Jamie Cureton to control and shoot into the net at my end of the ground. The away side replies within two minutes when Tommy Miller converts a corner at the far post – it was headed out but deemed to be over the line.

All square at the break then, but City soon get into their stride as we get under way once more, and go ahead thanks to a terrific 30-yard strike from Liam Sercombe. Five minutes later a deep cross from the right falls to Scott Golbourne on the far side, and his shot beats Nicky Weaver at his near post. On 72, Cureton runs on to a threaded pass and slots number four under the keeper. Then near the end, it becomes a nap hand when substitute John O'Flynn, unmarked in the box, nets from 10 yards. A gilt-edged chance at the death represents Wednesday's only real effort in a half in which the home side has dominated, and as a spectacle it has been fantastic to watch.

Given the qualities of their opponents on paper, this has to go down as one of the best performances I've seen in all the years I have been coming here. If all Football League games were like this and the other one I saw back in August, I would probably go more often. To be honest I think I may have been fortunate in my selections – I definitely was today. Up the City!

# Monday, December 27

Christmas time, which for the football fan means the tradition of going to a game on the 26th. Mind you, if I had my way they would have had games on Saturday even though it was Christmas day – an opinion I suspect wouldn't be shared by many out there! Thanks to the weather, though, I failed to attend a Boxing Day fixture this year – the first time in 16 years I have not done so.

According to my records, I have been to two matches on December 26 for each and every one of those times, bar one. Most of those occasions have involved local games, although I do recall one instance when I decided a Southport/Hyde double was a good idea, and in my defence it was a good day. There was no chance of me repeating such deeds yesterday, though, but no matter as I have looked at what is on offer this afternoon. The answer is not a great deal, especially in my area, and I am just beginning to resign myself to another day at home when Martin rides to the rescue.

It may be a long, long way to Tipperary, but Hayle isn't exactly a hop, skip and jump from my place. I didn't fancy making a 200-hundred mile round trip in the current weather conditions, but my good friend has no such qualms and offers a lift that I willingly accept.

It's a journey that passes well, and we arrive with ample time to spare – mainly down to my misjudgment of the time it would to get there. Martin does not drive like an old woman, as I invariably do, so my estimate of a two-hour run is wide of the mark. My excuse is that it is better to allow too much time than not enough, but there's no getting away from it – I'm a slowcoach.

Trevassack Park is at the top of a hill overlooking the surrounding countryside, with St Ives bay in the distance. They have a medium-sized car park, and entry is attained via a concrete-block hut that brings you out behind the goal in the corner. Ahead of you down this side is a small seated stand with blue and white plastic seats. Turn left upon entering and directly behind the goal is a gable-roofed building that holds the clubhouse, with the dressing rooms in an annex on the far end.

Along the side opposite the stand is a more recent addition in the form of some covered standing with a wooden fence behind. I can only assume that was erected as a wind-buffer, as it's quite open here. The far end, along with the areas either side of the seating, is open with no hardstanding. The pitch is railed all around and the playing surface ensures that matches are rarely called off, so there were no worries on that score on the way down.

Opinions vary of course, but I think this is a splendid little ground. Last time I was here was for the groundhop game against Camelford, when heavy showers gave us a good soaking. It is dry today, though, and Perranporth are here for a Peninsula Division One West fixture.

The visitors won the title last season but because their facilities were not good enough they were unable to go up. There are similarities to this venue as it is in a nice setting with hills in the background and the harbour not too far away. The one notable landmark at Ponsmere Valley is the single china clay chimney that stands alone as you enter the car park, and I don't think any other venue can boast that.

Possibly as a result of Perranporth staying in this division, they have lost some of their players and, like most at this level, operate on a budget, so look unlikely to retain their crown. Looking at the table, though, makes it easy to see why Martin sees this contest as a promising one.

The opening salvos of this match do indeed provide credence to my friend's pre-game thoughts as both sides look good. It is the away side who break the deadlock when the ball is pulled back from the left byline for Ross Maynard to slot in at the near post. On the half hour Hayle draw level as Matt Thomas's run and cross from the right falls to Dan Bell, who shoots low into the corner from 15 yards.

Thomas then makes a penetrating run through the middle, only being prevented from striking towards goal by a tackle from behind. The resultant penalty is duly tucked away, as Gary Bell sends the keeper the wrong way from the spot. Perranporth come close to restoring parity just before the break, but at the interval the home side are still holding on to their advantage.

The refreshment facility here is contained within the clubhouse, so the two of us head there and make a purchase. Martin and I take it in turns to buy the teas, and it's my round today. An historic event happens here, though, as I splash out on a pasty and chips as well. This happens about as often as Halley's Comet passing the Earth! It's not that I dislike food at non-league grounds, it's just me minimising my costs – although I am sure my friends think I'm a bit of a skinflint. Perish the thought!

With our bodies refuelled, we resume our places for the second half. From the get-go it is an open affair as the visitors press for a goal that will salvage a point. A brace of counter-attacks see the hosts spurn opportunities to seal the win, but a third one is more productive; Thomas once again being the instigator with another dribble down the right before crossing for Kieran Harris to convert from 10 yards. Having contributed to all three goals, the man of the match could so easily have got one for himself, but he has to contend with the starring role in his side's victory.

At the end, Martin and I agree that an highly enjoyable contest has made the journey down worthwhile; after going a whole nine days without a game, this has been a good way to get back into the swing of things.

# Thursday, December 30

My last game of the year and, unusually, the first time this season that I will attend a Peninsula Premier Division game. This is not something that normally happens, but of course it has not been intentional. It's just the way things go sometimes and has absolutely nothing to do with the quality, that's for sure, as games are just as enjoyable as you can realistically expect to see, and compare favourably with other leagues.

In fact, I'd go as far as to say that in the years since its founding in 2007 the league has been a success story, made even sweeter by those who slammed its conception being forced eat their words. Of course, not every game is going to be a classic and, just as at any level, you get matches that are dull. But while the levels of skill shown on the pitch may vary, there is no doubting the high standards of the way in which the Peninsula is run.

This is mostly thanks to one man in particular: Phil Hiscox. Most groundhoppers know Phil as the organiser of the three-day excursions that enable them to tick off Peninsula grounds while cutting down on those long south-westerly journeys. Certainly those I have spoken to have nothing but praise for the way it has been run, so it should hardly surprise when I remark on his forte as the league's secretary.

Apart from the usual stuff like player registrations and so on, Phil must be the first person to issue the following season's fixture list. He also does the league website, which always gets positive feedback when I am somewhere and this topic is raised, although I do wonder if it is realised just how much trouble he goes to in order to keep it updated.

One example is when he took the train to Penzance for a midweek Peninsula game, when he brought the site up to speed after returning home in the early hours before going to bed. I'm sure no one would have blamed him for leaving it until later that morning, but that's the way he is. While the league has other good people, who I'm sure do a great job, there is no doubt in my mind that Phil is the main cog in the well-run machine that is the South-West Peninsula League.

He, along with Martin and others I know, are present at Edge Down Park tonight as Witheridge take on Buckland Athletic. This is a village about 10 miles west of Tiverton and is just off the main road as you enter the built-up area. Entry to the ground is by a pathway to the right of the building that houses the clubhouse and refreshment kiosk, with the changing rooms at the far end. There is a small paved area to the fore, with a path leading from here down to a hut, where payment is made to enter in one corner of a spacious pitch.

To your left and behind the goal is some covered standing, then open hardstanding leading around to a bench-seated stand on halfway that is flanked by the dugouts. Beyond here is inaccessible, as is the far end, which is backed by a hedgerow. Down the near side it is partially railed at present, with an expanse of grass behind. Floodlighting comes from four corner poles, but due to the size of the playing area and the space between them, the light provided is patchy.

The pitch has been moved, so down the stand side there is quite a distance from spectators to the touchline. As a result, viewing from the seats is partially blocked by the dugouts, with the technical areas not helping either. However, this is a good club whose progress on and off the pitch echoes that of the league itself.

So to the game, which starts dramatically as inside two minutes Liam Moseley's chip is handled outside the area by keeper Mike Searle, who is sent off (yes, this is the same Searle who played in the Bodmin/Poole game. Maybe I'm a jinx!) Sub keeper Mike Taylor saves the free kick, but moments later he is picking the ball out of his net when Moseley rounds him and rolls the ball in.

The home side respond well to this double setback and equalise when Aidan Harper-Penman stabs in at the third attempt after Jordan Charran's free kick is half-stopped and David Hood's follow-up is blocked. Twelve minutes later, Mike Booth makes an unchallenged run down the right before slipping the ball under the keeper and into the far corner.

A succession of corners for the hosts is fruitless, and indeed the ball is manipulated up to the other end. From 40 yards out, Shane Gill lobs the keeper, who gets a hand on the ball but cannot prevent it going in. On the hour, Booth makes it four with an angled shot before player-manager Antony Lynch comes on and scores at the second attempt, tapping in after his initial effort somehow hits the bar from close range. Gill gets his second with a low first-time shot and Lynch follows him thanks to another Booth assist that sees him shoot low into the right corner.

Witheridge's night is summed up by the final goal of the evening, when Simon Revell rounds the keeper and sees his goal-bound effort hacked off the line, only for it to hit the hapless Richard Groom on the back of the head and go in for a comical own goal. The referee seems to take pity on the home side and blows the final whistle after 87 minutes, but this does not take away from an emphatic showing by the champions who, if this is anything to go by, will be in with a great shout of retaining their crown.

It has been nice to finish the year with a few goals, although it would have been better if it had been a closer scoreline. Still, it improves the ol' goal average – I'll settle for that!

# Saturday, January 1

I am not one for making New Year resolutions as the likelihood of me following them through is, well, unlikely – in fact about as probable as me watching two games today, which is what I had in mind initially.

Given the enormity of the journey I had thought of undertaking, especially today of all days, I have decided to give it a miss. Besides, I had a few drinks last night, and while I'm not hung over, I don't think it's in my best interests to go.

Instead, I make the much shorter journey down to Plymstock and once again have Martin with me, this time as a passenger. He was with me the last time I saw a game on this day and it's to be hoped that what lies ahead will be a lot better than what occurred then – a scrappy game in which the only goal came from a dubiously awarded penalty.

My first ever game on New Year's Day *was* part of a double. First I saw Arsenal win at Southampton then caught the train down to Bournemouth, where I missed the start (and a goal) thanks to a signal failure. Another double saw me go to Bristol City in the morning and on to Cheltenham in the afternoon. Trouble was, though, that on arrival I found the start time had been altered to the evening! I had a third game in mind, so started off for that one, but changed my mind and doubled back to Whaddon Road for my first game there.

Looking at my records, I see that both games were fairly low-scoring affairs, but there has been the odd time when I have started the year with a goal-fest. A 4-4 draw at Plymouth springs to mind, although I missed the last goal to catch a train to Torquay for a game in the afternoon that was called off! Not one of my better decisions.

That scrappy game I mentioned saw Martin's team on the wrong end of the scoreline, but I did see them win 5-3 on this day a few years ago. What that proves is that like most aspects of watching football, it has its ups and downs. It's a bit like a tube of pastilles – until opening them you never really know whether you'll like what's inside or not.

I do know that Holsworthy are at Dean Cross this afternoon in a Peninsula Division One West game, on a pitch that was rotated from its original layout in the summer. The clubhouse and changing rooms are still in one corner, but now when you walk past the front and straight ahead you are strolling along the side of the pitch, and on the only hardstanding here. This, along with the far end, has a metal railing, with the remainder of the perimeter being roped off. These two sides are open, expansive grassy areas that form part of a public recreational spot. This includes a tennis court behind the near side, where the dugouts are.

With no cover (unless you view from afar via the clubhouse windows), this is a ground that will not rank among the best in this league, but for some reason I am fond of this place. I suspect that is due to my liking of the club, as this tends to make you look at a ground in more favourable terms than with others where logic rules. At least I think it does.

Four weeks ago I saw Plymstock in action and they have not played since then, thanks to the winter weather we have been having. Perhaps that explains their sluggish opening that should have seen them fall behind, only for Dan Jenkins to miss an absolute sitter. Colleague Craig Allen makes up for this blunder moments later, bundling in after the keeper spills a free kick. The hosts seem to have needed that setback as they gradually find their way back into the contest and get back on level terms; Aaron Hulme turning in from the left and firing low into the near corner of the goal.

The visitors attack from the restart, with an attempted through ball that would have put Allen in on goal being stopped by the hand of Ben Alcock, who only receives a yellow. It's not long before he badly mistimes a challenge on the edge of the box, though, and he is off. Four minutes before the break, the 10 go in front when Hulme on the right sets up Joe Jasper, who cannot miss. With the last action of the half the roles are reversed, Hulme scoring at the second time of asking after his initial effort is saved.

They say you can wait ages for a bus only for two to come along at the same time. Well, a similar trait can be seen at half-time as, for the second time this week, I am making a food purchase! Apart from being hungry, I believe a visit to this club is not complete without the consumption of one of their delicious pasties, so purposely delay my lunch intake so that I can have one.

Along with a nice, strong cup of tea, it sets me up for the second half and once it's under way it's the home side who continue to impress. The same cannot be said for their finishing, though, and in the end the only goal of this period is given to them on a silver salver with ribbons attached. Adam Fuller tries to throw the ball out but it hits Chris Ward on his back, looping up over the keeper and into the net.

That typifies Holsworthy's showing in the half but should not take anything away from a fine performance from Dave Baskwill's boys. He is delighted, that's for sure, as the usual welcome we received pre-match mixes well with the action that has ensued. It all makes for a great start to the year, and hopefully it is the shape of things to come.

# Monday, January 3

One of the banes of the groundhopper's life is when you make a journey to your intended game only to find it has been called off. This is what happens to me today as I make the short run down to Teignmouth for their intriguing cup tie with St Blazey.

Their pitch is not the best, so with less than an hour to go I ring the club to check – no answer. Plan B sees me ring the secretary, only for him to be out, with whoever I speak to saying they do not know if the game is on or not. Next tactic is to ring his mobile and this goes to voicemail, so as it is a small ride I take the chance.

That ground is not called Coombe Valley for nothing; it can be sighted from afar. With this knowledge, I turn off the main road and into a side one where I can see it. With 20 minutes to go I would expect to have seen players warming up or some activity, but clearly no one is there.

At this point, I do what I should have done at home and ring Phil on his mobile. He confirms my fears, but at least tells me of a game I could go to. It means going all the way back to Exeter, but it's better than doing nothing whatsoever.

I like to think I have a good record when it comes to avoiding wasted journeys like this – which was only 20 miles or so – but there was the one time when this was not so. It all began on a Friday night in November, when I bumped into a friend who asked where I was going the following day. I told him I was going to

Kidderminster to see them in a Football League match (I'd already visited for a Conference game) and somehow he got me to change my plan and go to Crawley. This seemed like a good idea as I had not been there – and of course I'd have a passenger too – so I picked him up the following morning.

The game passed an early-morning pitch inspection, so we made our way up through the downpours, arriving at two to find that it was off. Nothing for it, then, but to dash off to another ground and up the M25 to Hayes. We got there with five minutes to spare and the game was on, but not for long as we entered to see the referee testing the pitch with a ball – with little success. Splosh! It's off, but at least they gave us our money back.

In desperation, we headed west to Slough but that was postponed, so there was no option but to make our way home. We stopped at a service area near Reading and my passenger went in but I stayed in the car where, after making sure no one was around, I let out a yell or two in sheer frustration. Why did I allow myself to be talked into this when 24 hours previously I had had a completely different agenda?

The moral of this story is never to change your mind at the last minute unless it is completely necessary. Oh, and there is a footnote: not only did Kidderminster play but four months later I went to Aggborough and saw a goalless draw! I have not been back since.

This afternoon I am returning to Devon's number one city to see Exeter Civil Service play Exmouth Town in Peninsula League Division One East. This is a sports and social club based in the Exwick area of the city who have overachieved in the recent past but nowadays just about hold their own in this league. In fact, it was only two seasons ago that an unexpected last-day home loss to Bovey Tracey gifted them the championship of this division.

The facilities here have not changed a great deal over the years, so perhaps it won't surprise if I say that the social aspect of this place is very good. As for the ground itself? Well, it is entered at the end of the car park with a refreshment hut directly to your right and entry to the changing rooms in the main building beyond this. At this point you are behind the goal, with a path snaking around behind a garage-type building to your left that leads along the side of the pitch to a covered standing area flanked by concreted dugouts. This cover is a recent upgrade and is sturdy, unlike its predecessor, a leaky, wooden one.

On the other side it is possible to stand behind the rail that runs along this side plus part of the near end but the far end backs right on to a high wire fence with allotments on the other side, thus off limits to spectators. The club share with cricket here, so the other side is open with the cricket square roped off. All in all it's not too bad.

This is a derby fixture that sees the hosts make the running early on. Civil's build-up play is very good but lacks an end product, so it is ironic that when they do score it is more through luck than judgement. Dave Wilkes undoubtedly over-hits a ball in from the left, but it strikes the underside of the bar and is ruled over the line despite the desperate attempts of a defender to prevent this from happening.

A series of saves from Adrian Pullin keeps Exmouth in contention as we go into the second half, whereupon his teammates start to show much more of a threat. Going into the last five minutes it looks in vain, but thanks to a silly foul in the box, Ben Shephard levels the score from the spot. Three minutes later the scorer puts Andy Jones in on the right and he crosses for Adam Turner to put the visitors ahead. A dramatic finale concludes in added time when Ben Murby hits the ball hard across the six-yard area and Stuart Coombs inadvertently puts it past his own keeper to give us a draw with the last kick of the game.

I attended this fixture last season, when both sides scored in added time, and as then it was a draw from an open contest that neither side deserved to lose. Ultimately, while I am disappointed to have missed out on the game I wanted to see, things have worked out well today, and I am pleased.

# Saturday, January 8

Having gone a whole four weeks since doing my last new ground, I really feel the need to do one today. Sadly, the rain has its say, though, and after a phone call it results in my planned trip being cancelled.

I have to look at an alternative and in the end plump for St Blazey's much postponed FA Vase tie with Bemerton Heath, which finally gets the go-ahead. It's a place I have been to a few times before, so my next new ground will have to wait a bit longer.

Trips to venues I have not been to before are the high points of my season, and I do not really like going this long without getting one in. The one thing I have learned, however, is that this so-called worry should not lead to me going somewhere just for the sake of it.

January last year taught me this, as after more than five weeks of visiting 'old' grounds I travelled up to Walton & Hersham and had to suffer one of the dullest 0-0s in history on a ground with an athletics track, followed by the long trip back being made even longer by what I had seen. The programme was a full-priced reissue from the original date three months before and, of course, under my self-inflicted rules I have to go back. What is it they say about rules being broken? In this case I think that saying is one I will put to good use.

Not quite as far to go on this day, and it's a journey that passes with no traffic issues – in this instance no traffic full stop. I end up arriving about an hour before kick-off at a ground that is easy to locate, being just off the main A390 north of St Austell. The clubhouse is directly ahead of you as you drive into a small car park, with the entrance to Blaise Park on your left and an iron double gate, painted green, next to it.

You enter at one corner with some more parking along this side leading up to the seated stand, whose roof seems to be a bit high for its size. On the other side of this is open hardstanding that leads around the far end and along the far side. Here it cuts into a steep grass bank with a fence at the top separating the ground from the railway line. As a consequence of cutting into the bank, there is a retaining wall at its rear and wood has been attached at the top of it, giving you the option of sitting along this side.

Straight ahead of you when coming in there is an open-sided tunnel along which the players enter the field from the changing rooms, then beyond this an old-fashioned, lean-to covered standing area with a flat corrugated roof held by wooden posts. The dugouts, which nestle into the banking either side of halfway, are of a solid construction and are unsurprisingly the only parts of the pitch perimeter that are not cordoned off – this being your standard rail and post set-up. The same can be said about the floodlighting here, as four poles are sited on each side. For me this typifies your South-Western venue which offers its best viewpoint from the top of that banking.

St Blazey go into the game as underdogs as their opponents play one level higher and are going well in it, lying second in the Wessex Premier. It is the Peninsula side who have the better of a goalless first period, though, and they are unfortunate not to be in front. Will Cherrill strikes an upright with a crisp strike, and Chris Reski hits the bar with a header as the Quins hold on.

Needless to say, it's the visitors who break the deadlock a mere 30 seconds into the resumption of the tie. Jack Slade bears through on the left and is thwarted by keeper Blackler as he tries to go around him, but the loose ball falls nicely for him to square back across goal for fellow frontman Joe Sanger, who taps in.

Thankfully, this early blow does not sap confidence in the home side, which is made evident seven minutes later when Reski's free kick is flicked on to Mamsie Sabo, who nods Blazey level. This in turn seems to fire up the Wiltshire outfit, who are rewarded for a spell of pressure on the home goal with what proves to be the clincher on 71. Sanger takes advantage of a defensive slip on the left and crosses to an unmarked Graham Mankin, who makes no mistake. Late attempts to force extra-time are almost rewarded, but a fine save at the death is as good as it gets.

No matter, at least Blazey have gone down gallantly and can take consolation from their performance in a good cup tie which – unlike their last one – was at least played!

# Sunday, January 9

That phone call preventing me from making a wasted trip yesterday was not all bad, as it was another contest which suffered due to the bad weather and, I'm glad to say, has been rescheduled for this afternoon. I'll not have to wait that long after all, then! There is a morning inspection and it gets the go-ahead, so my intended fare of footy has merely been put back 24 hours – or, to be precise, 22 as it kicks off at 1pm.

That destination is Westfields, who tackle northern-based Billingham Synthonia – don't you just love these exotic names in the FA Vase? Westfields is on the north-western outskirts of Hereford and not far from the racecourse. As it's a Sunday, my drive up is not too bad and I arrive in good time to park in one of the few spaces available.

As with Pegasus, I have to pass along Edgar Street past Hereford United's ground. I well remember my last visit there, as it was a relegation shoot-out between them and Brighton. Driving past that stand I remember standing on the terracing sited underneath, from where I saw Robbie Reinelt smash in a superb equaliser in front of the away fans. This kept their team in the league, but I also recall a last-gasp chance missed by the Bulls that would have given them the win they needed.

Looking at the current state of these clubs, you can't help but wonder how different things could have been if it had gone in. Would Brighton be where they are now? Maybe not, but I have to admit I was glad they stayed up because of the loyalty their fans showed during those troubled times. That faith is being rewarded now, with the new stadium at Falmer being built at last after so much faffing around, and I look forward to going there.

Allpay Park hosts Midland Alliance football and apparently used to be part of the nearby Mansion gardens. Entering in one corner, you have the clubhouse to your left, smaller inside than it looks from the out. There is open hardstanding behind the goal at this end that carries on along the far side and the far end.

That side has a good-sized seated stand bridging the halfway line, while on the near side there is a smaller covered standing area. Once more we have four floodlight poles on each side, although these are not as tall as your orthodox versions. Tucked away in a decent location, this is a good set-up.

After acquiring the team line-ups I bump into a familiar face: Kerry is in town to see his friend again. He had this cup tie down as his choice for yesterday as well and, like me, went somewhere else instead. We catch up on the latest gossip, although more of that comes from him as he is much more up to speed with things than I am. He has been here before, as is the case with so many other venues that I will probably never get to.

Kerry has done well over a thousand grounds, a figure way that is beyond my capabilities unless I live to be over a hundred! Even then I am hardly likely at that age to be travelling around the country. Also, unlike my friend, I have never seen either of these sides in action, but we have in common our belief that this game could go one way or the other.

It's a promising beginning to this match as the teams show why they are having good league campaigns. Richard Kear rattles the upright for the hosts, who open the scoring when Craig Jones's left corner is met by Phil Glover's downward header. The Tees-siders restore parity just before the break in a similar manner, this time the corner met by a near-post header from James Magowan.

The second period sees the Northern League side gradually take control, but with no luck in forcing a winner that means extra time. Time to grab a cup of tea, with Kerry's purchase of the half-time brews at Pegasus meaning it is my turn to cough up.

Less than two minutes into the extra 30, Billingham take the lead when Colin Iley sets up Nathan Jameson on the left, his angled drive just evading the keeper's dive and creeping inside the post. Westfields try to hit back, but with both teams tiring on a heavy pitch no further goals are scored, and the away side run down the clock for a fine victory.

While not a classic, this has been an absorbing cup tie in which the stronger side have come out on top, with the home team running out of ideas on how to penetrate the opposition's defence. I think they call it northern grit.

My route home takes me back on a similar trail to when I was last up this way, but this time I don't try to be a smart Alec, and I end up on the right road to Chepstow. Just before there I take the chance to visit a pub in Tintern where I have been meaning to go for a long time.

Back in the 80s, Courage brought out a series of booklets that listed pubs from where you got the book stamped, and when enough were obtained, you sent the sheet off to get a T-shirt, sweatshirt or tie. I, of course, trailed around and completed three books. My doing the Rose & Crown means I have finally completed another one, even though it is no longer a Courage pub. Better late than never, though, and it rounds off a good weekend that has provided the unexpected bonus of two Vase games instead of one. Great stuff.

# Tuesday, January 11

It's funny how your attitude towards certain things can alter drastically due to circumstance. My friendship with Martin is one of those instances.

Before this, my opinions of his club Taunton were, shall we say, less than favourable as I enjoyed watching their Western League rivals at the time on a regular basis. Tiverton Town had a terrific side back then – one that vied with the Somerset club for the title every year until gaining promotion into the Southern League, thus leaving Taunton a clear run to the title before coming up themselves. While my comparative thinking about them hasn't completely turned around, it has to be said that I am no longer willing Tivvy to success like I used to.

My first game at Ladysmead was on a Sunday in the 90s – one that saw me enraptured by the home side's style of play and the quality of some of their side, which included current boss Mark Saunders. Nowadays, talk is rife about the system that uses a third frontman behind two out-and-out forwards, but back then Saunders was very effective in this role and scored a lot of goals. This inevitably led to him joining a Football League club, where a solid career ensued in the lower leagues until he suffered a broken leg which, in the long term, has brought him back home, so to speak. Long-standing followers of the club talk of him being Tiverton's best-ever player, an opinion I couldn't possibly dispute.

Along with a successful spell in the league, Tiverton have had a sizeable number of victories in the Devon St Luke's Bowl and seemed to win it every year back in the Smith/Everett/Saunders days, although this competition did not involve non-Western League clubs at that point. It has only been in the last 10 years or so that the Football League clubs have made a significant mark in it, which perhaps cannot be said for the Peninsula Premier clubs so far, although it's early days.

This is why I am attending tonight, as the Royal Marines have come up for a first round tie. They were drawn at home but have no lights, so the tie has been switched. With Tivvy being three divisions higher, a home win looks a formality, but I have a sneaking suspicion that a combination of the away side raising their game and their opponents taking it lightly might make for an intriguing contest. I have seen the Ambers lose in this competition under similar circumstances, so the prospect of a repeat showing definitely warrants my attending tonight.

When I first came to this ground there was not much here, but it's a lot better now. As you drop down into the car park, the clubhouse, which can only be entered from within the ground, is ahead of you. This can be done through a turnstile in the near corner and a walk alongside the pitch, where there is terracing. The centre section of this is covered, with some seating directly in front of the clubhouse doors. Once through those doors you have a choice of going left or right, as both provide matchday hospitality.

At each end there is some more terracing, with the areas directly behind the goals being under cover, while opposite the clubhouse is a stand with amber-coloured plastic seating. This runs two-thirds of the way along before there is a gap and then the dressing rooms, which are a reminder of days past. There are four floodlight poles, each with three lamps, down each side, sitting alongside the pitch perimeter formed by a concrete wall with a metallic covering. The metal fence that encloses this venue rounds off a tidy ground.

I have been here many times now and have seldom seen a dull game, with most of these occurring in more recent times. I have already mentioned Tiverton's halcyon days in the Western, which yielded quite a few comfortable home (and away) wins. Looking back now, I find it odd that I didn't mind seeing such so-called contests. Naturally, the home faithful relished seeing them win by four, five or six every week, but there has to come a time when it gets a bit much. Promotion to a higher and more competitive division was a blessing in that respect.

Strangely, the Western League game I remember most was against Backwell as the visiting front two gave the hosts a rare roasting. It was 1-5 until Tivvy snatched two injury-time consolation goals, thus making it a tad respectable, but it was a big shock at the time. I went to see Tiverton's back-to-back Vase wins at Wembley which, despite their goalscoring prowess, only finished 1-0 on each visit. Pete Varley and Scott Rogers were the respective marksmen who, as a result, etched themselves in the club's history book (written by Kerry Miller).

Since the club moved up, two memories spring to mind. The first was an end-of-season game against Hinckley that was goalless at the break but 7-2 at the end, with the home side scoring at will. If five more minutes had been played I am in no doubt that it would have been double figures. The second was the Dorchester play-off game that decided who would become one of the founder members of Conference South. This was played at Exeter City as the club had pre-booked a concert at their ground and were unable to use it.

Even now I find that baffling, and in all probability it cost the club a Conference place. Throwing away the advantage of playing at home is not the cleverest of strategies, and it was one that saw them lose to the better side on the day. Since then Tivvy have been unable to get close to a shot at redemption, and I'm not sure if they have ever recovered from that setback. They have only themselves to blame, I'm afraid.

The same could be said if they lose tonight, as the home side have rested a few of their first-choice players. Word must have got out, because there is a sparse crowd here this evening. Those who are here see Tiverton go in front early, as a poor defensive clearance results in Liam Ellis scoring with a low shot. Marines hit back, with Stu Morgan and Simon Bochenski going close, but it's the home side who find the net for a second time. This is thanks to a Colin Marshall penalty, given for a handball just inside the box, and by half-time the home side are in control.

After the break, the Peninsula outfit show little sign of pegging it back but deserve some reward that in the end never comes. Tiverton, whilst unspectacular, look solid and composed. They at least spare us a goalless half, as a defender's slip allows Adam Mortimer a free run on goal. He duly slots home a third goal – one that puts the icing on the cake of what has been a comfortable passage into the next round.

It's a pity the Marines players haven't shown as much precision as in the as yet unheralded pre-match competition that in my opinion should be in the next Olympics. It requires the player to smack the ball with his foot towards the back of an unsuspecting spectator's head – a feat accomplished in gold medal-winning style here, as I can personally testify. It hurts, although not quite enough to justify bawling and squealing like some of those Premiership divas. On the other hand, it does prove that the adage 'No sense, no feeling' has some credence, which could also apply to my somewhat inaccurate instinct on this game.

The home manager's decisions have been justified by the result, which is one of the many reasons why he is in the game while I am a mere onlooker. From my point of view, though, tonight was a bit of a let-down. Never mind.

# Saturday, January 15

The Beatles once sang about the long and winding road, which today will lead me to the door of Hellenic club Flackwell Heath – one of the two grounds I need to do to complete the Premier Division.

Despite a minor hold-up on the drive up, I arrive just after two o'clock. Flackwell is to the south-east of Wycombe and is reached by a twisty (but not that long) route from there. Once in the village, you access the ground via a small lane just off the main road to the left, but I only manage to spot the turn just after passing it. I stop to reverse, only for a bus to be right behind me. With him being unable to pass I have to drive on, then turn around at an appropriate spot and go back for what is now a right turn.

That's the trouble when you do not know exactly where the venue is, although I have gone through worse scenarios than this before. Finding Roman Glass St George is one case I have already mentioned, and another was when I drove past the narrow entry between houses for Winterbourne.

Turning into the car park, you have the clubhouse in the corner on the left, with entry next to it. Parking is on coarse gravel – of which I am not a fan – but at least it's not a nightmare when it rains, unlike some places I could tell you about. I spend some time in the clubhouse, which is bright on the outside but as dark as the Black Hole of Calcutta inside! This is one of those that can only be accessed from outside the ground before the match, and is pretty much average for this league.

Soon it is time to hand over my cash and enter Wilks Park. Straight ahead of me down one side is a covered area with seating and standing divided by the players' entrance from the changing rooms at the rear. Spectators have to go around the back of this if they wish to reach the covered standing and the open area beyond this that leads behind the far goal, where there is some cover. This is replicated at the car park end, while opposite the players' entry to the pitch is a reasonably-sized stand with plastic seating.

# DIARY OF A SEASON

Twin lights are on each of the four floodlight poles on each side of a venue that is enclosed by a mix of housing and trees. It's not quite your typical village setting but it is all right, albeit with a run-down feeling about the place.

This afternoon's visitors for league action are Shrivenham who, like the home side, I have seen only once before. The Flackwell game was that goalless match at Wantage, while my visit to Shrivenham saw them come from behind to win a fine FA Vase clash against Dawlish – a trip I recall more for what happened afterwards than anything else. I would certainly have taken a repeat of the score from that day here, but not the aftermath.

At 3pm it is a case of wait and see. After 40 minutes of this clash I am still waiting for any sort of decent chance, as the hosts struggle to put any moves together against opposition who are content to stifle them. Flackwell go close before the interval, but this match deserves its goalless scoreline at this stage.

On my way to the tea hut, I hear the gateman tell the secretary how much money he has taken. Without giving a figure, I will say it is a double-figure total. It is indeed a sparse attendance, confirmed by my headcount of 25! You have to wonder how they will pay the officials here, as the sum gathered clearly will not cover that. Presumably they have other sources of income that will cover the shortfall, but it's a shame most of the locals seem reluctant to support their club. Mind you, if it's been as bad on the pitch as the opening half here, I'm not surprised!

It never helps, of course, when the physical aspect of the game goes too far, which has been a telling factor up to now. Upon resumption, I hope that a breather will have calmed things down a little. No such luck, though, as a tackle by Dan Conway is deemed bad enough to warrant a red card and, by retaliating, Adam Paget restores parity in player numbers as well as the score.

Nine minutes later Shrivenham lose Chris Flanagan to two bookables, which triggers a good spell of pressure from the home team. This pays off when a crossfield ball finds Lee Thompson free on the right, and his strike beats the keeper at his near post. Craig Shand's late challenge reduces the visitors to eight before Flackwell get a second goal to wrap up the league points through Adam Harman, who is found with acres of space on the right to score at the second attempt after his first effort is smothered. He should bag another at the death, but at the final whistle I am just relieved that I have not made it two out of two goalless Flackwell games.

Overall, this has been a poor advert for the Hellenic, with the issuing of four red cards pretty much summing up the contest. These things happen, though, and I cannot expect every match I see to be a colossal classic – this has been a long way from that!

It's an uneventful ride home, which is more than can be said for the aforementioned occasion when I last saw Shrivenham. I got away promptly after the match, but near Swindon my accelerator pedal decided not to work any more. A call on my mobile resulted in my waiting around about an hour before I was towed off to a side road. Here, I had to sit for another hour or so before being loaded on to the back of an RAC truck and taken home.

Touch wood, this is the only time I have broken down like this, and thankfully it occurred after and not before the game. Nonetheless, it is not something I would recommend, and I am keeping my fingers crossed that there will be no repeat of such instances or similar. I have broken down in works vehicles as well, but at least you get paid for the inconvenience of the extra time spent on the side of the road then! I think it's safe to say I will take watching poor games if it means getting there and back without any hitches – which is a precise summing-up of my day today.

# Saturday, January 22

Rain is on the menu again this week, so once more I go seven days without seeing a game. In recent years this has been a rare occurrence throughout my campaign, but this time round it seems to be happening quite a lot. Part of this is due to the weather, but another factor is my being not so keen on the long midweek runs that get me home in the early hours.

I have to say the latter aspect is creeping into my Saturday thoughts a bit more these days, but it's the former that ensures I will not be going far this afternoon. With it being Devon Premier Cup quarter-final day, I have the bonus of getting a new ground in, as the draw has given Sidmouth a home tie. The Devon & Exeter side have been pitted against Liverton, so once more I will be watching a Peninsula club travel to a lower divisional team in this competition.

Sidmouth's ground is located in the northern outskirts of this coastal town and is not too difficult to reach. Given how close it is to where I live, it's been quite a while since my last visit to a place which, contrary to rumours, does have some form of nightlife.

A director of the company I worked for had a pub crawl on his birthday and invited me among others to tag along. I'm not sure we sampled all of the town's hostelries, but we must have done most of them. In one of the last ones there was a piano which, for some unknown reason, the director asked me to play. I must have had a few as I obliged, even though I had never played this instrument, and got some cheers although I suspect this was drink-related! Goodness knows what it must have sounded like, but we weren't thrown out so I suppose it couldn't have been that bad.

Who knows or cares, as it was a great night out with a top bloke with whom, sadly, I have lost touch. He does not like football, so the odds of me seeing him at the ground today are about the same as me finding Prince Charles in attendance. As it is unlikely that our future king is a Sidmouth Town football club fan, I think it's safe to say that the chance of this occurring is remote!

You enter this ground off Manstone Lane and drive along a narrow path, with the pitch to your right and the clubhouse/changing room building to the left, reaching the car park just past this at the end. This building looks fairly modern and has good facilities, but the big surprise is the issuing of a programme, which is extremely rare at this level. Apparently the first ever issued by the club, it comes with the £2 entry fee and is a welcome bonus I had not been expecting.

It's nice to get a programme from every ground I visit, but at games like this I have presumed there would not be one and have not been wrong — until now. Naturally, it would be great if clubs put out a team sheet but I understand why they fail to do so: the costs involved make it unviable. The Peninsula League has a rule that some form of programme or sheet must be put out for games, with clubs paying a fine when they fail to do so — something I definitely agree with, although some may think otherwise.

My feelings on this subject are not as extreme as they once were, so I do not now consider getting a programme at a place I have already been to as a must. In the past I have resorted to asking strangers if they will part with theirs when I have been unable to get one myself, which I didn't really like doing. Sometimes you would get a cursory or even nasty response, which was uncalled for in my opinion, but there we are.

Another example of my eagerness to get a proggie came when I went to what I, and many others, thought would be Burnley's last League game against Orient. I arrived over an hour before to find programmes had sold out, so ended up asking at the main entrance if they could get hold of one from somewhere on the basis that I'd come up from Exeter and it was my 92nd ground — well the first bit was true — and they came up trumps. Interestingly, I was told of one guy who bought *12* copies, so after the game — which the home side won to stay up — I wondered what he could have done with all those spare ones. Serves him right for being so greedy.

It is a sell-out today as well, with my new friend purchasing the last copy. We get acquainted when he asks me if that A5 mini-booklet in my hand really is a programme for this match, which I confirm, and from there we seem to hit it off once he recovers from the shockwaves I also feel on this momentous occasion! He is a first-time visitor here as well, having made the journey west from Dorchester, and tells me that he is the football club's announcer.

We take the short stroll across to the pitch, which is part of a recreational area that has no cover or hardstanding, with the playing area being roped off on all four sides. Temporary dugouts are on the far side, with a tarmacked enclosure behind that has bumps and ramps used for skateboarding. The far end has a metal fenced perimeter that divides the ground from the road, while at the near end it is tree-lined with a public footpath in between.

Speaking to one of the people here leads me to news that hardstanding is in the offing, along with permission being sought for a stand to be erected. This is just as well, because in the ground's current state the club have little chance of going up into the Peninsula League, so I can only deduce from this information that they will be ready if this were to come about — I hope so, anyway.

As underdogs, the last thing you want to do is concede early, but that is what happens when Liverton score inside a minute. Rob Farkins is at the far post to meet a cross from the right with a header that loops over the keeper and into the far corner.

This establishes a lead that his side hold on to without any concerns up to the break.

Chances missed in that period prove costly, though, as the home side level three minutes into the second half with their first real attempt on goal. A free kick on the edge of the box deflects out to Andrew Thomson, whose shot is going wide before Wes Tarr sticks out a foot at the back post and prods it in amid vain calls for an offside flag. This sparks an end-to-end contest in which both teams have fantastic chances to win. Josh Oak pulls off a marvellous double save for the away side, while Luke Ashford pulls off a fine stop to deny Liam Ford.

Extra time is called for, then, and Liverton soon have a gilt-edged opportunity to go in front, only for Shane Shobbrooke to fire over from the penalty spot. Teammate Ben Carter shows him how to convert a set-piece moments later, saving his blushes with a fine winning strike via a curling free kick that clips the right post on its way in. Another good save by Ashford denies the visitors, who in the end run out worthy winners.

This has been a highly competitive cup match from which Sidmouth deserve credit for playing their part. This view is shared by my new pal Terry, who gives me his number to ring if I should visit his club – a fine offer, although one I am unlikely to take up any time soon, but you never know. I do know that the day has been an enjoyable one not marred by the absence of the Prince of Wales who, ironically, has put his royal seal of approval on Dorchester's ground. Maybe he'll be here for the next home game? Mmm, probably not. I know I won't be.

# Wednesday, January 26

Seemingly not content enough with having loads of grounds to do in this country, I have recently started doing venues in Wales too. By this I mean the Welsh League, as I have already done the clubs who play in the English league's top divisions.

Martin is the person who has got me interested in this, which has gradually become an pleasurable experience even though the standard on the pitch is not that good. I do enjoy going with him across the Severn Bridge to these places, so his apparent wish to visit Bryntirion for their First Division fixture against Cardiff Corinthians is one I am happy to go along with as a passenger.

The ground is located on the outskirts of Bridgend and is one Martin has been to before – not that he can remember the way to our destination. He has brought along a piece of paper showing directions taken off the website, which turns out to be as much use as a chocolate teapot, and it's only through good fortune that we find the ground. In my friend's defence, it is hard to find, especially when you are relying on a load of nonsense. While my memory of routes to venues is quite good, I'd have to say this is not one of the easier ones to recount.

We still get there in plenty of time, as our guesswork has been accurate enough. I'm putting it down to my intuitive thinking and fantastic sense of direction, while others just call it luck! There are plenty of spaces in which to park, especially near where we need to be. It's only natural, then, that our means of transportation should be positioned at the far end – Martin needs the exercise – before making our way to the clubhouse, a large area contained within a building just outside the confines of the ground. It has two entry points, with one of them coming out next to the entrance sited behind the goal.

There is a metal perimeter boundary fence all around, which is painted green and thus is not such an eyesore. Other venues could learn from this idea when doing something similar, as the unpainted silver version has a visually negative impact. Open hardstanding runs all the way around the playing area behind a metal railing, with sporadic advertising boards attached.

The left-hand side has shallow grass banking with a covered stand at the top that has three rows of blue plastic seats. Quite a good set-up, then, with four poles on each side for the lighting and very good viewing from the stand looking down on the action. On the whole I'd say this a good venue under lights – something that can be said about several venues, Cadbury Heath being an example. Unlike that one, though, I can't comment on what it is like here in daylight hours, and it may well be a nice setting. It's definitely OK at night.

So why do floodlit matches produce a much better atmosphere than those played in daylight hours? After all, it's the same sides on the same pitch playing in the same competition but played under artificial light. My theory is this: because that lighting is produced specifically for the pitch and not everywhere else – unlike during the day, of course – it somehow registers in the mind that it is special. This light is for *our* game and that alone.

There is just something about a pitch being lit up that creates that extra feeling – one that a crowd somehow picks up, thus producing a better backdrop to the action than for an afternoon game. Even in the big cup games the difference is notable, and it would not surprise me if more cup upsets were registered under lights than not.

The last time I saw Corinthians it was a game I remember for the wrong reasons. This was an end-of-season match at Caerleon that undoubtedly goes down as the worst game I've ever seen. There was only one effort on goal, and that was hit with so little power that the keeper could have popped behind the goal to the nearby clubhouse, downed a pint, returned and still had time to save it!

Things are never going to be a bad as that this evening, although by half-time a goalless game looks on the cards as the home side are unable to penetrate a resolute back line. Within two minutes of the restart, they do break the deadlock as a cross-field ball puts Jon Cuss in on the right and his low-struck shot beats Rob Bloor at his near post.

The visiting custodian pulls off a brilliant stop, somehow tipping a close-range strike around the post, before being beaten again just past the hour; Rhys Llewellyn's centre headed in at the near post by Cuss. Having netted twice, the scorer turns provider on 78 when his cross from the right is met by Brian Burke's downward header. The visitors can only muster one real half-chance in the period, and they are a well-beaten outfit by the end.

Ultimately, Bryntirion's patience – a lot better than mine was at the midway point – has paid off. That's the one good thing about pessimism – when your prophesies of doom and gloom on the pitch are unfounded, it feels so much better – and I have a warm feeling on the way back afterwards. Which is more than can be said for the weather this evening. Boy, it's freezing!

Martin takes an unexpected detour on our way home. We have to come off the M4 near Newport, going down the slip road and rejoining on the other side. This means taking the third exit off the roundabout, but for some reason he takes the first one. Now we are on a dual carriageway heading north for several miles before we are able to turn back.

Cue red face from the driver, whose digression results in a later return home. Never mind, we are all prone to making the odd *faux pas* – I certainly have – and it hasn't spoilt a good night out.

# Saturday, January 29

A long day is in prospect as I look to tick off the second new Football League ground at Morecambe – a journey that's made a tiny bit smaller by my departing from my friend's place near Bridgwater, where I'm staying for a few days. I start out with a sense of apprehension, as the cold snap has returned to our shores this week. It has affected the whole country, with several games already called off as I make my way up the motorway.

The Shrimpers are due to take on Macclesfield, so I tune in to the radio at regular intervals to check if it's still on. Things look good as I join the M6, but half an hour later bad news is transmitted: a frozen pitch means I will have to wait a bit longer to visit the new arena.

Luckily, I have set off this morning with a plan B, which is not a bad alternative as Fleetwood are at home to Forest Green Rovers in a Conference Premier clash. Having found out in time about my original choice, there is no need to turn around; instead I turn off a tad earlier and hook up with the main route into a town just to the north of Blackpool. I arrive at about 1.30 to find the game is definitely on – phew!

There is plenty of street parking to be had, so with oodles of time to spare I take a stroll into the nearby town centre. From there I have a walk along the seafront on a road that, I believe, leads on to the fabled Golden Mile. There are good views across Morecambe Bay and the Cumbrian fells in the distance, but there is a cold breeze coming in. As catching double pneumonia is not on my agenda, I head back to what I have actually come here for.

Fleetwood play at Highbury, which, of course, is also the name of Arsenal's old ground. They play in a similar kit as well, but it is there that the coincidences end.

I have certainly never felt the same way upon entering this version as I did on that day back in the 70s, although I would hardly have expected that.

The new stand on the far side is a sight to behold – one that is not quite finished. It has a shallow, arched roof with two levels of seating and some hospitality boxes. Both ends have covered terracing, with a gable-roofed clubhouse located behind the end where you come in. To your right on this side is a seated stand that goes to up the halfway line. This is where the players enter from the dressing rooms sited behind in what remains of the old stand.

Beyond this point is the area that could do with a little improvement, with an old building that seems to be a social club not really fitting in with what would otherwise be a perfect venue. The pitch certainly falls into that category, and it is easy to see why they rarely have postponements here. In the corners we have floodlight poles that fit nicely with the arena as a whole.

With programme and team sheet in hand, I settle down to watch the match in the lower seats of the new stand, which are seeing their first use today. It is inadvisable to sit too close to halfway, as the dugouts obstruct views from the lower rows of seats, but I find a good spot. From here it is clear that the home side are edgy in the opening exchanges, and Forest Green seem to sense this. As a consequence it is they who have the best chances of a goalless half, which must please their manager.

At the interval the hosts' boss, Micky Mellon, makes a couple of changes that have an immediate impact on his side's showing. On 55 a corner flighted in from the right is punched out by visiting keeper James Bittner to Junior Brown on the far corner of the box. Taking a touch, he strikes a sublime effort that arcs past the goalie and into the far corner. Bittner denies Sean Clancy with a great save, but on 78 the latter notches Fleetwood's second, heading in the rebound after Dan Rowe's strike comes back out off the underside of the bar. The away side deserve a goal for their efforts and almost get it, but a fine save ensures that the home custodian keeps a clean sheet.

I half-expected the home side to secure the three points today – no surprises there, then – and the best team has definitely come out on top in what has been an absorbing encounter.

This is not the first time I have had to revise my plans for the day. Once I drove up to Bedworth and found the game was off on arrival. Luckily for me, their secretary was on hand, and he told me of a game nearby that he was going to. I followed him down to Rugby Town for a visit which, like today, I had had in mind for a later date. The thing I remember most is the short run down the motorway, which was done rather fast as I tried to keep up with the Formula 1 imitator who had instructed me to follow him. I did not know the way, so with little time to spare had no alternative unless I wanted to miss kick-off, which would never do.

It all worked out well in the end, and I ended up doing the Oval at a later date instead, which is exactly what will happen as far as today is concerned. If I made a list of grounds I wished to do in order of preference, then my original choice for this afternoon would be number one and my actual visit number two, so it was hardly a let-down going where I ended up.

Better than nothing, that's for sure, with the long drive back to my friend's feeling shorter than it actually is. On my return I am able to partake of my pal's excellent single-malt whiskies, which put the seal on a very pleasant day.

# Tuesday, February 1

Never say never is the saying that springs to mind when I look at my options for this evening, as Dorchester Town have a home match that meets with my interest. I say this because of the offer given to me by Terry at Sidmouth the other day – one that I didn't feel was necessary at the time but has now come in rather handy. A quick phone call results in him proving as good as his word, so it's game on, so to speak.

It is not one of my favourite drives, but I am sure it will be worth it as Chelmsford – the only team I have not seen in this division – are the away club in a Conference South fixture. For once, I have quite a good run along the A35 and arrive in good time, although this does not stop me from parking in a side road nearby so that I can save the pound it will cost me to park at the ground.

Is there nothing I won't do to save a few pennies? I suspect there is, but in this instance the small walk required is worthwhile as far as I am concerned. Call it an excuse if you like, but I am not a fan of paying to park at grounds like this.

My attitude has not been helped by what happened at Northwich's new ground, where I was told that if I did not pay the £2, my car would be vandalised on the approach road where I planned to park. Of course, on the way out after there were plenty of cars parked there, with a brief glance telling me that no harm had been done. I felt foolish in the knowledge that I had effectively been conned. No one likes to waste money – I don't, anyway – and there is no doubt that what occurred at the Victoria Stadium has had an influence on my way of thinking as far as parking payments go.

The Avenue Stadium is one I have been to twice before. I remember the second occasion as being an FA Trophy game against Woking that was refereed by Mike Reed. Earlier that week he had given Chelsea a controversial penalty that gave the Blues victory and, lo and behold, he gave a similar decision here – at least I and many others thought so. On the way home I tuned into the radio phone-in show 606, on which comment was made about it.

Come Monday, though, and a browse of the match report revealed that the player who conceded the spot kick had confessed to his mistake, therefore proving Mr Reed's call to be spot on, if you'll pardon the pun! Ultimately, what this proved was that officials do tend to make the right decisions at crucial times and the story here, as a whole, also establishes that when they do err, as humans are prone to do, the media grab hold of it and blow it up. Who'd be a ref? Not me.

To be honest, this is not one of my favoured venues. The stand dominates, with two levels of seating divided by a centrally-based walkway and the roof incorporating a triangular dormer in the middle with the club's logo on it. The changing rooms and hospitality area are located beneath the only part of the ground that I like. There is some uncovered terracing either side of the stand, while the dugouts sit at the front.

The opposite side has covered terracing with metal crush barriers and a gable-type roof that has miniature dormers akin to that which is on the stand. There is a gap on halfway where you enter the stadium on this side, while the covered scenario continues along the bypass end. The town end is similar but without the cover, which effectively forms a span between what can only be described as square turrets.

These are the main culprits as far as my liking of this ground is concerned because, while I accept their uniqueness, I cannot see the reasoning behind them. It makes the ground seem more like a modern-day version of a castle, and I suppose you could say that this club has literally made their home into a fortress! With its four corner lights, this venue has a sort of evenness about it that was lacking from Saturday's visit to a Conference stadium.

After he has carried out his announcing duties, I meet up with Terry, who invites me into the PA box, but I decline as I'm not too keen on watching games from behind glass. There is an embarrassing moment when he welcomes my presence over the tannoy, provoking an enormous round of applause – not! I bet that has gone down well with the small but loyal away fans behind the goal, who have travelled a hell of a lot further than yours truly on a cold Tuesday night.

They are certainly not clapping their side off at the break as the hosts deservedly lead by a solitary goal. It comes when Chris Flood makes a run down the left and crosses to the far post, where strike partner Ryan Moss controls the ball before stroking home with an angled shot. Indeed, the homesters could have been further ahead as both forwards have had chances but failed to take them.

Terry invites me down into the hospitality area for a bite to eat and a cup of tea. I have a chat with some of the home officials, who all seem to agree that Dorchester have done well so far, with an unexpected win a possibility. I do not tell them that on my previous visits the away sides have triumphed, so on resumption just hope that that run will not continue.

Things look ominous, though, when the visitors equalise on 52 minutes; Rainford's high ball in from the left sees Rob Edmans beat the keeper to it and, having knocked it skyward, he gets to the loose ball first and taps into the net. Chelmsford are on top now and press the home side back, but to no avail as they stand firm and nearly snatch it with two breakaways in stoppage time.

Come the final whistle my belief is that as a game of two halves it has warranted a share of the spoils. No away win this time and third time lucky as I say my goodbyes and head home. Thanks, Terry.

# Wednesday, February 2

Back in October, Martin made a trip to a Welsh League game that went somewhat awry. Thanks to his work commitments he was on a tight schedule and, as most drivers know, when that happens it's Sod's Law that you get held up and arrive late.

So it was then, as my friend turned up at the ground only to see the lights go out! Abandoned after just over half an hour with him having seen but a few seconds of action. He's a pretty philosophical kind of guy, but that must have tested him in that respect. From a selfish point of view, I was relieved not to have accepted his invite to go along that night.

The dreaded floodlight failure is one most hoppers must have encountered in their lives – I certainly have. Most of the time these have been at local venues such as Crediton and Dawlish, but not always. I have already relayed the time at Lydney, when we played out the contest with one light pole switched off, but I have had a couple of other close calls too. Barnstaple saw the lights go out as we were due to start, with the match being delayed for nearly an hour and a half before we restarted and completed the match at a late hour. The other was at Portland with a similar outcome, only then the game was played with the end light of four on the stand side being out of action.

On one occasion when the lights failed it was met with cheers, as Exeter's cup tie with Swansea was called off with less than five minutes to go – well, we were losing – although justice was done in the restaging. The only thing gained by the club in the end was the extra gate revenue, but I didn't mind because it gave me another game to watch.

The odds on the same game being abandoned in the same season are remote, so when Martin informs me of his decision to have another stab at ticking off a Welsh ground, I take him up on his offer and meet up with him. More time is allowed on this occasion as we head off in his car to Aberaman, and naturally we arrive with oodles of time to spare – Sod's Law again! The club have four floodlight poles along each side of the pitch, which this evening appear to be working – hip, hip, hooray! Mind you, that would have been the case for the original staging, so no time for celebrations just yet.

This ground is not too dissimilar to Bryntirion in that it has open hardstanding all round behind a railing, along with a seated stand on top of what is a steeper grass bank. This stand has more rows of plastic seating as well, with a medium-sized clubhouse attached to the rear and a refreshment kiosk tagged on at the end, next to where you come in. There is just about enough natural light to determine that the surrounds make this a reasonable setting, making this a venue that goes under the category of good under lights.

I can only assume that the pitch cuts into a slope, as on the opposite side it falls away slightly, and the tree-lined ends are definitely not on a level plane. The end nearest to where you come in could do with a tidy-up, but apart from that it is good here.

Pontardawe, in town this evening, are put under pressure from the start as the hosts force a succession of corners, but it proves to be a false dawn. With their first attack the away side open the scoring, although whether it is intended only the scorer knows. A free-kick is won on the left touchline, which Garry Taylor swings across and ultimately into the net off the far post.

This ignites the away side and it isn't long before they score again. Luke Borelli grabs it by getting on the end of a centre that is headed back across goal for him to apply the finish. On the half-hour, Matthew Hibbs' header from a cross whipped in from the left goes in off the underside of the bar to emphasise his team's dominance at the break.

After acquiring teas, we head into the clubhouse and bump into a couple of familiar faces – one who, like Martin, was at the first encounter, only in his case from kick-off. It's always nice to have a natter and catch up on any gossip, and it makes for a pleasant 10 minutes.

On resumption, we sit in the stand and with our neutral hats on hope for a turnaround. No such luck, as Hibbs is unmarked in front of goal for a tap-in before making it five on 68 with a cool finish. Lessons are not heeded as two minutes after this he finds space in the box, but is pushed over in an attempt to get on the end of Hoskins' right centre; Steve Cox slamming the resultant spot-kick down the middle.

By now, Aberaman are probably hoping the lights will fail again, but their suffering is not yet over. Hoskins tees up Andrew Stokes, whose low angled drive nestles in the left corner to complete an emphatic win – a surprise, really, when you consider the clubs' respective league placings.

Despite the lopsided score, there have been parts of this encounter that were good, with the lights having the good grace to stay on until the end this time. For the record, Aberaman were leading in the original contest – talk about rubbing salt in the wound. I am sure Martin is happy to have made the trip tonight. I know I am.

# Saturday, February 5

Once upon a time, not so very long ago (well actually quite a long time), I could name all the Football League grounds, but I don't think I'd be able to do that now. This is not because of a loss of memory due to old age but because so many clubs have sold their ground name to sponsors.

Indeed, I can think of one or two that do not have a name of their own, and while most of these are new-builds, such as the one I did in August, there are those that have been around for a while – Huddersfield being an example. Since moving from Leeds Road it has been called after different companies, and my sad brain wonders what it would be named if not for these people.

Don't get me wrong, I am certainly not lambasting the notion of ground sponsorship as this is obviously a valuable source of revenue and in some cases actually plays a big part in the ground being built. I guess that I am just a sentimental old fool who likes to call Accrington's venue the Crown Ground and such as like.

The latest club to join this group are Thame United, who eight weeks ago moved into their new stadium after ground-sharing at nearby Wallingford. They had been doing this since the loss of their own ground, which was a short walk from the centre of town. After my first attempt was frozen off, I was able to see a game at the Windmill Ground – a Southern League game versus Bedworth. I recall it as a venue with a stand on halfway and some covered standing behind one goal that was at a slightly higher level than the pitch. The lights were on tall, thin poles like those at Bodmin, and all in all it was a decent ground, although sentiment may be clouding my judgement here.

Next to the ring road to the north of town, the ASM Stadium is easy enough to find after a relatively trouble-free drive that sees me arrive with just under an hour to spare. Time, then, to visit the clubhouse based within a white building with wooden cladding. Inside it is spacious, although I cannot understand why the ceiling is so high.

Given its recent opening, I shouldn't have been surprised to see another person who is on the same wavelength as me – in other words barmy – and I have a natter with him. He hasn't come quite as far as I have, although like me he is completing the Hellenic Premier grounds with this game.

To enter the ground, you walk past that building from a large car park and enter at the far end. Looking back to your left you see a seated stand that is attached to the modern complex, with the players' entry from the changing rooms in the middle. It is set well back from the pitch with a roof that is a bit on the high side, which means that the quality of shelter from the elements really depends on how windy it is.

With the remaining sides being uncovered, a coat is almost a necessity, as this ground is set in an open location. Hardstanding is a constant and there is a vacant grassy space between it and the prefabricated concrete boundary fence. A single rail separates spectators from the playing area, while Perspex dugouts flank the halfway line opposite the stand. Both sides have three floodlight poles with twin lamps on each. Refreshments are available from a built-in kiosk at the far end of the stand, with a hospitality area accessed through glass sliding doors next to this. Both of these have a tarmacked area to the fore, which extends along the front of the stand.

I cannot get away from thinking that this venue serves its purpose as a functional ground built merely to satisfy the Step 5 grading criteria. It would help if more cover were added in future, that's for sure. The programme is disappointing – too glossy and overpriced – and from it I note the second line of the club's address is Meadow View Park. Presumably, if the auto recycling company were to end its sponsorship, this would become the ground's name.

Wantage Town are the visiting club this afternoon. One of the better sides in this league, they, like the hosts, are on a decent run. A good contest is on the cards, but this doesn't seem apparent during the first 45 minutes. Thame never get near the away side's goal and could so easily have been behind. Tom Austin is blatantly fouled in the area, but the referee fails to award the spot kick despite having a good view. I am close to where it occurs and simply cannot understand why it is turned down.

Richard Claydon then goes close, but as we go into the second period a goal seems inevitable. It nearly comes from Thame's first chance when a cross is met by Stuart Braun, whose header is well saved. Wantage pile forward in the latter stages, with Tom Butler hitting the crossbar with a 20-yard strike followed by Ellis Langford's header that is tipped over by Milan Barisic. Butler and Claydon are denied as the official plays over seven minutes of added time in which yet another effort is cleared off the line, but somehow the homesters hold on for the dreaded goalless draw.

Thame seemed pleased about the point gained, which is an attitude that, at times like this, I cannot get my head around. Given their form going into this game it is baffling to see them play in such a negative fashion. They seem to play a 5-4-1 formation, with the added flavour of a 9-0-1 line-up at times, and this has definitely spoilt the match. I understand that defence is an important factor of course, but this is going a bit far, especially as they have been at home.

But it is what it is – a fact that stops me from feeling frustration as I travel back – not just because I have seen my first goal-free match of the campaign, but also for feeling let down by what I have witnessed. To be frank, I am not over-eager to go back, but may do so depending on the circumstances. Martin may wish to come here, meaning I can tag along with him, but we'll see. Hopping has its good days and bad, and today has been one of the latter.

# Tuesday, February 8

As well as selling off ground naming rights to companies, there is a tendency in football to do likewise to cup competitions. This is good news for those who participate, with prize money up for grabs that can add up to a tidy sum if you go on a good cup run. The FA Cup is the prime example, with massive rewards if you reach the latter stages sitting alongside the smaller sums given out in the qualifying rounds that can be a lifeline to non-league clubs.

Unfortunately, the Southern League Cup cannot attract as much sponsorship for obvious reasons, and has had more than one backer in recent years. This time around it is called the Red Insure Cup, and tonight I will be attending a quarter-final tie between Taunton Town and Chippenham.

Cup ties in this competition lend themselves to upsets, as the Premier clubs often field weakened sides in order to concentrate on what they consider more important matters. If the visitors do likewise here, the home side are in with a great chance of making the last four.

I am meeting up with Martin tonight, which is hardly surprising. Apart from the fact that I am in his territory, so to speak, there is the small matter of him being the home club's secretary. This is a duty he has undertaken for quite some time now, along with his role as a director.

Martin is, of course, a good friend whom I have known for a few years, although my memory draws a blank as far as our first encounter is concerned. I have no idea why, as I can recall meeting most of my other mates for the first time. One of those, from Essex, I met at Crewe station on our way to Chester nearly 30 years ago! It's funny how things turn out sometimes – if my travelling companion hadn't missed the train at Euston we'd probably never have met. For some reason, Garry is the only one of the lads I knew in my London days that I have kept in touch with, and I'm regretting that now.

Wordsworth Drive has some similarities to the Ladysmead home of Taunton's rivals Tiverton in that they have terracing behind both ends with cover directly behind both goals. They have the same floodlighting set-up too, but there are seated stands on both sides here. The one on the near side is on the right as you enter, with open standing on the left. On the far side is a small stand, with open terracing on its left and a thin line of open standing in front of the clubhouse to the right.

Behind the goal at the town end is some official parking accessed through a gate in the corner, which you pass upon entering the fans' parking. In that corner are the changing rooms, with the hospitality area and club offices next to this. The dugouts are on the far side, spaced at about the mid-point of each half, while the pitch stands up to the weather in a much better manner than may appear to the naked eye.

Not that playing conditions are a factor as, for once, things are good in this respect. Prices have been reduced in an attempt to attract people to this game, and while it's not a full house by any means, there seem to be a few extra here. Crowds were bigger in the Western League days than they are now, but this is almost certainly because Taunton were a winning and, thus, successful side. As a rule, this tends to attract more through the gate, although Somerset is not what you would call a football hotbed.

Like a lot of others, TT find themselves struggling to make ends meet. Budgets have to be adhered to at this level and as a result, clubs like Taunton find it hard to put together an 11 that will push for honours on small wages. I have heard some of the loyal regulars moan about the club's lack of ambition, which I find annoying.

How easy it is to criticise others for not putting enough money into their club. 'Get your chequebook out' is a phrase I have often heard and my message to those people is 'why not get *your* chequebook out?' The saying 'talk is cheap' has never been more apt.

After a tentative opening, it's Chippenham who go in front, as Guthrie's corner from the right is touched into the far corner of the net by the head of Shaun Lamb. The home side hit back, with Jon Vance going close with a drive that shaves the outside of an upright, and Rod Marsh has an effort saved. But the visitors double their advantage on the counter; Scott Lye makes a penetrating run only to be tackled in the act of shooting. The ball spins out to the left wing, from where it is whipped into the box for an unmarked Alan Griffin to net with a low shot.

After the break, the Premier outfit look to add to their tally, hitting the woodwork twice before the hosts' Alexis Piper sees his free kick from the edge of the box go just wide. The half finishes with Taunton huffing and puffing but not blowing the away back line down, and at the final whistle I feel disappointed, not just because Taunton have lost but because it has felt like a low-key tie, especially in the final throes.

Still, the home side have done well to get this far and can now focus on retaining their Southern League status, which I fully expect them to do. It's a shame they are having problems in their quest to move to a new stadium, as this would undoubtedly aid them. In the meantime, they will soldier on and this will be due to people like my mate, who work hard behind the scenes and don't make a song and dance about it.

Martin goes to all the games including friendlies, and his commitment is second to none (I'd carry on singing his praises, but I believe in value for money and he's not paid me that much!) He's a realist and knows that Taunton will never be a Conference club as things stand. Staying where they are will be a success in itself at present. I wish him luck.

# Friday, February 11

Of all of the grounds I visit on a fairly regular basis, I tend to have a mix of those where I see good matches, those that are average and those where I do not fare so well. Liskeard definitely falls into the third category, and it is here that I will be visiting this evening as they entertain Plymouth Parkway in the Peninsula Premier. Martin is going too, so he picks me up from my place and, after an hour or so, we are parked up outside the ground.

Lux Park is to be found to the north of town and has two ways of being entered. We take the option of the entry next to the main road that brings you in at one corner, with admission paid to someone in a small concrete hut. A similar means of access is attainable at the far end, coming from a car park that's shared by the nearby leisure centre.

Between these two is the refreshment and hospitality area, followed by some covered standing behind the two dugouts. Both ends are uncovered, with a concreted path at the road end and a tarmacked surface at the other. The building at the rear holds the changing rooms, accessed via steps, and a social club on the first floor.

On the far side is a seated stand and some more open hardstanding, with a wooden perimeter fence at the rear separating the ground from the facilities behind it. The four pylons on each side are vintage, with two box-type lamps on each that provide much better light than you may think. Mind you, given this ground's name they ought to be good!

Martin goes in before me and picks up the last programme. In the past I would have found this frustrating, but not now as I don't feel the need to acquire one anyway. It is not the best and does not vary from season to season. Instead, I have one of my self-designed team sheets and write out the line-ups on that, just finishing in time for the start.

Mind you, I might as well have done it throughout the opening half as there is little to watch in the way of goalmouth action. Parkway come close when Shane Krac's 20-yarder is tipped round the post and Glynn Hobbs is denied by a fine save, but it's goalless at the break.

Not for the first time, Mr Hobbs comes up in conversation as we wake ourselves up with a cup of tea. Here we have a classic example of a player who has failed to utilise the talents he so clearly has. This is a guy who, not so long ago, was offered the chance to train with Manchester United and turned it down!

Why he chose to do that is a question only he can answer, but I am not the only one who is baffled by his refusal to go. It may have been personal reasons, but how could any player turn away from a once-in-a-lifetime opportunity like that? At least he could have had the experience to savour, but there we are. Unfortunately, Hobbs suffers from off-field problems too, and one cannot help but think of what might have been.

A similar instance occurred with a player from Torquay called Mark Loram, who at least gave it a go at QPR before returning to Devon, and I suspect that both of them feel that at home with their mates is where they feel comfortable. Whether he regrets it in later years remains to be seen, but for now he appears to be content, and you can't argue about that.

Upon resumption, the only debate for me is whether Liskeard can get within 20 yards of the visitors' goal. They must have read my mind, as the hosts press forward and eventually find a way through on 66 minutes; Chris Maskell receives the ball from the left, and when his low shot is parried by Ben Elphick it's Sam Cooper who is first to react and prod home.

Parkway then make what proves to be an inspired substitution when Andy Sargent comes on and promptly scores with his first touch – a low strike into the left corner after good work from Hobbs on the right. Less than two minutes later, an attempted clearance from a cross ricochets skywards, and when it drops, Sargent beats keeper Gary Maule to the ball to head the winning goal.

The hosts lay siege to their opponents' goal in stoppage time but Parkway hold out to conclude a contest that has improved greatly in the second period. Overall, though, it has been one to add to my list of average games seen at this venue, and I will not be in a rush to return any time soon.

# Saturday, February 12

Today I am making the relatively short journey to Wincanton as they tackle league leaders Hamworthy Recreation in a Dorset Premier League fixture. It is only the second game that I will be attending in this division, having done my initial one at Westland Sports at the end of the previous campaign.

I have had it in mind for a while to do this venue as it is one of the easier places to reach, but have not got around to it until today. As it is, after just over an hour behind the wheel I am parked up in the club's car park.

The Wincanton Sports Ground is set in an out-of-town complex to the south and my way in is, thankfully, not made harder by the town's one-way system. Entry to the playing area cannot be found easily, and is done by means of entering through the main entrance and going right, passing through a cafeteria, then left for a short stroll down a path to the gate. The changing rooms are reached by going left inside that main front door, with the players walking to the pitch via a more direct route.

Once in, you are immediately struck by the main feature: the box-shaped stand on the opposite side, with steps within on which flat plastic seats are attached. The remainder of the pitch surround is open with no hardstanding and a white metal rail perimeter. Dugouts are placed either side of halfway on the open side, while a hedge runs behind the stand with a gap that leads you through to another pitch – one that is used by the reserves. There is a decent enough programme issued as well, and that is pretty much indicative of this venue as a whole.

I get the player numbers from the referee's team sheet beforehand and find an unexpected bonus: there are three officials for this game, which is at the same level as the Peninsula East and West divisions. These operate a club linesman policy that applies to almost every game now, and is the one negative aspect of this league.

While I can understand the clubs need to cut down on costs by having only one official, it does raise the question of possible bias when it comes to making crucial calls such as an offside or whether the ball has crossed the line for a goal. I am not saying they cheat, but it's only human nature to favour your side in a 50-50 call. Even when a club linesman makes an unbiased decision, he can be derided by supporters of the team against which he has given it – as I saw at Shirehampton – so in many ways they cannot win.

I did see one blatant example of cheating at a Devon & Exeter game, when the away side were denied a good goal by a phantom handball seen by the home official, and the subsequent abuse saw him walk away to be replaced by someone else. In the Peninsula I have certainly seen instances of the flag going up for an offside that was, to say the least, a tad dubious, and one does wonder whether the call was a genuine error – as it is in most cases – or not.

Mind you, I once saw an instance at Liverton where the home centre-half's header was cleared off the line only for it to be given as a goal by the visiting assistant – a crucial call as the hosts went on to win 6-0. Now there's honesty for you. I have already commented on them being a necessary evil, and this is an opinion that I cannot see changing any time soon.

The game starts well and on seven minutes Mike Notley chips the ball over the keeper from the edge of the box to put the visitors ahead. The home side miss a great chance to level before Notley adds a second by chipping Leach from 25 yards after being put in on the left. Six minutes later he is gifted another when a mix-up involving keeper and full-back leaves him with an empty net to roll the ball into, and there is little to trouble his side as we go into the second half.

When a cross from the right is knocked back for Dan Blackburn to score, it is game over with 40 minutes still to play. Wincanton do get one back thanks to a fumble from the keeper, who can't stop Dan Golden's right centre going in. Jamie Moore bursts through the middle and rounds the goalie to net number five for Hamworthy, and it's not long before Notley draws the home custodian out and unselfishly sets up Mark Dykes for an easy tap-in.

With 12 minutes remaining, the homesters bag a second consolation as Matt Hann curls the ball into the top corner, but it is the visitors who have the final say as substitute James Osborne plays a one-two with Notley and strikes low into the bottom left corner. Somehow, Wincanton miss an open goal with the last action of a game that, despite the emphatic scoreline, has been a good contest defined by the high ratio of chances converted by the victors.

The home side will play worse than this and win games in future. What a contrast to seven days ago, and I feel as good today as I felt bad then – that's football for you.

# Wednesday, February 16

Wales beckons again as Martin is making another excursion into dragon country for Ton Pentre's game against AFC Porth, which is a top-of-the-table affair. It will be a new venue for both of us, and for me a first taste of Second Division fare in this league.

Located in the Welsh valleys, this is not a straightforward ground to reach, but all goes well at first as we head north from the M4, following directions we have been given. It's too good to last, though, and we have to ask a local if we are on the right road; he says no, and that's all I can understand because of his thick accent.

Martin takes the bull by the horns and instinctively chooses an alternative way that gets us there with less than 10 minutes to spare. I dash off while he finds somewhere to park, and on entering am able to snaffle the last two programmes. When he follows later to find none left, I wind him up by saying he's missed out before handing over his copy. Ha! Ha!

Now we need the line-ups as the game is about to start. The secretary here says he'll photocopy the sheets and give them to me later, and at some time during the half he does just that. I expected him to do it at the break.

Not every club official is as helpful, though. I asked for a copy of the team sheet at half-time at a Football League ground and, despite there being a surplus, was refused. Mr Jobsworth seemed to take pleasure in quoting me some nondescript policy that he was determined to adhere to no matter what. I'll not say what club it was, as it would be unfair on the majority there I'm sure, but it was all rather petty.

For the record, I got one from another source anyway, which proves the point I have just made. Nonetheless, it's a shame that some people seem to revel in an authoritative role in such a manner.

Ynws Park has a stand on halfway directly to your left as you enter. This has shallow steps and plastic seats, a recent addition. To the right is covered terracing behind the goal with the remaining sides open, narrow grassy areas. Between the entrance and the cover is a stone building, where the players go up an exterior metal staircase to reach the changing rooms. The playing area has an orthodox railed perimeter, with lighting provided from the poles located in each corner. Although this venue is old-fashioned and has seen better days, there is an air of character about the place.

Jordan Coles misses the best chance for the hosts in a goalless half, which concludes with a sending-off as Porth midfielder Josh Owen is harshly penalised for a foul. Within minutes of the restart, Adam Wright's curled strike comes back down from the underside of the bar and out, but this fails to inspire his teammates as the match became a little scrappy.

Ton Pentre take their turn to hit the woodwork, with Chris Colvin striking the base of a post, before the breakthrough comes with just over 10 minutes remaining; Wayne Antoniazzi makes a run down the right and crosses for Chris Vardon to force the ball in. Despite another attempt hitting the bar, it looks as if that will be the only goal, but out of the blue a long ball puts Wright in on the left for a chance to level things up – one that he takes by beating the onrushing keeper to the ball for a calmly taken finish.

A deserved share of the spoils is denied, though, as deep into added time Antoniazzi is again the provider, squeezing out a great cross from near the right corner flag for Vardon to head in a dramatic winner. Quite a finish, then, to a good derby game in which both sides have given everything, which is all you can ask for.

# Saturday, February 19

Since Scunthorpe became the first Football League club to move to a new stadium at the beginning of the 1988/89 season, I have made a point of attending a game at each new venue in its first year. Two clubs have made that move this time round, and having done one in August I have decided to get the other one done today. My initial attempt fell foul of the weather three weeks ago, but there will be no such problems this afternoon as I make the long drive north to see Morecambe play Oxford United in League Two.

If I am honest, this is a case of needs must, as after looking at my schedule this appears to be the only realistic time for me to go, and while it would not be disastrous if I left it, I would like to keep that record of mine going if possible.

A long and tedious journey of almost 300 miles passes without any problems with traffic, unless you count the 50mph Middle Lane Annies overtaking nothing on the M6, and I am parked in a nearby side street with over an hour to spare. It is not that far from the old ground and is easy enough to find. There is parking available at the venue itself but, as seems to be the trend, it requires a pass to enter. This can be a bind in some instances, Shrewsbury being an example, but thankfully not up here. It's bad enough with the time it takes to drive up without adding to it with a long walk back to the car afterwards.

On the way up I could only hope for better luck than that I had visiting Christie Park. My first trip saw me call in on the way back from a job I did in Scotland, and this match was a goalless draw. Seven days later and another job north of the border saw me replicate the journey in the knowledge that I would surely see a goal this time. So much for my perceptive thinking though, as it was goalless again! I did not put the third time lucky theory into practice so, along with the National Hockey Stadium at Milton Keynes, these will be places where I will never see a goal scored.

Even now, I find it hard to believe that I saw 0-0s on consecutive Saturdays at the same bleedin' ground! What makes it more annoying is that I should have taken advantage of my situation and done a couple of Scottish League games instead, but there we are. This especially applied to the second Saturday when my revisit proved to be a waste of time, although if there *had* been a goal, I'd have seen my decision in a different light.

The Globe Arena is located to the south of town and has a similar layout to the old ground. There is a large seated stand ahead of you when walking up the approach road, and this has hospitality boxes with the changing rooms underneath. Both ends have covered terracing, although not as much as the old place.

Opposite the stand is a narrow run of open terracing with a space in the middle where you enter and a building in one corner that houses a sporting facility. This side is where I will be watching the game and, bizarrely, it is cheaper on this side than it is behind the goal. Floodlight poles are sited in each corner of a ground that looks good apart from that open side which, compared to the others, seems out of place. From a TV perspective it isn't visible, with the cameras being on this side, but it would be nice if the club could do something about this part of the ground in future.

With both teams playing a pleasing brand of passing football, a free-flowing half is the result, although it is a set piece that gives us the opening goal. On the half-hour, a free kick on the right edge of the box is squared to Steve Maclean, whose mishit shot falls nicely for Asa Hall to fire in from close range. At last I have seen a goal at Morecambe! Six minutes later, the away side double their lead from another free kick that is touched to Paul McLaren, who proceeds to curl it into the right corner of the net.

Oxford continue to dominate as we go into the second half, and on 65 they wrap things up with a third thanks to Hall's low strike from 20 yards. The home side's fortunes are summed up five minutes after this, when Tony Capaldi's fine run sees him fouled in the area. Regular penalty taker Phil Jevons has just been taken off, so responsibility lies with Lawrence Wilson, but his spot kick is well saved by Ryan Clarke. Opposite number Barry Roche pulls off a brace of fine stops in stoppage time and at the end you have to say Oxford have been good value for their victory.

This has been a good game to watch as a neutral, and with programme, team sheet and goals seen on this occasion, maybe it is third time lucky after all. Certainly the long drive home is made to feel shorter by the satisfaction gleaned from this visit, and it definitely goes down as one of my better days on the footballing trail.

# Tuesday, February 22

I have always liked the notion of attending the first-ever competitive game played on a new ground, and have done this a few times. The problem, of course, is that other like-minded people turn up and as a result it can be a little hectic pre-match. Hinckley's opening match at their new home was such an instance, with over 2,000 present when their average crowd was way below that. To be fair, the home club handled things very well, but this is not always the case.

AFC Totton started life at their new Testwood Farm home on Saturday and I did consider going, but am glad I chose not to. Apparently it was chaotic with such a large crowd, although having seen the layout on my visit in November I cannot say that I was surprised to read this. My decision to stay away was made easier in the knowledge that within days they are at home again, and having done Morecambe it's a handy bonus.

Gosport are in town this evening, so another good attendance is anticipated, hence my allowing enough time to get there and arriving with ample time in hand. I roll up about an hour before kick-off and grab the last parking space in an area that is clearly not big enough to handle bigger occasions. Goodness knows what it must have been like here three days ago, and I guess the only consolation is that times like this will not come around often.

I could say the same about access to this venue, as the only way in is via two turnstiles that are next to each other. This results in there being a lengthy queue to get in. Upon entering, one has to hand over a sizeable amount of cash, and I'll wager it is the most expensive in the Southern League, while the programme is acceptable but a little pricey. In those respects I'm glad this will be my sole visit here.

Once inside you cannot help but be impressed by what you see. Directly to your left is a large clubhouse with hospitality incorporated, and straight ahead is some open terracing leading up to a seated stand that is narrow in length but large in depth, with excellent views from the upper seating. Beyond this is more open terraced standing, which runs behind the far goal where it is narrow, as indeed is the near end.

The reason for this stems from an error in the original build that caused the delay in this ground's opening. There was a misunderstanding that resulted in a failure to provide enough space for the length of the pitch, hence the delay as both ends had to be narrowed to accommodate the minimum pitch requirements. Even now it is apparent how tight it was, as there is barely enough room to put the goals in between the pitch and the perimeter fence.

The opposite side to the main stand is similar, but the seated cover is longer and narrower, with bench seating. Floodlighting comes from four poles on each side each having twin lamps.

It is certainly a lot better than the old ground, that's for sure. Testwood Park, much more centrally based, had a narrow entry into a small-sized, tarmacked car park (no change there, then) and had an old-style clubhouse. There was an old seated stand down one side while the remainder was open, especially down the far end. I saw a Wessex League game there, and it is one of the good number of places that I have taken my dog to. Reggie the amazing groundhopping hound has been to at least 50, which is more than some humans have done, I'm sure – and no, he has not been to Barking!

The last time Totton entertained Gosport in a league game was a title decider that saw the away side win the league despite losing on the day. In the end it was so tight that if Totton had scored one more goal they would have clinched it.

No such dramas here tonight, although a good contest looks on the cards as we get under way. What unfolds during this half is undoubtedly one of the best 45 minutes I have seen from a side for a long time. Mike Gosney gets the ball rolling with an early penalty, and inside 10 minutes Totton are two up as Nathan Campbell exchanges passes with Michael Charles on the left before converting with a shot that goes in off the far post.

Twenty-three minutes in and Mike Green's cross is punched out by keeper Mark Brown, only for Charles to head it back over him and into the net. Ten minutes later, Jon Davies and Brown combine, with the former striking low past the keeper's near post. Less than a minute on it's five, Gosney letting fly from the left, his shot deflecting off a defender and looping over the hapless Brown. Ian Jones has a half-chance just before the half-time whistle, but when it goes his side are shell-shocked – as indeed am I and many others, I suspect.

It's a case of after the Lord Mayor's Show on resumption, as the hosts ease off. Just before the hour mark Gosport get one back, Justin Bennett turning his marker on the edge of the box and scoring with an angled shot into the right corner. A second comes four minutes later when he is pushed in the area; James Taylor tucking the penalty away with aplomb. Although no more goals are forthcoming it is competitive, with both sides carving out good chances until the end of a splendid contest that has been well worth the admission.

Plus marks must go to the secretary, who went out of his way to get me my team sheet and partake of an interesting conversation that was informative and pleasant.

It has all made for a great night out, and justified the round trip of over 200 miles on a Tuesday night – at least that will be my excuse if my sanity is ever questioned in such matters!

# Wednesday, February 23

My sequence of new ground visits comes to an end tonight with my eyes fixed on a Throgmorton Cup quarter-final tie. Rain means a slight change of plan, as the match I wanted to see has been postponed, but the alternative is not too bad – at least I hope it won't be. Martin is coming along as well, so I have someone in my passenger seat as I head down to Plymouth to see Parkway take on rivals Saltash United.

The home club have a settled base in Bolitho Park now and it is easy to reach, being about a mile from the A38 dual carriageway. The downside is having to negotiate the 101 speed humps to get there.

In the past Parkway played for a couple of seasons at Brickfields, and before that were at Ernesettle. The latter staged a hop game – which I attended – while I visited the former twice even though it was sited inside an athletics track, a bête noir of mine. One season actually saw them play their rivals twice away as they had no ground of their own. They managed to pull through that, and the club's future now looks bright.

Based in the Manadon area, this ground is at the far end of a car park that is shared with nearby communal facilities. You pass by two Portakabins that hold the temporary clubhouse and changing rooms before passing under some fir trees to the entry hut. Directly inside there is a grassy area behind the goal, with a hardstanding path taking you left and along the side to a covered standing enclosure – a decent-sized area with a flat roof and two levels of concreted standing within.

The dugouts are placed either side of this cover, while the uncovered path takes you all the way round to a small seated stand on halfway. The pitch is railed all round, while the ground has a high wire fence perimeter with trees providing shelter on three sides behind this. Four poles on each side provide good lighting to a pitch that is not the best when it comes to absorbing precipitation. Thankfully, it has held up for this evening's encounter.

The good news is that the changing rooms will shortly be moving to a building sited within the ground's confines to the right of entry, with further plans in the pipeline for a hospitality area on the left. This will convert a decent venue into a really good one.

I am not one for predicting scores, but based on the two matches I have seen between these two clubs here I am confident of how it will finish tonight. The first saw Saltash edge a close game thanks to a solitary first-half penalty from Marc Thorne, and the second produced an identical outcome – what are the odds on that? Thorne is playing, so a hat-trick of scores remains a possibility, and the prospects of a tight match also favour this outcome.

A heavy surface is never going to be conducive to good football, but both sides do well enough, with solid defensive play keeping the scoreline blank. On the half-hour Thorne nets with a header that is ruled out for offside – well, it wasn't a penalty, so how could it count? – and from the restart John Heveran crosses to Danny Brook, who turns inside and strikes a low shot past the keeper. Four minutes later, the scorer feeds Glynn Hobbs, who jinks past two defenders before teeing up Lee Doel's thumping strike into the bottom corner – a goal that puts Parkway in control at the break.

By this time I have bumped into a local reporter friend of mine who is the Peninsula League's press officer and a freelance journalist. Mike Sampson is someone I have known for a while and I see him at various games, mainly in the Plymouth area where he lives.

Larger than life and with a wicked sense of humour, he has been in his line of work for quite some time. There was a rumour that he covered the 'white horse' Cup Final at Wembley, but I'm not so sure about that! I do know that if you try to outdo him in the banter stakes you will lose, as he has a witty line on hand for most things. As you would expect, he has a good line of contacts so is well informed on the local league scene and, seeing as they are his local league club, he favours that lot from Home Park. Well, nobody's perfect, are they?

The second half gets under way and Saltash make a promising start. Sadly for them, the opportunities they create are not taken, and as we approach the three-quarter mark they suffer a blow when Toby Clark is stretchered off after a hard but fair challenge, resulting in a delay in proceedings.

Fifteen minutes from time the hosts make sure of a semi-final spot when Brook's cross from the right is turned in at the near post by Andy Sargent – a goal that completes the scoring on a night when the home side have won with relative ease. Not quite the result I thought it would be – so much for coincidences – but a deserved one.

# Saturday, February 26

A combination of poor weather and the amount of travelling I have been doing recently leads to my settling for a local game this afternoon, and what could be better than to see the league leaders in action? This takes me east to Ottery St Mary, who have the ominous task of trying to stop Liverton from adding to their bulging bag of league points in Peninsula One East.

At least it is a short drive and I find a dry spot in the car park, which I failed to do on my last visit in similar conditions. Basically, I drove beyond the solid areas on to the grass, which was boggy enough to ensnare my rear wheels in the process of reversing. Fortunately, an acquaintance of mine was there, and he attached a rope to his vehicle and pulled my stranded car out after the game.

This was not the first time I had done this, though. A trip to Verwood for a midweek Wessex game saw me drive around the rear of the clubhouse and towards the pitch. In the dark, I assumed you could park there and, after finding this not to be so, made to turn back. In attempting this I drove into what you would call a muddy lake and was as stuck as you could possibly be. Two friends of mine tried to push me out, but this merely resulted in a pair of muddied pals, and it was a stranger who saved the day, pulling me out with his 4x4. Needless to say, I have been 'reminded' of my *faux pas* at regular intervals since!

My first visit to Washbrook Meadows didn't pass without incident, either. I rode my pushbike there and, on a sharp ascent, in the town my gear cable snapped. In the end, I left the bike in an outer shed and got a lift back to Exeter with one of the Ottery players. The next day I went back to retrieve my stricken machine and, looking back now, I am amazed it was not stolen. That outhouse had no door and my bike was unlocked, so I'm guessing no one felt that desperate; it was hardly a lean, mean racing machine. I treasured it though, and after all these years it still hangs on hooks at the back of my garage, along with the mountain bike I can no longer use. Ride to Ottery? Hell, I'd struggle to ride to the end of my road!

The home side lost heavily that night, and the smart money is on a repeat this afternoon. On a heavy pitch. the visitors camp in their opposition's half and eventually break through when Ben Carter plays Dan Broadway in on the right and his low cross is tapped in at the far post by Robbie Bowker. Six minutes later Derek Fields slams home a penalty that has come from a needless handball, and Liam Ford then nets from a Broadway assist. Ottery go down to 10 as Jamie Jones feels the need to abuse the referee, who sends him off for his troubles, and soon after Ian Down crosses for Liam Jones to make it four with a low drive into the right corner.

At the break, I buy a cup of tea from the refreshment hut next to the clubhouse, which has a raised patio area at the front. Entry is to the left of this building, and if you go left at the end there are two steps down to a path that runs behind the goal, with a metal rail pitch perimeter. In the corner, where an old cricket pavilion sits, there is a gap before both path and rail resume their course along this side, with a small row of uncovered seating near the halfway line.

The opposite side has railings flanking both ends of the wooden bench-seated stand that provides the only cover here. From the clubhouse, another hardstanding path leads to this, which is accessed on this side only and has the dugouts in front at each end. To reach the open, grassy standing beyond means walking behind the seated area, and along this small stretch you are hampered by some small trees.

The far end is open, with dense fir trees dividing this playing area from another behind that is used for lower divisional games. The changing rooms are in a rectangular, flat-roofed structure that you pass in front of just before reaching the stand, and the four floodlight poles, each with two lamps, do a surprisingly good job on an expansive pitch that, as today shows, holds up very well to wet conditions.

With the game effectively over, the sides resume and through a mix of the visitors easing off and a show of pride from the homesters a competitive half ensues. Only one more goal is added – Shane Shobbrooke and Bowker combining down the left, with the latter crossing for Broadway to score from close range. Ottery could have got a consolation with the last move of the match, but in the end it bears a resemblance to what happened at Totton in the week, only nowhere near as good quality-wise. In fairness, the outcome is pretty much as I expected, so disappointment is not the order of the day.

# Wednesday, March 2

An upturn in conditions means that, unlike seven days ago, I can make my once-a-season visit to Dartmouth as they take on the might of Bodmin Town in a Throgmorton Cup quarter-final that was rained off then.

It's not the most straightforward of journeys down from my place, hence my reluctance to go there more than once a year. Most of the drive is all right, but no matter how many times I do it the last five or six miles seem to go on for ever. Then there is the windy section from the A38 to Totnes, with the alternative being shorter but time-consuming.

The consensus seems to say that Appledore is the worst Devon club to reach, but I tend to disagree. There are parts of that northbound trip that are irksome but the rest is OK, especially on a sunny day when it becomes a relaxing drive up. Going to Dartmouth always seems to be a race against the clock somehow, even though I have never arrived late or cut it fine for making kick-off. I guess it's just one of those oddities in life – at least in mine, anyway!

The club has an arrangement with the nearby Lidl that enables you to park at the store. It is but a short stroll along the road, past a BP garage and through an iron gate, bringing you in behind the goal. The building to your left is the clubhouse, entered from an outer door just past the gate. A refreshment facility is on the end and there are a couple of benches at the fore where you can sit and watch the action while eating or drinking.

To the right upon entering is a path that trails around to a wooden covered stand with old-fashioned bench seating and a flat area in front. With the dugouts flanking this, it makes for poor viewing, especially near the front. There is a gap in the middle where the players come out from the changing rooms underneath. The area beyond the stand is open and grassy, which also applies to the far end and the opposite side. This has a hedge line that divides you from the road behind, and being on a small ridge, has a small seated area cut into it near halfway.

Behind the far goal is a grassy area where you used to park, and there is a wooden rail pitch perimeter. The recent addition of floodlights down each side has enhanced this venue, and plans are on the table to replace the stand which, at night games like this one, is very dark inside. The drawings look impressive but, of course, the costs of seeing this project through will be astronomical for a club like this and it may well not go any further. I hope it does.

# DIARY OF A SEASON

My visits to Longcross have produced a mix of good and not so good. The hop game against Newton Spurs was the first, and a Devon League title decider the second – the hosts beating rivals Stoke Gabriel and thus giving the championship to Budleigh. In that game Stoke missed a penalty when it was still level; ironic, as earlier in the month they had lost the cup final on spot kicks and as a result took second place in both major competitions for the year. A couple of years later, the Darts won their last league game again, but this time it was they who clinched the league crown with a nervy single-goal win.

Under the astute management of Garry Lobb, they were one of the better sides during the Devon League years. Peninsula success has eluded them, at least in terms of trophies, but in my opinion they have done well to maintain their Premier League status – one that has never really been threatened – and that is a victory in itself.

Dartmouth had a good win at the weekend, and as underdogs this evening I can see them taking the fight to their opponents. What actually happens is a case of attack versus defence as they are made to sit back. The back line holds firm until the 40th minute when Chris Luxton sets up Steve Colwell, who strikes home from 15 yards.

Now behind, the home side come out with a more positive attitude after the break, but cannot find a leveller. Dan O'Hagan misses a sitter when the keeper spills another effort from Colwell, but soon after Bodmin do get a second. Steve Ovens has just come on, and his first touches see him take the ball from a throw-in on the right and head for goal, evading two tackles before shooting low into the net. The same player finds himself onside on the left and he presses on, rounds the keeper and calmly slides it in.

A quick-fire treble is only denied him by the crossbar, before a comfortable win is secured near the end – a move that begins with Lewis Reed's threaded pass putting Luke Hodge through one-on-one. He hesitates enough while going round the goalie for a defender to get back on the line, only for the visiting forward to place the ball past him and into the far corner.

All in all a solid if unspectacular showing from the Cornish outfit, who are in the semis yet again – they certainly know how to get the job done – and whilst they're not pleasing to the eye, you cannot knock their effectiveness. Personally it's just not the kind of football I would enjoy watching on a regular basis, but as an idealist I guess that's easy to say. Bodmin fans won't be complaining, that's for sure. They say there is more than one way of skinning a cat, and that applies to the methods used to find a winning formula in this game. It's what makes it what it is: fascinating.

# Friday, March 4

I team up with Martin once more as he is off to watch Goytre United play Afan Lido in a Welsh Division One fixture. As it's a Friday night game, he feels the need to allow enough time for traffic hold-ups – his Aberaman experience taught him that lesson – and I have no qualms about that.

So it's up the M5, across the Severn Bridge and into the inevitable traffic bottleneck around Newport – only there isn't one! As a consequence, we arrive at the ground an hour and a half before the start, which could have been a tad earlier if the driver had been able to remember where we should exit the motorway. Then, after going through the village, he passes the turn into the ground and, as we are in a narrow lane, a three-point turn proves tricky. Just as well we do have time to spare, as I've seen ships turn around quicker! Martin, though, has yet to perfect the art of getting stuck in a lake, unlike some!

Finally, we drop down a steep slope and right into the large parking area, with the clubhouse to the left at the point of entry. Here, we kill time by perusing the trophies of old, along with pennants and photos. The club appear to have a good history if this is anything to go by, although I can only go on more recent times.

Strangely enough, we were at the game played between these same two clubs – one that decided the title – last season. Goytre travelled to the Runtech Stadium, and in front of a large crowd won the league in a dramatic finale, Lido going ahead and looking like winning it themselves, only for the away side to snatch it from their grasp. It was terrific stuff on a night I'll recall as one of those 'I was there' moments.

Glenhafod Park is set in a fine valley location, and with our early arrival I can at least appreciate that, as it's still in daylight. There is a stand on the car park side that is accessed by a set of steps and has three rows of plastic seating. It has a slightly raised position, so views are good from here. Elsewhere is basic, with open hardstanding all round behind a metal railing.

The dugouts are on the opposite side to the stand, while a refreshment facility is at the near end, which does have cover of sorts. Four floodlight pylons are on each side, with three lights apiece lighting up a tidy venue which, while lacking in certain things, makes up for them in others. I think it is a really pleasant set-up.

This is a derby fixture, and going into it the visiting side are challenging at the top again while the hosts sit in mid-table. We have been informed in a conversation with some home fans beforehand that this is due to a player exodus. Whatever the cause, I am expecting it to be a keenly fought game, but by half-time those thoughts have altered somewhat.

Afan attack from the off and score inside 10 minutes, Nathan White netting from a narrow angle after Scott McCoubrey's shot is only half-stopped. Just before the break, a foul on the right edge of the area sees Andrew Mumford curl the resultant free kick over the wall and into the top corner – a fine strike that would not disgrace any game played at a higher level.

Cups of tea in hand, Martin and I bump into a couple of hoppers we know well, one of whom I last met at Welton. They are not surprised to see us and the feeling is mutual. We are all impressed with the away side but hope for better things from Goytre. I am the only one of the group who has not been here before, and my comments on the ground are met with nods of agreement, so my assessment must be fairly accurate.

The second half gets under way, and at last the home side threaten to get back into the match. All to no avail though: the away side are able to see off whatever is thrown at them. With 14 minutes remaining, Goytre force a succession of corners, but a counter-attack sees Afan clinch the points with a third goal. From a left-sided cross, Mark Jones's header at the far post hits the bar and, when it drops, White reacts first to nod it in. He could have had a hat-trick, but by the end the hosts are well beaten, looking a million miles away from being an outfit capable of retaining their crown.

It has been a fine performance by Afan Lido though, and it completes a league 'double' over their rivals. It hasn't been as dramatic as that encounter last May, but my second sighting of both teams has been part of a delightfully spent evening.

# Saturday, March 5

They say one good turn deserves another, and so it is today. I repay Martin by taking him in my car to a ground he has not been to but I already have. The role reversal sees me pick him up at his place and head up to Banbury to see Easington Sports play Lydney in a Hellenic West encounter. There is a touch of déjà vu going on, as on the last Saturday when Taunton Town did not have a game we attended a game in this division, only then it was me attending for the first time.

As a rule I do not revisit grounds unless they are local, or in those horrid instances when I see a goalless game. Apart from helping Martin to tick off another ground, my reason for going today lies in the events of my first visit last season.

This was a midweek game that resulted in me arriving five minutes late due to an accident on the motorway. I didn't miss anything of note, but in the closing stages it was so dark that the referee had no option but to blow up with a minute or so plus stoppage time still to play. While the game was decreed to be completed, I still feel that a return is required for it to 'count' (this was the night when Ardley was the alternative). It was not one of my better nights.

Today there are no hold-ups on the M5 or on the roads I take to reach this ground, which is located in an housing estate to the south of the town. Being the sad person I am, I recall how long it took me to rush across from the motorway back then, and work out that this afternoon it has taken me all of five more minutes to cover – so much for making up for lost time! The outcome, then, is an arrival with about three-quarters of an hour to spare.

On the way up I have prepared Martin for what he will find here, as I thought it a necessity. Driving down to the end of Addison Road, you wonder where on earth the ground is. With a sports establishment straight ahead, I assumed it to be in there – it isn't. Instead, you go left and down a track. Even on approach it's easy to think you are in the wrong place, but after passing through an old gate on to a grassy area, you glance left and see the pitch.

We park up in a large playing field and walk back to the clubhouse, which you pass on the way in. Since my last visit it seems to have had a new roof fitted, but inside it is the same – an old-fashioned but perfectly acceptable place.

The changing rooms are attached to the far end and the facilities are, shall we say, somewhat basic. To the front of this building is some cover, with a row of padded plastic chairs placed at the back. This is sited behind the goal, while the two sides are open and non-hardstanding with a rusty rail that passes for a pitch surround. The dugouts face each other on halfway, with the far side being off limits to spectators, as is the far end, which is tree-lined while the other side is open, of course. Obviously, there are no lights and the playing surface is awful.

Martin concludes that I must be mad to want to return here, and under different circumstances I would have to agree with him. Just to add to the silliness of it all, the lad at the gate gives us a programme and charges us a pound each for entry, which is ridiculous really, but there we are.

Despite lying second in the division, Lydney seem to have a mental block as far as the pitch is concerned, and start poorly. Mind you, I can see where they are coming from. If the Ordinance Survey people did a contour map of it they would have a field day, if you'll pardon the pun.

No such worries, though, for the mid-table hosts – who must be used to it – and on 29 they take the lead; Dan Watkin starts it off with a run through the centre before finding Luke Bedding on the left, and he scores with an angled drive. Within minutes he is on hand at the far post to meet a deep cross from the right and knock down for Tom Foley to net with a shot keeper Mike Reddan should have prevented from going in.

On the stroke of half-time Bedding should make it three but misses an open goal having charged down an attempted clearance from the keeper. Nonetheless, by the interval the sprinkling of home supporters have every reason to be content with what they have seen so far.

Five minutes into the second period Jarred Liddington finally gives the home custodian something to do, and moments later the same player forces a good save from him. Easington are by this stage starting to live up to their name, and the game drifts until 12 minutes from time. Having blazed over when clean through, Watkin shows himself to be a better provider of goals when outstripping the left back and crossing from the byline for Jon Danby to score from 10 yards.

Lydney get one back on 83 when a mini-game of head tennis ends with Steve Jones nodding over the keeper, who cannot prevent it crossing the line. Matt Timmins misses a chance to make things really interesting in the final throes, but in the end his team get what they deserve.

This has been reasonable fare considering the state of the playing surface, and

DIARY OF A SEASON

at least this time I have seen a full game, accompanied by an up-to-date programme as well. I have to say that, despite my reservations about this place, there is more to it as they run youth teams at various levels, and the fact that they are a sports and social club means they are an integral part of the local community. The secretary here is a nice fella, and we have been made to feel welcome, but Martin and I are united in thinking that only a good bribe will make us come back here. Ever.

# Tuesday, March 8

My selection of certain games can lead me to question my sanity at times, and none more so than this evening as I make my third visit to Almondsbury. They now have UWE attached to their name, thus making them in effect a university side. I can only assume this to be a cost-related issue, as student players will not be demanding silly money and, of course, will not need to take time off from their jobs. It does not seem to have favoured them on the pitch, for they are a low mid-table side and have been since joining the Western League.

This venue resides right next to the M5, near the M4 interchange, but, unlike others in the same situation, is extremely easy to reach. Parking is just off the A38 and you walk down a dirt track to the ground. Since my last visit a number of changes have come about, most notably the playing surface being raised, although I do not know why the club felt this necessary.

I do know it has given them endless problems as the drainage is laughable, and I have passed the ground on several occasions when the pitch has been under water. My understanding is that the job was not done properly, and I can see it being extremely costly in the long run. I cannot help but sympathise with the players and particularly the officials here, because it must be frustrating for them. Frankly, it's all a bit of a joke.

I certainly wasn't laughing after my first visit here, which was goalless, although a return six months later was much better. The gable-roofed building housing the changing rooms in the far corner of the near end is still here, while open hardstanding remains – only now at a higher level, of course. Cover is provided by a small stand with plastic seating and a covered standing area next to it.

The open sides are now tarmacked and there are three floodlight poles on each side, one doubling as a mobile phone mast. A refreshment hut sits to the right as you come in, and there is a single windmill beside this which, I presume, is a source of power. Apart from the pitch, I would say this ground is much improved.

Tonight's visitors are Hengrove Athletic, which explains my reasoning behind coming here – they are the only Western League side I have not seen away from home. I have had fun and games in trying to 'qualify' their venue on my records, that's for sure. The first game there was a goalless draw and the second abandoned at half-time. I thought I would settle for having seen a goal in that 45, but a third occasion came about when Phil wanted to go and see Truro there, which produced five goals in a full game. Job done at last!

To count or not to count – that is the question as far as abandoned games are concerned. My belief is that you can put it down as a game seen if it reaches the midway point, but not earlier. I did count that second Hengrove match, but the hop game at Lydney that gave us less than half an hour of water polo couldn't possibly be in the same category. Phil *did* count it as a visit and has not gone back, while I chose to see the restaging. I guess we all have our own rules on this, and while I may have a playful dig at him about it, I understand his way of thinking, even if it is cheating!

Anyway, when I went back I took my programme with me and got free admission for my troubles – I don't know if anyone else did that, but I thought it was a good gesture by the club, and one that was appreciated. Clubs do not give any refunds or some sort of discount voucher, which I think should happen in some cases. I do recall going to Torquay once when the game was called off just before it was due to start, and when it was restaged seven days later I did not pay. I assume I got some form of readmission ticket issued on exiting Plainmoor, but I can't remember. I do recall the club issuing another programme, which I did not purchase.

The game gets going, and I take a stroll around and end up sitting in the stand. Here I meet up with a friend who assesses the referees in this league and whom I have not seen for a while. He makes notes over the opening 30 minutes, which is more than I would be doing if I were a match reporter here. Nothing really of note seems to happen as the half ends goalless, albeit with the promise of better things to come.

Over a cuppa I catch up with my pal, who has obviously been busy during the action but, like me, believes things can only improve once the game restarts. Indeed, it's not long before James Hughes's cross from the right is met at the far post by Ben Crewe, who taps Hengrove in front. Five minutes later the hosts win a corner on the right, which is swung into the box by Sam Peplow and fumbled into the net by keeper Richard Jenkins. All square then, and now a much more entertaining contest that, alas, brings no more goals despite the away side having two great chances to win it near the end.

A draw is just about right from a game played in cold conditions that has hardly scaled the heights. I am not too downcast, though, as my pre-match expectations were not great. In future I will pass by this ground many times I'm sure, but that is as close as I will get to seeing a game here again.

# Saturday, March 12

For once, I am letting the train take the strain today. There was a time when virtually all my trips were done in this fashion but times have changed, especially since I belatedly passed my driving test. Before that, all my journeys were done by rail with few exceptions, and there are various reasons why I rarely use this mode of transport to get to games now.

For starters, I had a railcard then, which had its benefits; an example being a deal by which you could go anywhere for £12 return in March only. I certainly took advantage of that offer, the biggest being my trip to Berwick-upon-Tweed. This was in the days of British Rail, when cheap day returns were not as restricted as they are now under private companies. In short, it is much cheaper for me to go around the country in my car which, along with the convenience factor, makes it more viable.

For today's trip I booked the tickets about two months in advance, and, while I'm committed to a specific schedule, it works out cheaper. I would do this more often, but the inconsistencies of our climate, along with the no-refund policy, make it a gamble I am not prepared to take.

Apart from the weather, I also worry about the train being late and me missing kick-off. This has happened before, with one day springing to mind. All had started all right but then we were delayed near Weston-super-mare, and when we stopped I suddenly realised I had left my hat – which had sentimental value as it was given to me many years ago – on the platform at Exeter. Eventually we got to Bristol, and my connecting train to Swindon was late too. I ran to the ground, arriving on kick-off only to have to queue for a ticket (it was a play-off semi). The end result was a goalless game, which meant that, for the first time, I had seen 10 0-0s in a season – not my greatest day ever. Just to round things off, I never saw that hat again. I was hoping someone would have handed it in to lost property, but no such luck.

Like then, my journey today requires a change of train – this time at Reading – but unlike then it all goes smoothly. My final destination is a tad further along at Maidenhead, where I face a steady walk north to Holyport's Summerleaze Park home. On the way out of the station I look across to the entry for Maidenhead United's ground, and they are at home this afternoon.

I did a similar run to get that one done last year in a game that the home side won with a late winner, and their match today was my back-up plan if things went awry. That's not the case, and I start walking, only to find the ground to be further away than expected.

Eventually, I branch off the road and down a track that seems to go on for ever and bleedin' ever. Just when I am starting to despair, the ground appears magically behind some trees – hooray! – and I pay to get in with a mere 15 minutes to spare.

Then I have to go back out again, as the player and spectator facilities are just outside on the right as you come in. Having acquired the teams, I collapse onto one of the chairs placed outside the refreshment hut beside the entrance. If ever I needed an indicator of how I am getting on in years, this is certainly it.

Expectation can lead to disappointment, and this applies to this venue. I thought I would find a tidy venue, but it is open with no cover. Hardstanding runs all around behind a rail, with the dugouts either side of halfway, slightly set back from the perimeter. The opposite side and the far end are literally open, with a large population of swans gathered in the distance – something to watch if the action on the pitch is dull, I suppose.

Foundations are in place for a stand on the dugouts side, so that is a step in the right direction I guess, even though it's odds on that it will be another of those metallic Atcost jobs that are springing up everywhere these days – I call them Meccano stands. It's understandable that, due to the current financial climate, this is happening. They have lights here in the form of three floodlight poles on each side. I guess with it being a Hellenic East ground, I should have expected it to be sub-standard, but there we are. If I were to come back in a year or two I am sure my opinion would be different.

Woodley Town are here this afternoon and, along with the hosts, they are unbeaten away from home. Mind you, they have only played five, with the last of those being way back on October 2! However, they start well against the league leaders and are unlucky not to score in a goalless first half. On the other hand, Holyport have a goal disallowed for an alleged foul on the keeper, at which even the away players are amazed.

Four minutes after the break Woodley go in front, with Sam Cripps sweeping the ball home after a fine run and cross from Paul Holloway. The lead does not last long, as the dubious award of a spot-kick sees Jamie Handscomb restore parity: a classic refereeing example of trying to make two wrongs into a right. From here it is anyone's game to win, but with both teams failing to take chances, it looked odds on for a draw.

Then, five minutes into added time, Adam Jeffrey whips a left-sided free kick into the box, where Danny Isaiew helps it into the net with a flick of the head for a dramatic winning goal. Barely seconds after the restart the referee blows the final whistle, thus rewarding the visitors' positive approach to this contest – one that merits the three points as far as I'm concerned, in what has been a good game.

The late finish gives me the problem of getting back to the station, which is touch and go by foot. Thankfully, I have struck up a conversation with a long-standing local supporter, who offers me a lift. Apart from being a Good Samaritan he is a pleasant guy and, not for the first time, it's a welcome addition to the trip which, overall, has been a 'rail'ly good day.

## Tuesday, March 15

After much thought, I have decided to find out what the Gloucestershire County League scene is like by attending Tuffley Rovers' game against Hanham. Barring reserve teams, this ground is the only one that has lights and, being handily located on the southern outskirts of Gloucester, it makes for a straightforward car journey up – or at least it should do.

A drive of just over 100 miles turns into a somewhat shorter one as I head out towards the motorway. At this point there is a loud bang and a tinkling sound that clearly means a spring has broken. Upon examination, I discover the suspension on the right front is lower than it should be, so I have to crawl back home.

Despite the disappointment, I console myself with two thoughts: one, it happened close to home and two, I was going slowly at the time. I dread to think of what might have happened if it had gone while I was blasting down the M5, so while I have missed out on doing a new ground tonight, at least I am still in one piece.

A phone call to my mechanic friend Mark will get the problem fixed, hopefully in time for the weekend. If not, I'm sure I will find a way to get to a game – we'll see.

## Saturday, March 19

It's all systems go as my vehicle was repaired within 48 hours thanks to Mark, who really epitomises the saying 'a friend in need is a friend indeed'. Being the eternal pessimist, I did not make plans for today until I got my car back. When I do, I make up my mind to sort of make up for losing out in midweek by doing a bigger drive than that which I would undertake in normal circumstances.

This means heading east then up the A1 to Biggleswade, where the Town's side are at home to Northwood in a Southern League Central Division encounter. It is one hell of a long journey, but in terms of traffic it's heavenly, so my arrival comes with an hour in hand.

The Waders are in their third season at this ground, which sits right next to the main trunk road. Getting there is not as easy as it may appear, though, and you are taken into the centre before doubling back, so to speak. Mind you, I cannot comment on the degree of difficulty as I choose to exit the dual carriageway to the south and pass through a village on a road that takes me straight to the ground, thus saving a bit of mileage.

Unsurprisingly, this venue has a modern feel to it, although this does not extend to the approach road into the car parking, which is a mix of stone and gravel. Coming in, you see the clubhouse directly ahead with the parking to your right. This is the side where you enter the ground.

Passing through the turnstile, you see open hardstanding behind the goal, which is replicated at the other end. Down the left side is a metal cantilevered stand with plastic seating that backs on to the clubhouse and runs along most of the pitch's length. These seats are in blocks of green and white and have a gap in the middle where the players enter from the changing rooms.

On the opposite side at halfway is a small Atcost-type standing enclosure with open hardstanding either side that links up with both ends. Three floodlight poles are on each side of a ground that is tidy enough but nothing out of the ordinary.

Biggleswade are a team I have not seen before, which is not the case with today's away side. I recall the day I saw them well, as it was a goalless FA Trophy home game against Winchester that I thought was a reasonable match. Martin did not agree, which is highly unusual as it is normally the other way around.

He is the kind of person who can take the positives out of games, whereas Mr Jonah here sees it a different way. On our return home he remarked on a return to Chestnut Avenue, but like me he has yet to do so. Northwood Park is one of a mere handful of grounds where I have not seen a goal scored, but to be honest it is not high on my list of priorities at present.

With the hosts, on the fringe of the play-offs, up against a side in the bottom two, a goal-free match is not really on the cards this afternoon. No one really expects the lower-placed side to get off to the better start, but with five minutes played it looks like paying dividends when Romaine Walker's run into the box sees him tripped; but home keeper Dean Bull saves James Bent's penalty low to his right.

It's a wake-up call for Biggleswade, who end a good spell of possession by opening the scoring halfway through the half; James Freshwater swinging in a free kick from the left that is met at the far post by Paul Barnes, who smashes it into the top corner. Six minutes later he loses his marker to meet a cross from the right with a header into the right corner, and by the break he has four goals to his name. Goals three and four come in a quick-fire burst, with the treble attained from a deflected 15-yard strike and the last through another header, this time from Freshwater's corner kick.

Northwood push forward after the break and pull one back on 56 when Sledyn Grant scores after an initial shot from Walker has been saved and Scott Orphanov's follow-up cleared off the line. However, it's not long before Barnes gets in on the act again, making it a nap hand by converting Harry Hunt's pass at the far post.

With 20 minutes still to play, Craig Radcliffe runs down the left and centres for Hunt to grab a goal for himself, and the scoring is concluded for the day when the visitors get a second through Orphanov, who bursts through the middle and slots under the onrushing keeper. He could have bagged another but for Bull, who saves his second spot kick of the day, while at the other end Brett Donnelly – on for Barnes – misses a close-range free header with what turns out to be the last move of the match.

The final whistle brings to an end a thoroughly entertaining game from my perspective, although an away fan doesn't quite see it that way. I comment on his loyalty to a struggling side and receive a cursory response. Presumably he thinks I'm a gloating home fan, even though my accent should tell him otherwise. As I drive out I see him walking, and if not for his attitude I would have offered him a lift, so he has lost out, which is a shame. Thankfully, this is a rarity and does not mar what has been another pleasurable day out.

## Tuesday, March 22

The downside of my one-visit-a-season policy rears its ugly head this week with the Devon Premier Cup semis taking place. The Budleigh/Galmpton one looks the better option but, alas, is being played at a venue to which I have already been. The other, though, is at Exmouth Town and, as I have not been there, I will attend this match, which sees Liverton take on Bickleigh.

Having seen Liverton make heavy weather of overcoming lower-division opposition in the quarters, I see it as a chance of a mini-upset: Bickleigh have pulled off some good results to get this far, whereas Liverton have had an easier run on paper, from which they have done just about enough to win every time.

Driving down to Southern Road is not one of the best journeys from my place. It is only about 11 miles, but with a maximum speed limit of 40mph it can feel like 111! Despite this, it is a well-worn route, not just when I have seen Exmouth play but also when my nan lived in a bungalow on top of a hill not far away from the ground. Combining the two was ideal, although this did not happen that often.

Mixing family and football can be a lethal cocktail. Many a time I have had to make a mad dash to make kick-off on time and, in the process, feel bad about leaving so abruptly. Nan has passed on now, going less than six months before reaching her 100th birthday – a mark she was determined to reach so she could get a telegram from the queen. We were close, and every time I go down there, memories of the times we spent together come flooding back. I miss her.

Reminiscing about past visits to the ground is hardly going to bring a tear to my eye. My first visit was one of the handful of occasions on which I travelled on a train, as I couldn't drive at that time. The railway line passes the ground and it's a short walk back in the direction from which you have just come.

This was the year when, as a Western League outfit, Exmouth reached the semi-final of the FA Vase before losing out to Fleetwood. Around 2,000-plus were at the home leg, which I did not see; it was a much smaller but decent gate that witnessed a tight encounter with Bideford. I was there when Exmouth had their record crowd (2,395) for a pre-season game against a Liverpool XI, and I've seen other league clubs such as West Bromwich Albion, Watford and Chelsea there.

Ironically, I saw Exmouth's last-ever Western home game against Bideford before they dropped out and took up the reserve team's spot in the Devon & Exeter League. They earned promotion to the Peninsula East Division, which is where they remain.

Turning in off the road, you have the clubhouse building directly ahead, which can only be accessed from within before the match. Parking is around to the right, while the entrance is on the left in between it and the changing room complex.

This is a wood-slatted, unusually shaped structure, which is impressive. Passing through, you come to a grassy area with the refreshment kiosk directly right and the clubhouse door beyond this.

To the fore of the changing rooms is a covered stand with blue plastic seats which, alas, gives obstructed views, especially at the back. On the other side is an old wooden enclosure with large steps that, frankly, has seen better days. Now utilised for standing, this has Exmouth Town's name across the front of its roof. Thanks to the dugouts, which are positioned at each end, sightlines are once again limited in places here.

All other parts of the perimeter are open concreted standing behind a breeze block wall. The far end has a hedge line that divides the ground from a playing field, while the near end lies close to the main road. This has a grass ridge and a triangular paddock that has some donkeys in it (there have been times when I swear they have masqueraded as Exmouth players!) Four floodlight poles sit on each side, two of which are the main culprits when watching from the seats. With just two lamps on each one, the light is not that good but is sufficient – a term that sums up this venue.

Liverton play in blue, but it is the opposition who are feeling that way inside 20 minutes as they are already two goals down. In the sixth minute, Dan Broadway's speculative effort from 20 yards should be saved but Chris Garnsworthy allows it to go under him and in. Here we have a keeper who blows hot and cold, and this incident falls into the latter category. Ten minutes later comes another silly goal when Liam Ford's free kick on the right is headed out to Ben Carter, whose goal-bound shot takes several deflections before going in, Robbie Bowker claiming the final touch.

Kieran Rapo hits the upright for Bickleigh just before the break, and two minutes into the second period he is denied by a good defensive block. This, though, is as good as it gets for the men in yellow as Liverton stroll to a comfortable win without ever threatening to add to their goal tally.

The term 'winning ugly' springs to mind, and it hasn't been exactly the best semi-final I have ever watched. It has been my first 'neutral' match seen here, and I have to say that if this is anything to go by, it will also be the last.

# Friday, March 25

Since becoming what I would call a hardened groundhopper, I have undergone a drastic change in the way I go about attending games, and over time I have developed certain habits. Of course there are the orthodox ones such as getting a programme and perhaps noting the players' numbers, but some of us take it a step or two further, which in my case means doing a lap of the pitch perimeter during the game.

I have absolutely no idea how it came about, but as Martin does it too, I am going to blame him for it! That is not to say that I did it before, but if so it would not have been intentional, as it is nowadays. I have recently made second trips to places such as Odd Down and Brislington just so I could do a circuit, and tonight another instance arises as I am off to Westbury. In fairness it is only because of Martin, who asked if I wished to come along, that I am going. I would not have gone on my own as it really isn't that important ... honest!

It has been over 15 years since my sole visit to Meadow Lane, so my memory of the way to this ground is a little vague. Without meaning to boast, I can recall routes quite well, but as we enter the outskirts of this town the changes throw me a little. My mate is at the wheel, though, and he has been here more recently. Even so, he is not 100 per cent sure of where we have to go, but gets the turn-off for the road leading to the ground correct, rightly ignoring my suggestion of going the other way. I am sure he'll admit to not having the greatest navigational skills, but what this has proved is that we can all get it wrong at times – some just do it more often than others!

Having got here early, we drive in and opt to park behind the goal instead of down the side. A stroll down to the far corner at this end takes us through a covered standing area – in need of repair – to the clubhouse, which is a typical old-style place with a refreshment hut next to it. Down this side you pass the changing rooms and come to a seated stand on halfway that is set back from the pitch with open hardstanding beyond, which continues around the far end and down the opposite side.

Here a small tree line separates you from the cars, while there are wooden benches at regular intervals, which give better views of the action than the stand. Four poles on each side provide the lighting on a ground that is acceptable but nothing more.

League leaders Merthyr are here this evening, which partly explains why the game is not being played tomorrow: Wales play England then. Looking at the table in a very good programme tells me the home side are up against it, that's for sure. If they're not outplayed on the field they'll certainly be out-sung off it, as several have come across the bridge to follow the Martyrs, and they will expect to see their side come out on top.

Apart from Martin and myself, there are other familiar faces that have used this game as an excuse to add to their tallies for the campaign. Kerry is one of them, and it's nice to see him somewhere other than Hereford! Another guy I know has travelled down from Norwich, and it is nice to see him as well. This is the great thing about hopping: you get around and meet new people who can become good friends, or at worst just make a visit more enjoyable. OK, there are exceptions, as I have already demonstrated – and it is why I like doing what I do.

Mind you, if all matches were like the first half of this one I would probably give up and start watching rugby or whatever. The word uneventful is the polite description, I think. Merthyr's fans may well have anticipated victory, but the players seem to feel the same way. With Westbury showing the kind of fighting spirit that belies their league position, they cannot find a way through in a goalless half.

Once we're under way again, it's the visitors who almost score when Kris Leek strikes the crossbar, and home keeper Jason Grubb denies Luke Prosser twice with fine saves. The hosts do come close on a rare foray, but on 73 go down to 10 when Ashley Groves is a little too enthusiastic – his challenge on keeper Joe Perry is somewhat mistimed. Five minutes later, Merthyr finally make the breakthrough when a corner on the left sees Prosser head back across goal for Ryan Dorrian to tap in the team's 100th league goal of the season.

It's not long before the lead is doubled as Craig Stiens bursts through the middle and, after holding off a stiff challenge, slots the ball into the right corner of the net. Grubb saves well from Leek and Prosser (that sounds like a firm of solicitors!) as the champions-elect finish well in what has not been the greatest of games.

At least I have got my lap of the pitch in along with Martin, who has stepped it up to one in each half now. Naturally, I have taken it one step further and go clockwise in one half and anti-clockwise in the other. My excuse is that you view the action from a different perspective, but in reality it's perhaps a tad obsessive. Before long I will be taking photos and other such things – some people already do; still, what's the harm? It's all part of the hopper's life and it is great. Really, it is.

# Saturday, March 26

The quantity of football one watches varies according to one's personal choices. I guess most football followers go once a fortnight with the odd midweek jaunt, while those who loyally follow their team go every week, or even twice in that period. Hoppers, though, take this on to a higher level, which can see them do more than one in a day.

Bank holidays are the most common occasions on which this is doable, but in more recent times the international schedule presents another opportunity – and today is one of those days.

For people like me, the chance to do a 'double' stopped becoming a novelty many years ago, although it is unusual for me to go this long into a campaign before doing it. Indeed, a look at my records tells me that prior to this season I have done two in a day on Boxing Day for the last 10 years.

It is certainly easier to do this when watching non-league: the professional scene seldom lends itself to such luxuries. Even the Sky games give you little chance, as the timing is so tight. Bank holiday games tend to start at similar times as well, although, if you are so inclined, a mix can be done, of course.

My first double-fix was on New Year's Day 1980, when I saw Southampton play Arsenal in the morning and Bournemouth take on Torquay in the afternoon. The Plainmoor outfit went through a phase of Saturday night games during the 80s, and I travelled down after seeing Exeter in the afternoon. In the 90s I went one further, with a triple consisting of Bristol City, Kidderminster and Hereford, and have done these kind of days a few times since then – mainly on organised hop days.

Many fellow devotees will have done four and even five in a day – a feat that I now regret missing out on. Nowadays I feel that three is an ample number of games to be seeing in 24 hours. Even that can be tiring, although the levels of fatigue can vary according to how good or bad the matches have been! Maybe it's because I'm getting old that I find the occasional 'double' is sufficient these days.

The first of my dynamic duo of matches takes me east as Axminster Town kick off at midday against Stoke Gabriel in Peninsula Division One East. It is a reasonable journey that takes about three-quarters of an hour, and I arrive in good time at a venue located up the hill from the town centre. At least it has been an untroubled drive up, whereas last time I came by rail and had to walk it.

You drive in past the clubhouse and the dressing rooms located to your left, then on into the parking, which is behind the goal and around to the far side. Most of this side, however, is grassy and uneven, whereas the near side has a narrowish track with a view overlooking the pitch, which cuts into a slope. The dugouts are carved into this on halfway, and this incline shallows out at the far end; this being the only side unrailed and off limits to spectators, with a mix of trees and shrubbery to the rear.

There is no cover here, unless you count the overhang at the refreshment kiosk attached to the changing room building. Viewing is not that good from its set-back position, what with the cars parked and the high netting positioned directly behind this goal. Pretty basic then, although plans are afoot to relocate in the not too distant future to a site just to the north of town.

With the hosts being at the bottom and Stoke fourth, it is perhaps not too surprising that the away side make the early running in this encounter. Kevin Wills comes closest when he is denied by a fine Chris Higgs save, but on the stroke of half-time the home custodian is beaten by a brilliant piece of opportunism. Dave Worthington seems to threaten no danger when receiving the ball 35 yards out, but with his back to goal he flicks the ball up, turns and smacks it into the top corner.

After the break, Axminster came out with more purpose and find a leveller just past the hour mark, when Jamie Barfoot beats the offside trap on the left and places his shot into the far corner. All of a sudden it's anyone's game as it becomes an end-to-end contest that, thanks to stout defending, looks like finishing all square. Worthington has other ideas, though, as his penetrating run down the right and low centre sets up Wills for a simple finish that, ultimately, costs the home side a deserved share of the spoils. Like the programme issued here, it has been decent yet unspectacular.

With time at a premium I dash off to my second helping, which takes me most of the way back before heading south across Woodbury Common to Exmouth – not to visit Southern Road again but to make my first acquaintance with the nearby Warren View home of Exmouth Amateurs. For once it is a traffic-free drive, which tends not to happen when you have little time in hand; not so here, albeit with an arrival 10 minutes from the 3pm start time.

The Ammies play in the Devon & Exeter Premier, a step below the level I watched earlier. To be honest, I do not make a habit of seeing games in this league and it will be only the third time. The first of those was a title decider at St Martins, while my second was a Feniton revisit, having seen a goalless cup game there first time round.

Ironically, the visitors that evening were the Ammies in an end-of-season nonentity that I did mainly because of the home side's impending relegation; I may resort to Premier games, but Division One is taking it too far as far as I'm concerned; I am not that desperate – yet! Indeed, similar thoughts have led me here today, as the hosts are in an identical position with games running out, and I have decided to get this ground done before the seemingly inevitable occurs.

Mid-table Heavitree Social United have made the short trip to be here today. This is the same club that graced the Western League with its two-and-a-bit sides of Wingfield Park and was the place to be if goals were your bag – the away sides getting most of them! Funnily enough. one game I recall seeing there was during one awful year when they let in over 200 goals, and I saw their one and only win late on against Barnstaple which, annoyingly, came without a programme as none were printed. OK, so it was hardly historic, but it was out of the ordinary that night. This was evident from the reaction of the home players at the end: they celebrated as if they had won the league.

It is a pity that they cannot get into the Peninsula as, apart from anything else, their pitch is too narrow and cannot be expanded – there simply isn't any room – so that is that. A few years ago an idea for them to relocate to a site a mile or so away was mooted, but it was turned down thanks to objections from local residents. Their reasons included – wait for it – the possibilities of rampaging hooliganism disturbing their peace and quiet! Mmm. Given the average attendance at Wingfield Park was three dozen or so, I somehow doubt if this would have been an issue. As far as I am aware, clubs like Shrewton do not have a rampaging hoard of drunken followers, so methinks this was simply a touch of nimbyitis.

Driving down the approach road, you see a white building ahead on the right, while to the left lies an open pitch where the reserve team are in action today. The near part of the building holds the changing rooms, with the remainder hosting a small bar and refreshment area from which the game can partly be seen. You walk past the changing rooms entrance and down to a railed-off pitch, which has a small covered standing enclosure directly to your left – one that also contains three wooden bench seats.

This is the only hardstanding area, as both ends and the far side are backed by shrubbery, with the dugouts at halfway on that side. The overall setting is in what I can only call a three-quarter bowl, with housing at the top and the more open end spreading out towards the estuary – hence the ground's name. I believe it to be a venue worth visiting.

While there is no programme, I get help in ascertaining player numbers from the secretary, who is most amiable. He scribbles out a team sheet for home games, and not only that but the numbers match the players too!

Getting the away team involves me asking the manager, which I am not keen on as he has his job to do, but as a lifeless opening half unfolds before me he is hardly preoccupied. A half in which brawn overpowers brains looks to be ending goalless, but right at the end Exmouth grab a goal when Norbert Taras strikes Jamie Williams' right cross into the corner of the net.

Tough on the Heavies maybe, but on the hour they restore parity with the full-back playing the ball down the left touchline for Ryan Crocker, who picks it up before turning inside and surprising the home keeper with a curled effort into the top corner. This fires up the homesters, who go back in front within minutes thanks to Liam McMahon's strike from 10 yards. On 74 Ryan Spring lives up to his surname by beating a woeful offside trap, scoring with ease after rounding the goalie. He bags another on 86, smashing the ball in from long distance for a fourth home goal.

There is still time for Williams to blot his copybook by getting sent off for throwing a punch that any boxer would have been proud of, but it doesn't detract from a fine second half showing by the hosts against lacklustre opposition. All that remains is the short, 11-mile drive home – one that completes a very satisfying day indeed.

# Monday, March 28

Life can be mysterious at times. How on earth, for instance, do crop circles really come about? How do some players manage to eke out a career in the Premier League with the measly amount of so-called talent they possess? And why do I look at going to games at Crediton in such a negative manner? Well, I cannot give a definitive answer to the first two questions and, frankly, am puzzled by the third.

It's one that rears its head this evening as the Lords Meadow outfit tackle Budleigh Salterton in Peninsula East. As with Exmouth and Dawlish, it is a short but painfully slow drive here, which does not help, but on arrival you find a decent venue and, personally speaking, I get on with the people who run the club. All in all, it barely reads like something out of a horror movie, but all the same I travel up to the game in my usual apprehensive mood.

The fact that I have been here several times in various competitions is a confirmation of me either being a masochist or just plain daft – probably a bit of both – and I suspect that most of those games were more than acceptable. The first of those games was a Western League game that Crediton blitzed 4-0, which turned out to be a flash in the pan from my point of view. Consequent trips there seem to have ended up with the away side winning most of the time, and some of the margins being of a fairly substantial nature.

A move down to the Devon League saw me attend more often as, thanks to a certain League secretary, they have had a lot of Monday night games. The merger of South-Western and Devon Leagues naturally saw Crediton join the latter, and they have continued keeping their heads above water (literally at times, given the large number of games called off there due to waterlogging!) whilst not getting close to winning any trophies; the two hostings of the Throgmorton Cup final being the closest they have got to having silverware at their ground. Despite all this they are a good club – aptly summed up by the first three-quarters of the town's name.

Located on the fringes of the Lords Meadow industrial estate, the ground's car park is a good-sized, tarmacked area with tennis courts next to it. Between the two is a path leading to the entry gate, with a small wooded admissions hut on the left opposite the refreshment kiosk. Beyond this is a hospitality facility, then, in this corner of the ground, a gable-roofed building that holds the dressing rooms.

Turning left as you come in leads straight into a covered standing enclosure with a couple of concrete steps within, then a gap before a cantilevered stand which has flat, wooden seats. The remainder of this side is open, paved standing, a trait that applies at the changing room end and all the way along the far side, but not the far end. Here it is tree-lined as, indeed, is the opposite end and far side, only these trees are dense firs.

Directly across from the refreshment/hospitality areas is the more recent addition of a covered enclosure of a similar ilk to that near the entrance, only with gravel standing. Apart from the front of the seated stand and the dugouts, which face each other on halfway, the pitch has a metal rail perimeter. The usual lighting set-up applies, with four poles on each side.

Upon arrival, I note that most of the usual suspects are here too. Martin's drive here makes mine seem like a cakewalk, as he has to undertake the far from straight route across from Tiverton, which takes for ever – especially if you get stuck behind a lorry, as I have found out in the past. Phil is here of course, as is Sammo, doing the press report. It's not like him to come all this way up from Plymouth, but at least it explains the trail of breadcrumbs leading up to the entry gate – after all, he might not be able to find his way back without them, having come so far!

Nonetheless, it is nice to see so many familiar faces – even his – and, like them, I get a welcome from the chairman and the secretary. Dave Blanchford seems to have been here for ever, and Mary Avery is another one of those who live and breathe their local club. Once again, this reinforces my bewilderment as to why I see coming here as torturous.

By 8.20, another puzzling question has arisen: how did that opening 45 minutes pass without a goal? I guess the response to that would be a mixed bag of good defending and opportunities spurned. Certainly both sides could have netted two or three times and both have hit the woodwork. What with Fred Tonkin pulling off two magnificent saves and his opposite number getting in one of his own, it has been far from being dull, that's for sure.

Worries about the standard dropping on resumption are soon quelled, and 12 minutes into the half a goal comes thanks to Ben Wooley's bullet header from Neil Pointing's corner. Within minutes, Phil Greenslade taps in an equaliser after Chris Wright spills Mike Broome's shot and he lobs his, and Crediton's, second two minutes later – a fine finish from 25 yards. On 77, visiting skipper Danny Williams wastes a chance to level when, after a foul, his poor spot kick is saved by Tonkin to his left. A point is gained, however, with a goal not dissimilar to their first, with Mark Lever providing the headed finish on this occasion.

An entertaining contest, then, with both sides deserving something from a match that has epitomised the strengths of the Peninsula League. Not for the first time, I return home in good spirits, but also with the knowledge that, come my next visit, I will go through the same ritual – a mystery indeed.

# Tuesday, March 29

Making long journeys to games being played in midweek is something I seldom do these days. Apart from the work factor, there is the small matter of getting home in the early hours, which can be tiring.

This was emphasised once when, close to home, I nodded off for a split second. As a result my car veered left and ran over that raised strip on the hard shoulder, which brought me to my senses. It was a wake-up call in more ways than one. The road was quiet but there must have been a solitary vehicle behind me, as less than 10 minutes later I got home to find a police car waiting. I was breathalysed for my one and only time, with the police officers apologising afterwards for the inconvenience – one that wasn't needed really as I understood why they had to do it.

I am not a fan of drink-driving so was unperturbed, although a little bit of me felt like I had been grassed up by some do-gooder. At this point I suppose the question I'd ask myself is: would I have done the same thing in their position? I don't know, but I do know this was yet another lesson learned.

Since that night I have made one or two long trips, although my biggest was not to football but to speedway at Redcar on a Thursday night. How on earth I managed to make the 350-mile drive back non-stop is something that, even as I write this, I cannot get my head around; whatever was in the tea I drank at the track must have been good, as I did not feel tired at any time on that marathon run. Needless to say, I have not repeated the experience and have no intention of doing so in future; it is not to be recommended.

Tonight's trip involves a drive of about half that distance as I head for Daventry Town, who are playing Leighton in a Southern League game. With no straightforward route, this means cutting across from the M5 via Evesham and later passing Leamington's ground before picking up the main road east. My cunning strategy means that I am able to avoid the rush-hour traffic and get to Daventry without a hitch. Luckily, I am approaching from the west, so I have the simple task of turning left off a roundabout on the outskirts of town – a road that leads me directly to the ground and a parking space half an hour before kick-off.

The Elderstubbs ground has a two-storeyed clubhouse that, unlike most, is only accessible from the outside before the match. It is impressive, with a balcony that gives good views of the game, as I find out later. Entry to this venue is next to the car park entrance, with two turnstiles available to take you in at one corner.

To the right and behind the goal is open hardstanding, which is replicated at the far end in a narrower form. Halfway down on this side is standing cover underneath the balcony, and it is here that a refreshment kiosk is found. The changing rooms are on the ground floor and entry to the pitch is at the far end, next to one of the seated stands placed either side of the building. On halfway opposite is a small covered standing enclosure that is flanked by the open hardstanding that links up with both ends.

They have corner floodlights here and a good pitch that is shared by rivals United, who play in the United Counties League from which Town were promoted. On the whole, it has a modernistic feel about the place, but is a ground I quite like.

While the home side are challenging for top spot, Leighton are outsiders for a play-off place. Unlike here, their Bell Close venue has an old-fashioned, cosy ambience and is a much more enclosed arena. I have to say that the first thing that enters my head when thinking of its features are the dugouts, which must be the worst I have seen at this level: wooden with little depth, they would be shambolic if seen at grounds two or three levels below. Of course, as my visit was over two years ago, it may well be that they have upgraded this facility. I hope so.

Tonight is a double-issue programme incorporating Daventry's game here on Thursday, which is a minor irritation. There are two line-ups on the back and features on both visiting clubs, although the rest of it is good. There is a brief but interesting historical account that, no doubt, forms part of every issue, and it costs a single pound. If you were attending both fixtures that would be a great deal, but for me it's an adequate part of my visit here.

I love it when an early goal is scored, as it eradicates any concerns I might have about seeing a goalless game. Here, Daventry do just that when Adam Confue's header from a right-sided cross is blocked on the line, only for Josh Blake to follow up and score after just 62 seconds. This puts the hosts in the box seat, and by the break the only surprise is that they have not added to their tally. Centre-forward Tom Berwick has had two great chances and veteran Howard Forinton has been denied by a good save by Kevin Marsh.

The ex-Birmingham and Yeovil man clearly hasn't lost his touch, and he goes close again in the early part of the second period. Winger Josh O'Grady hits the bar from a free kick, but the inevitable soon comes to pass when Confue strikes a 10-yard skidder past Marsh to double the lead.

With 10 minutes to go, the away side has failed to trouble the Daventry keeper, and I can't resist making a comment about this, which does not go down too well with a Leighton fan next to me. He is not aware, though, that when I say things like this the opposite usually happens! It almost does too, as the visitors realise they have to score a goal.

My vocal encouragement for his team gains favour from the guy next to me – not that I was looking for it – but his side cannot break through. They have three good chances, but in the end one can only look back and wonder why it has taken them so long to get going. For the hosts this has been their *15th* league win on the trot, albeit an unconvincing one on a pitch that is clearly showing signs of wear. The same can be said of me on my return home at 1am – knackered but happy.

# Saturday, April 2

Just now and again there are grounds that come within my radar but whose visit I keep putting off. Gateshead is a prime example. As the only Conference Premier venue I have yet to do, this ought to be high on my priority list.

At least with that one I feel I have good excuses, though. The 750-mile round trip should satisfy, with my athletics stadium phobia adding to it. Also, there is a story going round that Gateshead are moving to a new ground soon, meaning that I currently have three reasons not to make that long and arduous drive, which I am sticking to – for now.

There have been some other, not-so-far-away venues that I have eventually visited after a period of deferment. Lewes was a recent one, when I turned idea into reality after about half a dozen scheduled trips were put on the back burner. Quite why I chose to do this is baffling, as it is a decent ground and I enjoyed my day there. Another on that list is Braintree, and it is here that I am visiting this afternoon.

Since winning the Isthmian title the Essex club have figured in my plans for a bit and, unlike Lewes, this is one I had purposefully set out to do before. This was at the beginning of last season, when my drive up suffered considerable traffic delays. By the time I hit the M25 I was still just about OK, but a sign warning of an accident ahead resulted in my attending another game, as lessons learned from my M6 experience kicked in.

I ended up at Arlesey that day, which was a good consolation prize as I had wanted to go there at some point in any case. I saw only two goals that day but was thankful, under the circumstances, just to see a full game. After about 30 minutes the referee collapsed with an injury, but an abandonment was avoided due to there being a replacement on hand. Apart from that, I recall the second goal – a belter from the halfway line – and what a nice ground it was. Whether by accident or design, I would recommend a visit to Hitchin Road.

Thankfully, my journey eastwards is not as eventful, and goes so well that I drive the final hour of it at a slow pace. Even then I arrive an hour before kick-off at a venue within easy reach of the town's bypass. I park up in the club's large parking area, which is on rough terrain, and go for a stroll to kill time.

My initial reason for coming today was to meet up with Garry, who lives nearby. He, though, likes to attend Football League matches at weekends and has a ticket for a game. He rarely dabbles in anything else on Saturdays – which is his prerogative – but it would have been nice to see him. When I was working in London I saw him a lot more than I do now, but since then we have gone off in different directions, in more ways than one.

You enter the Cressing Road ground and find yourself in one corner with some Portakabins, holding the refreshment kiosk and club shop, on the left. It is in here that I acquire my matchday programme by means of a swap with a bag of similar ones from Peninsula games – a saving of £2! Beside this, and behind the goal, is open terracing, with the clubhouse directly behind.

Down the right side is a box-shaped seated stand that virtually runs along its entire length. At the far end there is some covered terracing that is replicated down most of the left side, where the concreted stepping is quite shallow. The dugouts are located on each side of the centre line along here, while four old, tapered-style floodlight pylons sit on each side.

At the far end of the clubhouse you will find the dressing rooms, which means the players enter the field of play in one corner. The ground has a tree-lined outer boundary on two sides, which contributes to its old-fashioned look – one that is perfectly acceptable at this level.

I am not the only one who has made a long journey to be here as today's visitors are Dorchester Town for a Conference South fixture. A handful of their fans are here, but Terry is not among them. Being a hopper like myself, he will be somewhere else today, and I would have been surprised to see him here. A glance at the league table seems to provide a reason for him not attending, but after seeing them give another high-flying Essex outfit a good game recently, I hope they can do likewise here.

Certainly the game starts well. The hosts like to play a passing brand of football and go close to scoring on a couple of occasions. In the 20th minute a lovely move sees Glenn Poole feed Cliff Akurang on the left, and he nets with a crisp strike into the top right corner. Strangely, the Iron fail to kick on from this and take that solitary goal advantage into the second half.

This proves to be a continuation of what happened before the interval as Dorchester resort to damage limitation. Their goalkeeper keeps them in the hunt with three quality saves which, going into the final 10 minutes, give his side the confidence to edge forward a bit more. Sensing a chance, they bring their centre-forward into play by knocking balls up to him and providing more support than before. As a result, Ryan Moss runs on to one such ball on the left before striking it across the keeper and inside the far post.

This stuns the home faithful, who have seen the Dorset side hold out for a draw despite the pressure forced upon them in added time. Put simply, it has been Braintree's inability to kill the game off that has cost them although, to be fair, the visitors' never-say-die attitude is to be commended. From a personal viewpoint, I am happy with the outcome as, at last, I have seen a game here.

# Wednesday, April 6

If at any time you derive pleasure from any experience, it is only natural that you would like a second helping. This can vary, of course. It may be an excellent book among a series of novels, or a visit to a pub, or whatever you fancy.

From a footballing perspective, this can come in having seen a side that you have enjoyed watching, which goes some way to explaining my reasoning for attending Hamworthy Rec's Dorset Premier game at Sturminster Marshall. Having witnessed their fine showing at Wincanton, I am hoping for more of the same, although with the home side being not far below them in the table it is not a foregone conclusion.

To my surprise, I have an untroubled drive up and arrive in ample time for a 6.30 kick-off. This is a village club located about five miles west of Wimborne, and although my expectations of what I would find here were low, I am still disappointed when I turn off into Churchill Close. In fact my first reaction is to wonder if I am in the wrong place, but I'm not.

Basically, the ground forms most of a green recreational area encircled by a road with houses on the other side. The only thing that marks it out as a ground is its railed-off nature, otherwise it would pass for a pitch on which kids knock the ball around, which they probably do when there is no match staged here.

The changing rooms are in the community centre beyond the far end, so a long walk is required that sees you cross the road which, thankfully, is not busy. Talking of which raises a question: why is it called a Close when it's not? I always thought a road's name defined it, whether it be street, road, crescent or, in this case, what should be a cul-de-sac. Maybe it used to be a no through road and they couldn't be bothered to change the name? I don't know (or care!) but I do know that, as a step seven 'ground', this is one of the worst ones I've been to.

I have been to Sturminster Marshall before, but for another reason. Speedway fans will be well aware of Poole manager Neil Middleditch, who also used to ride for the club in the 80s. I had the privilege of staying at his place overnight on the way back to London from a meeting at Weymouth. My plan was to head back the next day – a strategy that was to change thanks to him inviting me along to Poole's meeting that night. This was a terrific gesture given that I had never met him before, and it is something I have never forgotten. With Hackney being the opposition, I was able to get a lift back through one of their riders who I got on with, thus rounding off a memorable trip.

I have spoken to others about this and discovered that my tale is, unsurprisingly, far from a solitary one. Neil is a top bloke who still lives here, although it would never cross my mind to drop in and have a chat. After almost 30 years, he is hardly going to remember a one-off encounter among the many that he will have had in that period. Also, Poole are at home tonight, so he will be out anyway.

Given the openness of this venue, I had thought a programme might be issued to cover an admission charge, but not so. A freebie, then, but a hectic time as I borrow the team sheets from two busy dressing rooms so I can write the player names down. At least I have come prepared with a piece of paper on which to do this, although I cannot help but feel I am getting in the way – what with both teams psyching themselves up for a vital game – but I'd like to think I do not. Both managers are more than accommodating, which makes me feel a lot better, but I'm sure my interjection was not a part of their pre-match planning!

There is certainly a leisurely attitude about getting this game under way. At the scheduled kick-off time there is a distinct absence of anyone except the few who wish to watch the action, with a 10-minute delay the result. I am not aware of any late arrivals, with the Portland-based officials being present and correct along with all the players. I guess the reasons for our late start will, like the disappearance of Shergar, remain a mystery.

The league leaders stamp their authority during the early stages of the clash. Unlike Wincanton, though, the home side are more resilient defence-wise, and no goal is forthcoming. Mark Dykes flashes a header wide and Ashley Boyt sees his shot tipped around the post by keeper Doug Shear, while at the other end Scott Thomas rattles the bar with an angled drive. At the end of the half Mike Notley is denied twice by good stops from the home custodian, rendering the first 45 minutes goalless.

The competitive nature of the contest continues after the break. Dykes should put Rec in front and Dan Blackburn shoots wide as the hosts cling on. It isn't until the 73rd minute that the breakthrough arrives, and it's Sturminster who provide it. A corner on the right is headed against the bar by Luke Geddes, only for substitute Joe Wood to bundle in the loose ball.

Hamworthy pile forward in an attempt to gain the draw their efforts deserve – Notley going the closest with an effort that strikes the underside of the crossbar – but the homesters stand firm as the last five minutes of the match are played in really dark conditions.

Come the final whistle, the lights have gone out on Hamworthy's unbeaten run thanks to a loss that is only their second of the campaign, albeit against a side who have shown why they are in fifth place. As a neutral, this has been an absorbing match which has brought me two kinds of relief: one, that I have finally got a goal – one that resulted in: two, that I do not have to come here again.

# Saturday, April 9

Four weeks on from my trip to Holyport, I am making another run by train, this time to London and beyond as I travel to Dartford for their Conference encounter with Woking. There is a slight delay on the run up to Paddington, but not enough to prevent me from making my connecting train from Charing Cross – one that sees me alight in the Kent town at about two o'clock.

From there I have to head in a southerly direction towards the stadium, a stroll that turns out to be longer than expected. At least with time not being an issue there is no need for panic so, despite my slowness, I am there with half an hour to spare. It would have been much easier if I had come by car, as the motorway is within easy access, but an early arrival is to be recommended, as space appears to be limited.

Princes Park is an environment-friendly venue that is into its fifth year of use. The ground has solar panels and a system that uses rainwater to sprinkle the pitch. Inside, there is covered standing on three sides with the other side being seated – areas that are accessed from a continuous walkway that runs along the back. All of this has cover in the form of a roof with a slight curvature on each of the sides, with the floodlight poles positioned a little way in from each corner. An unusual feature here is a large sculpted statue that fits in amid the terracing between the halfway line and one end.

The dugouts are on the seated side and the pitch appears to offer a good playing surface. This is thanks not only to the irrigation but also to the gap down three sides between the roof and the rear of the terracing. There is a spacious clubhouse up some stairs behind the seated area, while the changing rooms and hospitality areas are to be found in the middle section. Dartford have a club shop within the ground which, frankly, feels cold inside, no thanks to its grey walls, but this is a tiny flaw to a highly impressive venue.

I did go to the club's old ground in Watling Street, albeit for a Maidstone home game. The Stones were ground-sharing there during their time as a Football League club, so I felt obliged to visit. From what I recall, it was a good venue with plenty of cover, but sentiment may be clouding my judgement here. I do know that I went there on a supporters' club coach, as Exeter City were the away side who lost 1-0 that day.

I never got to Maidstone's own ground before it fell victim to the bulldozers, and it's a pity that the club gone through hard times as a consequence. The good news is that they are close to having their own stadium built in the town's outskirts, which is great news as it must be soul-destroying making journeys to so-called home games elsewhere. For the fans this will provide light at the end of the tunnel – just as it did for Brighton and, to a lesser extent, AFC Wimbledon.

Oddly enough, the only time I have seen Dartford in action was at Exeter in an FA Cup replay which we won, unlike a couple of visits to Maidstone that resulted in embarrassing losses. I remember finding out about the first of these as it was announced on the PA system when I was leaving at the end of a game at Arsenal. While I like to see cup upsets, I would rather that my home club was not on the receiving end of them.

With programme and team sheet in hand, I make my way round to halfway and find a good spot where I can stand and watch the game. Woking are in play-off contention and start the game in a bright and positive manner – one that sees them rewarded in the seventh minute with a penalty, given after a push in the box, only for Elvis Hammond to place it wide of the left post. You could say that his teammates are all shook up as they concede a spot kick at the other end. Incredibly, though, Charlie Sheringham misses from 12 yards in exactly the same way. Unbelievable.

Two minutes after this, a dead-ball situation does give us our opening goal. Given what has just occurred, I suppose it was inevitable that it would come from a free-kick 35 yards out on the right touchline! Andy Burgess is the scorer, although I suspect his whipped ball in was not intended as a shot that went in between the far angle of post and bar, putting Woking ahead. With not much more than five minutes to go until the break, I make my way around to behind the goal that Dartford are attacking. They win a corner on the left, which is headed in at the far post by Elliot Bradbrook to level the scores.

From the restart, the hosts quickly regain possession and in the blink of an eye Sheringham is in on goal. His first effort is blocked, but he strokes in the rebound. Scorer turns provider as he puts Jack Pallen through on the right. Turning inside, he fires in under the keeper from 10 yards. Shortly after, the whistle blows for half-time with the home side having bagged three goals in a manic four-minute spell.

I retire to the clubhouse for a quick drink wondering if I will get a repeat of the same scoreline when I last saw Woking – a 4-3 thriller at Margate on a day on which I also recall asking a shop to reopen afterwards so I could buy a Mother's Day present, which they did. Here, upon resumption, it's the home team that are getting the gifts, going one man up as well thanks to Adam Doyle being sent off for two bookable offences.

Dartford miss some great chances to seal the win – the worst being an open goal missed by Rogers – and the 10 men respond by scoring their second of the afternoon. Another push in the area gives us a third penalty, with Craig Dobson converting to show the others how it should be done. This sets up a frantic finale in which the visitors press for an equaliser while leaving themselves exposed to the counter-attack, all of which concludes an enthralling game.

As I make the descent to Darenth Road and the walk back to the station, I feel that buzz one gets after seeing such a contest. It has to go down as one of my best matches seen this season, and I can't ask for more than that. Back at Charing Cross, I make the short walk across to the Chandos pub. Here they serve up my favourite beer: Samuel Smiths Old Brewery Bitter.

This is the one thing I miss about living in London, although time is not on my side today. There is just enough for me to down a single pint of a beer that slides down the throat with consummate ease. Alas, the temptation to have another must be resisted as I have a train to catch at Paddington. Shame. Chas and Dave once sang about Courage Best beating all the rest on TV adverts, but they were wrong. I say you can't beat a sup or two of Sam's. It's pure nectar and, for me, caps a delightful day out when even the weather has behaved itself. Happy days.

## Tuesday, April 12

My mini-run of new ground visits ends this evening as I make the short drive south to Liverton. They have a Peninsula Division One East fixture against local rivals Newton Abbot Spurs that, despite the huge difference in their league positions, has the makings of a feisty encounter.

It is a straightforward venue to locate, although heading for the village itself would be an erroneous act. Fortunately, a signpost indicates a left turn off the road just past the Star Inn, so an alert driver should not end up there anyway. The detour is one to be recommended if you wish to observe the pair of old brickwork pottery kilns, but not if your interests lie elsewhere, as mine do tonight.

After turning in opposite some cottages, you drive around to the right and past a building into the car parking behind the goal. This has some black matting placed over bumpy terrain. The left side of that building holds the somewhat cramped changing rooms, while the right has a small but efficient clubhouse that hosts a bar and a refreshment kiosk.

On the far side a short pathway leads to a rectangular covered standing area with flagpoles attached on top. Beyond this you have the dugouts, located either side of halfway, part of an open and grassy area with a hedgerow to the rear. This is replicated at the far end, which strictly speaking is out of bounds to spectators. A similar scenario beckons down the near side, but the ground gradually slopes away with trees at the back, along with a couple of benches. The far end is the only side not railed off, and there are no lights here at present.

It's not often that a club finishes ninth in the league yet gets promoted. This is what happened with Liverton though, as the reformation of the leagues in 2007 saw them join the Peninsula Eastern Division, where they have remained. I was present at the first game here against Buckfastleigh, in my initial visit to the Halford Ground – a game that finished in a 2-2 draw. Since then I have only attended this venue on a handful of occasions and the facilities have not really altered at all in that time – a description that could also apply to on-field results.

This season, though, has seen an upturn that has turned mid-table anonymity into possible title-winning credentials. Part of this has to go down to the manager Tony Bowker, who has previously done well at Newton Abbot and has put together a solid outfit here as well. He provokes mixed opinions about the way he goes about his business, that's for sure. Like Marmite, he seems to be either loved or loathed.

One person that doesn't provoke such opinions is the league chairman, who is here tonight. Mark Hayman is one of those guys who seems to get on with everybody and has a million and one friends. He comes across as a laid-back character and is someone I get along with. His daytime job is in insurance and, judging by the number of Chelsea games he goes to at home and abroad, it's something he is successful at. He is also a handful of grounds short of completing the 92, which is probably the sole area in which I can usurp him at present, but not for long.

Both of his sons have played in the Peninsula League, and one of them is on the bench for Liverton tonight. Mark used to be the Newton Spurs secretary and produced a lavish programme for their games, some with over 100 pages including lots of articles and not that many adverts. It did very well in the Wirral Programme Awards, which was not altogether surprising. It's a pity he can't return as a programme editor here, as the decent front cover belies the poor content within. It hasn't altered at all since Liverton joined the Peninsula, but at least it's free.

When we get under way, Spurs go close when Jake Elms chips over the keeper but just wide of the post. The hosts respond by taking the lead on 17 minutes thanks to Shane Shobbrook, who rounds Comerford before sliding the ball in. Despite this, it remains a tight encounter until six minutes after the interval, when a second goal arrives. It is Shobbrook who bags it, meeting a left cross from Simon Lewcock at the far post with a downward header.

On 56 he completes his treble, lobbing the keeper from the edge of the area after beating the offside trap. Robbie Bowker's low drive makes it four before the visitors get one back through Adam Dyson, whose fine volleyed finish completes the scoring for the evening.

With this win Liverton have effectively won the title as their goal difference is vastly superior. They have been given a good match here, though, in what has been a commendable game of football.

## Wednesday, April 13

With conditions a little on the soggy side, I decide to stay local this evening and attend Seaton's Devon and Exeter Premier Division clash with Clyst Valley. I am not a great lover of games at this level, mainly because of the pre-match issues I mentioned seven days ago, but the Seasiders do have a unique feature in this league: a programme. It would be nice to put one in with my collection as I do not get any from games I have not been to, barring some old FA Cup Final publications.

It is still damp as I make the 25-mile drive east to a ground that has no lights. Upon arrival I have to park in the road outside as there is no such facility within. The clubhouse lies adjacent to this road, with a pathway running between the two that brings you out at one corner of the pitch. The changing rooms are at the rear of this building, with a small, covered standing area at the front. There is a good-sized stand down the left side with three rows of plastic seating, although views from here are marginally obstructed thanks to the dugouts positioned at each end.

An uncovered path leads to this seated area from the entrance, but goes no further.

The opposite side and far end are technically out of bounds, with a small picket fence dividing the ground from the caravan park behind, but a tarmacked road immediately next to the fence means the game can be watched from what is, officially, outside the confines of this venue. That fence also runs behind the near goal, while a high wire version is down the other end. All in all, this is an impressive set-up.

There is no one at the entrance as I go in and, unbelievably, no programme tonight! Enquiries in the clubhouse lead to my finding out from the secretary that the club only issue programmes for Saturday games – aargh! I manage to get a copy of an issue from four days ago and will put my artistic skills to the test later by converting it into one for this game.

The annoying thing is that I could, nay should, have come here after my Axminster visit a couple of weeks ago – it's just up the road from here – and got a bona fide issue from a match that finished 6-3! Although I was happy at the time with my choice of going to Exmouth, it has turned out to be a bad decision on my part.

Not that it figures near the top of my list of errors in that respect; far from it. Undoubtedly the worst happened in the mid-80s, when I originally picked Plymouth's home game against Preston. The plan altered, however, when my friend arranged a blind date for yours truly that night. As I could not get back on the train in time I opted for Torquay's game with Peterborough, which was doable. It finished 0-0. By then I was already aware of there being three goals at Home Park and hoped for a goal-free second half there. No such luck: it finished 6-4. Six-bloody-four!

Not only that, but when I pitched up at my mate's place that evening he told me my 'date' had cried off. Apparently she remembered me from my school days. Bearing in mind there had been a gap of over 10 years since then which, among other things, saw me live and work in London, I think this was a lame excuse. I do know that it put the final touches to a rotten day. At least that's how it felt at that time.

Anyway, back here at Colyford Road I have to get the team line-ups. Getting the home one is simple enough, but Clyst's is acquired via one of their substitutes during the first half. Seaton have made a meteoric rise up the leagues and in their initial Premier campaign are challenging neighbours Sidmouth for the title. Sadly, this will not lead to promotion if they succeed, as the width of the pitch here needs to be lengthened to satisfy the Peninsula ground criteria. Plans are afoot to extend it, but this will not happen in the near future. There appear to be quite a few ex-Axminster players here, so they must have their eyes on going up soon.

From kick-off the home side go straight on the offensive and could have scored on two occasions before they do so on eight minutes. Alex Wheatley – one of the ex-Tigers – finds space on the right and finds the corner of the net with a low, angled shot. Seaton appear to be comfortable, but out of the blue Clyst find an equaliser. A through ball looks harmless enough, but a mix-up between Dan Stapleton and his full-back allows Justin Boult to nip in and tap into an empty net. Undeterred, the home side restore their advantage just before the break, Dan

Norman turning on the edge of the box and firing into the right corner.

Twelve minutes into the second period, the away side once again get on level terms when Elliot Weeks runs through unchallenged and strikes a low, crisp drive into the left corner of the net. On 72, Seaton go ahead for the third time, Jack Lamb-Wilson scoring with a low shot that goes in off the left post.

As the gloom descends, the hosts waste chances to seal the win and are made to pay in added time. A clumsy foul in the penalty area gives skipper Simon Coombs the opportunity to snatch a point for Clyst, which he duly takes with aplomb.

Disappointment for the home fans, then, but a thoroughly entertaining match. Hopefully Seaton will sort out their ground issues and go up to the Peninsula. That way I can return and get a proper programme!

# Friday, April 15

Peninsula Premier champions Buckland Athletic have brought their home game with Launceston forward to this evening, so I will make the short drive down to Homers Heath along with Martin, who is tagging along as a passenger.

The Bucks have been in residence on the southern outskirts of Newton Abbot since 2005, when they left their Homers Lane headquarters near Kingsteignton. This was a more difficult venue to find, being tucked away at the end of a side road. Its main features were an old-style clubhouse and a small standing enclosure on halfway. Surrounded by trees, it was lacking in car parking spaces but was a decent place to watch football. I saw Buckland's first Devon League game there, a 5-0 win over Ivybridge, and quite a few others including a 10-1 romp over Buckfastleigh.

One bad memory I have from there is a visit which saw the game kick off half an hour before it was supposed to. I missed a goal as well, so for a while Buckland were not exactly flavour of the month. Time, though, has healed those scars and I quite like them now. They are a good side to watch and it is no great hardship to see them on a regular basis.

Another reason for my change of heart could have something to do with the chairman who is, literally, a larger than life character. Roy Holmes and Buckland seem to go hand in hand, with his passion for the club coming through loud and clear. The same can be said about the volume when he gives out the winning raffle numbers; no need for a PA system here as Roy shouts them out from the clubhouse door. He would have been useful during World War II, standing on the Kent coast and warning London of incoming enemy planes! Who needs radar when you can have 'Roy'dar instead? Seriously though, he is a top bloke with whom I get on well.

Turning in past Sainsbury's, there is an irritating passage of speed humps to negotiate before reaching the right turn-off next to CLS laundry. It is well worth it, as you will see when reaching the top of a small ascent off the road. A wooden, garden outhouse-type facility is on the right at the top, while the white-painted clubhouse is unmissable to your left. The former is where you pay to get in, while the latter is a wonderful, spacious area inside. The building is L-shaped, with the dressing rooms to the rear and a refreshment facility to the fore.

In front of this is a bricked area with seats, separated from the parking by a thick rope held up by wooden posts. You park along this side, where it is gravelled. There is open hardstanding all round in the form of a two-coloured brickwork pattern – very smart. A single rail set in wooden posts forms the pitch perimeter, while the floodlight poles on each side are painted green and have three lamps on each.

The highlight of this ground, though, is the superb, award-winning stand located on halfway. Set into a grass bank, it has plastic seats at a raised level that enable you to see over the dugouts located either side of halfway. They are accessed via stepways at each end, while a walkway up the middle leads you to a standing area at the back. There is a gap in the centre that leads to a single line of seats facing on to another pitch. Views are slightly hampered by the struts and one of the floodlight poles, but it does not detract from a top-notch feature.

There are a few familiar faces here tonight. One of them is a local hopper who writes an article in the wonderful programme they issue here – a bargain at £1 – and talk inevitably leads us to our plans for tomorrow. I write in the player numbers on the back of the programme, which is the one let-down as it is glossy, hence difficult to write on.

Time to find a spot as the game begins, although the stand is where I will end up. Given their top of the table position, it's not altogether surprising when the hosts get off to a flyer. They open the scoring through a Danny Gaze penalty but spend the rest of the half trying and failing to score the perfect goal. In the meantime, Launceston do score on 26 when Paul Smith whips in a free-kick from the left for Sam Davey to head in.

All square at the break then, and time to head off for a cup of tea and a slice of cake. This is attained thanks to a certain Mr Holmes and is received with thanks. Yum, yum.

Having conceded from a set-piece already, you would have thought Buckland have learnt from that mistake. Eight minutes into the second half this appears not to be the case, as the visitors replicate the move to go in front. A disappointingly small crowd are stunned and their team push men forward in search of an equaliser. They get it on 73 as a long-throw is headed across goal by Antony Lynch for Gaze to strike home. Before long, Liam Moseley is crossing from the right for Mike Booth to put the homesters ahead with a 15-yarder, only for Launceston to level quickly through Gary Ashton's cross-cum-shot from the right.

As we go into stoppage time a draw looks like being the outcome, but a rash challenge in the area sees referee Lee Dudman point to the spot – a penalty that Gaze smashes down the middle to complete his hat-trick and glean three vital league points from what has been a breathtaking encounter.

Anyone who has not been here should earmark it for a future visit. It is a smashing ground, the programme's great and it is as good a guarantee as you'll get for seeing a good game of football. As a hopper, I should know.

# Saturday, April 16

Last night's pre-match discussions have led me to a decision I may regret later in the day. It is a time when my need to do a new ground is offset by not wishing to go too far so, in the end, I plump for an 80-odd mile drive to see Hamworthy Recreation play Sturminster Newton in a top-versus-bottom Dorset Premier clash.

Visions of a massive home win cloud my mind on the way. I like seeing goals but prefer it if they are shared out a bit, as happened yesterday. I had other choices but picked this one as it is easy to find. So it is, as I arrive just under an hour before the start.

The ground is just off the main road between Wimborne and Bournemouth and has a good-sized parking area. Given that it is part of a sports and social club this is hardly surprising, although the issuing of a programme is not such a foregone conclusion.

Thankfully there is one, which comes along with the £3 admission, and it is quite good. It has a reasonable amount of reading material, including one item that gives a potted history of the club. It explains why they are based so far away from Hamworthy itself, as they moved to Canford in the late 80s as Hamworthy Engineering and changed their name about 10 years ago. Mystery solved, but I cannot help but wonder if anyone has, without knowing the address, gone to Hamworthy and ended up at the Wessex League ground. Maybe, but probably not.

This is not the only club who do not play in their own town or village, of course. I have already mentioned Somerset County side Langford, then we have Grimsby playing in nearby Cleethorpes and, for a while, we had Wimbledon playing at Milton Keynes. They don't any more – or do they? Of course they do, only now they are MK Dons – how convenient!

What on earth made the Football League approve this nonsense? We were told at the time that bringing professional football to Milton Keynes was a good thing, and subsequent crowd figures seemingly back this up. Here, though, is a question I would like to ask any of their followers: if you were so fanatical about the game, why did you not bother with the local club you had in the first place?

Anyone remember Milton Keynes City? They are no longer around, finishing up in a ground-share arrangement with Wolverton – a venue that had a nice stand. No doubt our MK friends would have passed it on the train and not given it much thought. Perhaps if they had shown any interest, the club could have made their way up the leagues and, who knows, become a professional club in their own right.

Basically, MK Dons have cheated the system and one can only hope that it is a one-off. Of course, the irony is that AFC Wimbledon was formed from scratch and have risen up through the non-league ranks with a loyal following – proving that it can be done. Franchise clubs are prevalent in the United States, and that is where the idea should stay.

As they are part of a recreational facility, there is no chance of this club rising any higher than they are now. The ground is fairly basic, with no hardstanding and a single metal rail on three sides of the pitch. The far end is the exception, being tree-lined.

Entering from the near end, you have a large building to your right, with the changing rooms on the ground floor and a large clubhouse above it. This includes a balcony that gives splendid views of the pitch from its corner location. Down this side is a grassy bank, which shallows out to become level once you reach the far corner. The dugouts are on the far side, which is grassy, as is the near end, which is expansive. It is not a bad place to watch football, especially on a dry day like today.

It is a sunny afternoon as we get under way. The home side soon go close through Jamie Moores, who hits the bar with a header, and a Richie Sands shot that is superbly saved by visiting keeper Matt Robson. It is evident, though, that Newton are not just going to lie down and surrender. This is shown when they break out of defence and almost score when Stuart Frear's effort goes narrowly wide.

By the half-time break it is still goalless as the away side continue to belie their league position – a stance that the Rec find frustrating to say the least. Their pre-match mental attitude has obviously told them it will be a walk in the park, which is not clever at the best of times. Complacency is never a good ingredient to have in a footballing side – or indeed life in general – and it appears rife at times in the hosts' showing in the first 45 minutes.

Gareth Daniel, the Hamworthy manager is, I'm told, a stalwart at this club. No doubt his half-time talk has a lot of this passion because, upon resumption, his players show a positive yet respectful approach to the game. It is rewarded on the hour as a deep cross from the left is met by the head of Dan Blackburn at the far post, his effort looping over Robson and into the net. It is Hamworthy's 100th league goal of the campaign and it is almost followed by another as Mike Notley hits the woodwork. Robson keeps his side in it with two more stops and a fingertip save from Wayne Hole's piledriver, which then comes back out off the post.

It is only a matter of time before a second goal is scored, and it arrives nine minutes from the end. The bad news for the home faithful is that the visitors get it. There appears to be no real concern when Howard Batten's dribble takes him over the halfway line – a run that remains unchallenged until he decides to have a pot at goal. From 30 yards out his effort swerves past the keeper and into the bottom right corner for an equaliser that has come totally out of the blue.

Stunned, the home side push forward but are unable to find a winner despite intense pressure, with Newton holding out amid a succession of corners and blocked shots to gain a totally unexpected draw. Two hours ago the likelihood of that occurring was about the same as my becoming the next man on the moon! The goal rush hasn't materialised and I am pleased that I have seen a minor upset. It's not often I can say that about a 1-1 draw, but in instances like this I can.

# Tuesday, April 19

A virtual replication of my drive three days ago, only this time I go right at Bere Regis and continue along the A35 to Poole. Or nearby, to be precise, as I am to take in Poole Borough versus Parley Sports in another Dorset Premier encounter.

Located on the Upton to Poole road, the ground is simple enough to reach, although I do drive past the twisty, narrow lane that leads to the car parking, as it's unsigned. Luckily, I spot it away to my right, so turn back immediately. With over half an hour to spare, there is no panic anyway. Besides, I do not expect a large crowd as this is a mid-table clash at a venue that is closer to Hamworthy than Saturday's was!

Positioned at one end of a recreational area, this ground has a fairly basic set-up. The only hardstanding here runs parallel with the sizeable building sited on one side, next to where you park. This holds the changing rooms at the far end, plus a clubhouse facility at the other. To the middle is a refreshment cubbyhole, while an overhang provides cover on a rainy day. This will not be required this evening, which is just as well because you have a limited view of the pitch due to the dugouts located either side of halfway.

The pitch perimeter has a single, white-painted metal rail all around, with the far side and end being open and expansive beyond this. The near end has an artificial playing area to the rear – a high-fenced enclosure that looks as if it is rarely used. Even though this is an open venue, there is a spot between the car park and the hardstanding for someone to take an entry fee. It is only £2, which is hardly going to break the bank, and there is a programme thrown in for good measure.

The gateman, who also happens to be the secretary here, apologises for the standard of tonight's issue when I hand my money over. I don't know why, because it is perfectly acceptable. He must have worked out that I am a hopper because he goes away and gets me a programme from the last home game. Unlike tonight's, it has a colour frontage and more content, so I will take it home and take it apart so that I can combine the two into a programme that will be a more suitable souvenir for my visit to this ground. Mr Fussy strikes again!

There was a time when I looked to various means of having proof of attending football stadia. The programme is the obvious one, although not strictly kosher. By that I am referring to the availability of programmes at club shops and other sources. Basically, having one for a game doesn't necessarily mean you were there.

An example is when Arsenal used to put a small voucher in every home issue, which you could cut out and put on a sheet at the end of the season. If Arsenal were in the FA Cup Final, you could apply with a full set so, if you had not been to all matches, you could buy back issues outside the ground to remedy this problem or, some would say, cheat the system. It seems strange now to think that such a big club would adopt a method that is clearly open to abuse, but there we are. Given the limited number of tickets available, I cannot imagine much success was attained by this channel anyway.

On the whole, I believe a programme from each new ground is enough; let's be honest, nobody is going to be cajoled into providing evidence of them attending a game, are they? I'd presume not, but for the record I have been given a 'golden goal' ticket with my programme this evening, which means that, if accused of fraudulently claiming to be at this game, I have the proof that I was! Maybe it is me, though, who takes things to extremes.

When they're available, I like to get team sheets, and I show high levels of determination in acquiring one at times. And back in my Football League days, I bought a cheap ballpoint pen from each ground, of which I now possess about 50! I'm glad to say that, apart from the team sheet fixation, I regard a programme as enough now.

I know of others who collect pennants or fridge magnets, while one person is a purchaser of replica shirts – an expensive way of demonstrating your visit if ever there was one – and a metal badge. We all have our own idiosyncrasies, though, and I would like to think mine are harmless; baffling to some, but innocuous.

The same can be said of our late start to the game. Everyone of relevance is present in ample time, so the 10-minute delay in kick-off is rather puzzling. It happened at Sturminster Marshall two weeks ago, so maybe it's a Dorset thing – perhaps not.

However, once we're under way both sides show positive intent, with the opening goal coming in the 14th minute. It begins when Chris Squire is put through on the right only for him to lose his balance after rounding the keeper. His effort strikes the crossbar, but fortunately for Poole it falls to Jamie Holland, who is following up, and he bundles it into the net despite a desperate challenge from a defender.

Now behind, Parley press forward and are unlucky to go in at the interval without scoring. Paul Mitchell and Dan Merritt are the closest to levelling the scores, but two minutes into the second period they find the net. Adam Trimby's cross from the right results in a misunderstanding between keeper Ross Mills and his centre-half. Matt Newbury nips in and slots into a gaping net. Now it is the home side's turn to attack in numbers, with Andy Masson's fine strike bringing a fine save from Matt Harvey and Jack Mills scraping the upright with a low shot. Parley also have chances to win it as the game draws to its conclusion, but neither side can find a way through.

Honours even, then, in a contest that has turned out to be much better than I thought it would be. Bearing this in mind, I am a contented man on my drive home. And, in the unlikely event of me being injected with a truth serum and interrogated on whether I have been to Turlin Moor, I can say I have!

# Friday, April 22

Groundhop day. Yes, ladies and gentlemen, it's time to meet and greet like-minded persons from around the country – and in some cases beyond – who make me seem like a normal human being. I say this because some of them make me feel like a part-timer in comparison.

I have already mentioned Kerry and his ground total of over 1,000, but here he would find many others who have gone well into the four-figure category. Most of them, though, are making first-time visits to our triple helping of football fare today, while I have done them before.

It's nice to know there are actually venues I have ticked off before them, as it presents a minor victory for yours truly. Forget the fact that they have done millions of places that I have not and probably never will go to; this is a microscopic triumph for me. Not one to boast about to the grandchildren though, which is just as well because I don't have any!

The first port of call is Bovey Tracey. Martin is driving down, so I cadge a lift with him. Parking at the Western Counties Roofing Ground is limited at the best of times, so with a large crowd attending it is going to be full well before the start. We end up finding a spot a short stroll from the ground and, upon arrival, duly find it as I expected it to be.

The one thing I have not allowed for, though, is the heavy rain shower that envelopes the ground in the lead-up to the game. With no coat on, I take shelter in the refreshment area as the idea of catching pneumonia doesn't exactly appeal! While in there I find that a team sheet has been printed for this match – an unusual occurrence in this league, and I suspect done with this particular scenario in mind. Having taken the option on entering of not purchasing a programme, this is handy for me. No laborious writing down of names today.

This venue is certainly tucked away, being located off a cul-de-sac. When I came here for the first time I got to the end and wondered if I had taken the wrong turn. As it is, you turn right across a narrow bridge then left for the entry gate. There is parking before this and after, where you swing right and see the gable-roofed building that has the changing rooms at the near end, with the aforementioned refreshment part at the other.

There is an overhang at the front that, before this week, was the only cover available. Thankfully, two covered stands have been erected in time for this morning's contest. They are sited either side of halfway on the near side, with the first having plastic seating and the second of a similar ilk but used for terracing. Unsurprisingly, given their quick appearance, they are Meccano … sorry, Atcost constructions, which, as I have already stated, are becoming commonplace.

My first sighting of one came at Budleigh, and it seemed quite novel then. How times have changed, with Histon being a classic example. They dominate that stadium now, with three sides being occupied by them although, ironically, the only seated area there is in the original stand.

# DIARY OF A SEASON

Here, the twin structures are set back from the playing area, with an open hardstanding track running along this side – one that extends around the far end. An unusual feature is located behind this goal in the form of a pétanque club. This is a fenced-off area that looks neat and tidy, unlike the one at Cricklade, which is open and shabby. Mind you, people were playing on that one when I attended the hop game there, whereas this one looks as if it is hardly used.

Anyway, the near end of this ground is narrow with a tree line and a small ditch in between. You can watch the action on the far side by walking down here and go as far as halfway, but no further. At this point we have the two dugouts, which have shallow arched roofs to them – a smart piece of design work in my opinion, and pleasing on the eye.

Apart from the non-accessible part beyond these, the pitch is surrounded by a pair of wooden horizontal rails held up by wooden posts, with wire netting filling in some of the gaps. There are no lights at present, although this will change by the time next season starts.

Another standard item missing is a clubhouse, which resides at the club's old Recreation Ground headquarters in nearby Ashburton Road – a place that can be viewed on the way to this ground if so desired. That venue was used in the days before Bovey joined the Peninsula League. It was, and still is, an open facility that is shared with cricket and is less than a mile away.

Luckily, a series of factors enabled me to see a game there on a day when Phil and I had arranged to travel to another game. He turned up at my doorstep and came up with a new plan: Bovey's home cup game against Vospers. He said it had been switched to their old venue as the WCRG pitch was waterlogged. Given that it was a much shorter journey to a place I had not been to before, I jumped at the chance. And what a good decision it was, as the Devon Premier Cup tie finished 8-4. Wow! Not for the first time, Phil came up trumps with an alternative option that saw me hit the jackpot big time.

Buckland Athletic are the away side this morning, in a game that represents the closest thing Bovey can get to a derby fixture. The home side will need that local pride incentive for sure, as their opponents are looking for another three points towards retaining their league crown.

With the rain still falling, the match sees both teams start tentatively. Just past the 20-minute mark, the precipitation halts and a goal is scored; ex-Bovey winger Simon Revell swings a cross in from the left and Antony Lynch heads it in. Just before half-time Lynch is at the near post to nod home another Revell assist, putting the away side in the box seat.

Ten minutes into the second period, though, Bovey pull one back. Kenny Griffiths pulls off a fine save, but from Dan Taylor's corner on the left Mike Turner leaves him helpless with a bullet header. Undeterred, the Bucks go up the other end and restore their two-goal advantage. Revell is an unintended provider this time, as his 25-yard strike is parried by the keeper; Lynch, being the goal poacher that he is, pounces to complete his hat-trick.

Not content with this, he grabs another when snaffling a fourth after Buckler has failed to deal with a low shot from Danny Lewis. This turns out to be the final score, but only due to poor finishing by the champions-elect. Nonetheless, it has been a reasonable game watched by a crowd of just under 500.

We make a good getaway and I am home in no time whatsoever. Martin pops in for a cuppa as there is plenty of time in hand before we make our way to game number two. He gives me a slight scare by electing to sit on my garden seat, which is rather on the old side and has not been sat on for some time. Visions of him crashing through it and injuring himself come to mind, but he survives the experience. I keep shtum as the wood bends but doesn't break – it must be stronger than I thought – as Martin is a big unit! Anyhow, he heads off for this afternoon's match not knowing what a gamble he has unwittingly undertaken – at least not until now, if he is reading this!

After seeing to the dog, I grab a bite to eat and head off in my car for the short drive north to Bickleigh. I arrive with about half an hour to spare, then queue in order to park on the cricket field next to the pitch. This is a one-off as normally one parks in the Trout Inn car park, an area that serves its purpose on normal matchdays. We have not had much rain recently, so the parking is on firm terrain, meaning that I will not get stranded in any lakes this time!

No, it's a lovely sunny afternoon as I find Martin chewing on a burger (again!) and get the teams from him. Once more I have not purchased a programme, which means writing out the names on my trusty piece of scrap paper. I am tempted by the smell to join my good friend in burger munching, but decide that the opening of my wallet twice within the hour would be an extravagant gesture on my part – one that must be resisted at all costs. Besides, it's my turn to buy the teas at half-time. I'll let the moths out then!

Bickleigh's ground may be called Happy Meadow but the only people coming away from my past visits here feeling that way have been associated with the visiting clubs: they have come away victorious every time. On those occasions I parked in the Trout Inn car park before crossing the road to gain access to the ground via a gap in the trees.

After paying at the small wooden hut you find yourself behind the goal on a grassy area. This is replicated at the far end and, of course, down the open left-hand side. The only hardstanding exists on the right side, although the club have laid some black matting down at the near end. On the right side there are two buildings: the first an old-style cricket pavilion that holds the changing rooms, the other possessing an overhang that provides cover for the seating located at the front.

A refreshment kiosk resides in between these structures, while the dugouts are found on either side of the seating area. This side and the near end are the only ones with a railed perimeter to a pitch that slopes downwards from the right side. With its fine setting, there are not many better places to watch football, especially on a sunny day with the local vineyard looking over it to the rear of the pavilion, and the hills that form part of this riverside village scene. Not so good on a wet day, though, but I guess that applies to a lot of other spots too.

Thankfully, the weather is behaving itself this afternoon as Appledore are in town for a Peninsula East fixture. Funnily enough, the last game I saw here was the corresponding fixture from last season, which the visitors won by the odd goal in five. This is the Buzzards' second year in this division, having been promoted from the D&E, and when I see them on their travels they always seem to win.

In fact the only time they have not done so was in their first-ever game at Crediton. Even then they were three up with a few minutes to go before throwing it away in a frantic finale. Quite why I should habitually see them lose at home and do so well on the road is a mystery. It's not as if they have a fantastic away record, so I must presume that my attendance coincides with their good away days.

It's certainly not a stand-alone fact in this respect. My record at nearby Elmore tells me that, despite many visits, I have only seen them win once at Horsden Park. I could refer to other statistical oddities, but if you are not nodding off yet you soon will be! You'll have got the picture by now, I'm sure.

For large parts of the first half I would be tempted to fall asleep if I were sitting down. Appledore look as if they are having a jolly boys' outing and created nothing whatsoever. At least the hosts do come close to scoring when Kieran Rapo hits the post. Nathan Haskings also goes within a whisker through a header that is cleared off the line near the end of the period.

A crowd of 478 do get to see a goal seven minutes into resumption, when Rapo is sent through the middle to put Bickleigh in front with a cool finish into the right corner of the net. Having conceded, Appledore wake up at last and are unlucky when Russell Harrison rattles the crossbar with a header. Sam Fishwick goes close too, but prolific marksman Richard Hevingham does find the net on 66. A touch of fortune is involved, as a cross from the right is going nowhere until it ricochets off James Bateman and falls into Hevingham's path, and he scores with a low shot that goes in off the post.

Now it's the away side that look like winning the contest, but keeper Ben Mercy is not to be beaten again. In added time it's Rapo who has chances to score, but he snatches at two good opportunities. Perhaps a draw is the fair result of an average game, though, and on a personal note I am glad the home side haven't lost once more when I'm here.

And while the others travel on to Witheridge for episode three of today's football adventure, I'm going home. Besides the fact that I have already done my visit there, I am happy with what I have done today.

# Saturday, April 23

Day two of the hop sees everyone head west for another three games. Not me, though, as I'm travelling north for a single helping of Conference football. My destination is Alfreton Town, with Redditch the visitors in a Northern division encounter. The home side will win the title with a victory, which seems highly probable given that the opposition are at the foot of the table. No doubt those who know me will accuse me of goal-hunting, but there is more to it than that.

On April 24 last year I made a similar journey under identical circumstances to a place not far from where I will be this afternoon. Then it was the away side, Southport, who were going for the championship-clinching win at Eastwood. They won 3-0 and were presented with the trophy after the match amid wild celebrations. I am hoping for those scenes to be repeated today, as it would be quirky if I witnessed the same scenario at about the same time in around the same area of the country. Of course, another reason for coming is that it will cost more to see Alfreton at home in a Conference Premier game, so in the long term I will be saving a couple of pounds!

As it's Easter Saturday I think there will be quite a bit of traffic on the motorways, but it's not too bad. In the end I am parked up in a nearby street with over an hour to spare despite taking it really easy over the last 30 miles or so. This is an easy place to reach, being but a mile or two off the main A38, and it is nice to see that there are no blasted restrictions such as resident-only areas.

These have their uses, and I understand why they are utilised in certain spots, but they can be a pain. With virtually no parking available within the confines of this venue it would have been exasperating if I had to park a million miles away from the place I wanted to be. Not here though, and with time to kill I wander into the centre of this small town.

It is a short walk that brings dividends, as while perusing I spot a hairdresser that will cut my locks for a mere £3. Wow! I normally pay more than double that for a cut that takes no time at all. Let's just say that I am lacking up top (some might say in more ways than one) and as I am in need of a trim I decide to partake of this bargain, thus emerging a lighter, brighter person. After returning to my car, I cross the road and enter the ground in the hope that it is a portent of things to come in the next couple of hours.

After going through the double turnstile I find myself in one corner of the ground. Directly to the left is some uncovered seating behind the goal. To the right is a refreshment facility and the club shop. Straight ahead you come to a recent modification. The first part of this is raised, covered terracing with a separate walkway at the rear. This is replicated at the far end of this structure, while in the middle the pathway drops down to the front, with some red coloured plastic seating behind. This is mostly used for VIPs and has a hospitality area at the back.

Beyond this is open, raised hardstanding that leads around to the far end, which has concrete terracing with some cover at the back. On the far side is a covered, seated stand that runs almost its entire length, with open hardstanding areas linking up both ends.

For some strange reason, this stand has no dividing rail between it and the pitch – the only thing separating the two being a narrow tarmacked path – and this will certainly have to change if Alfreton go up. To be honest, I am surprised that they have managed to get away with it up until now although, from a viewing perspective, it is very good as it makes you feel close to the action.

The dugouts fit snugly into spots either side of the halfway line between the seating and terraced areas – which have your standard railed perimeter with advertising boards – while the four floodlights here are sited a little way in from the corners – as at Dartford – and have replaced more old-fashioned ones.

Given the raised areas on one side, it will hardly come as a shock when I state that the pitch slopes gently on a diagonal plane, which contributes to what is a decent venue – one that will produce the kind of atmosphere which will be ideal for a game like today's.

Not only is it my first time visiting the Impact Arena, it's also a first viewing of the home side for me. The same cannot be said for Redditch, whom I last saw at Team Bath. Remember them? Yes, that university club that appeared out of nowhere in the Western League, then progressed up the ladder before vanishing from the spotlight – a bit like Chico from The X-Factor. What a load of old nonsense that was (Team Bath that is, not the TV programme, although I'm not exactly a fan of that either).

I first saw TB in action at Chard, where they won 11-1 and could have got 20. One good thing that came out of it was Paul Tisdale, who has done a great job at my local club, so it's not all been bad. I am a great believer in clubs having to start from the bottom and work their way up. That's the way it should be.

The large crowd are almost stunned inside two minutes of the contest as a long ball sees home keeper Ross Turner and his centre back hesitate enough for Josh McKenzie to nip in between them and head the ball towards goal, but it goes narrowly wide. Nerves are calmed seven minutes later, though, when Nathan Arnold's cross sees Paul Clayton attempt to score via a back-heel. This is saved, only for the forward to lash in the rebound. Jake Bedford then denies the scorer with a fingertip save on to the right post, but on 26 he is beaten again as Clayton benefits from the result of the visiting keeper's fine stop from Liam Hearn's piledriver, the ball dropping for him to head into an empty net.

Not long into the second half the game is made safe, Hearn getting himself on the scoresheet after bursting through the middle and slotting under Bedford. Until this point it has been fairly competitive, but now it's a case of how many the hosts can add to their tally. In the end it's just the one, Hearn receiving the ball on the edge of the box, turning and curling it into the bottom left corner of the net.

Alfreton, who have certainly played like champions for the most part, are presented with the trophy after the game. As at last year at Eastwood, I stay behind to see it before making the long drive back. At the risk of repeating myself, it has been another satisfying day.

ADRIAN WICKS

# Monday, April 25

A few days ago I set my stall out to visit Simmons Park, home of Okehampton. After the weekend's Peninsula results, though, I have had a change of heart. Instead, I am heading down the A38 to Elburton, who play Buckland Athletic in a Premier Division encounter.

This could see me watch a title-winning performance for the second time in three days, as the away side need a victory to retain their crown with games to spare. Having missed out on them doing likewise last season, I really must be present this time around if possible.

It is a lovely sunny day as I arrive at the Haye Road ground and park up in an area that used to be directly behind the goal. In fact it still is, although that playing area is now used for non-first team action. Prior to becoming one of the Peninsula's founder members in 2007, Elburton played their Devon League games on that pitch. Now they ply their trade on one that is at a lower level beyond the far goal.

To get there you walk down a stony track on the right and pass the flat-roofed building that holds the changing rooms and small clubhouse facility, with an extension at the far end from which refreshments are purchased. Payment is made at a wooden hut, and you immediately look down from behind the goal to a venue that is still a work in progress. This grassed bank goes around to the left-hand side and shallows out by the time you reach the far end.

At the midway point on that side there is a cutting where a proposed stand is going to be. When it's done, it will be flanked by the already-present Perspex dugouts, while firm standing runs along here and the near end. The opposite side is an extremely narrow grassed strip bordered by a high wire fence, and the far end is tree-lined, dividing us from yet another pitch behind.

There is a single, unpainted metal rail all around the pitch, which is a lot better than the old one – a bumpy, stone-infested surface that must have been a nightmare to play on. With lights still in the planning stage and no cover, this has to rank as the worst ground in this division at present, but I think it will improve in time.

The same can be said for my opinions of this club as a whole. This goes back to a time when I drove down here with my dog in the back seat. I was not aware of the 'no dogs' ruling, so when I parked up I got him out to stretch his legs before promptly putting him back in the vehicle. In a flash I was accosted by the chairman, who treated me like a criminal and threatened to throw me out. At the same time a woman was walking her dog around, but nothing was said to her. A friend, maybe? I don't know, but I do know I was treated in an impolite manner undeserving of my so-called crime. He was on a lead (the dog, that is) and just outside the car for a few seconds.

I'm glad to say the secretary at that time, who is someone I get along with well, followed up with a calm and measured approach, so everything returned to normal. I do not hold a grudge – life's too short for that – but it has taken a while for my attitude to mellow in this instance. I am also pleased to state that this has been a one-off incident in my ground-visiting history, and long may that continue. The chairman has obviously forgotten the incident as I have encountered him since then and we are on amicable terms, which is good.

I wonder how many people can say they have seen a side score 14 goals in a game and concede that number in another? I can. Martin, Phil and I were at Elburton's romp against Crediton on the old pitch in an end-of-season encounter, while I was the sole member of the trio to see them lose 14-2 at Cullompton – a game where the referee blew for time three minutes early. As he came off the pitch I asked him about it and was informed that he felt sorry for the visitors!

That's all very well, but football is a 90-minute game, isn't it? And Cully were gunning for the title, which they could have lost on goal difference (they didn't), so an extra goal could have been significant. As a neutral I do not like to see such one-sided scores, but rules are rules.

The funny thing is that 52 weeks before that, I also saw a 16-goal game. That was at Teignmouth, and it was a game at which a local news photographer turned up and took one shot of a home player shooting towards goal. Later, the report related to the away side's 16 goals while printing that photo of the hosts' only effort to bag one of their own!

Unbelievable – a word that can describe my 24-hour period then: the night before I had seen a goalless game, thus going from zero to 16 inside that time. I cannot see that ever happening again.

The only contrasts on show this afternoon will be the playing styles of the two teams. Elburton are a more direct side who trouble their more fluent opponents in the early stages. Both Paul Baker and Mark Conday go close to finding the net, but just before the half-hour it is the yellows who open the scoring. A crisp move down the right sees Lucas Burgess lay the ball off to Simon Revell, and the winger produces an exquisitely curled shot that beats keeper Chris Waring and finds the top corner.

The home custodian keeps his side in the match as we enter the second half, with the likes of Liam Moseley, Danny Lewis and Antony Lynch all being thwarted. The feeling among the travelling fans is that one goal will not be enough, which proves to be correct as substitute Jed Smale is invited to have a pot at goal from 25 yards out. He strikes the ball with the outside of his boot, past the outstretched hand of Neil Montandon and into the net.

Now it's anyone's game as both teams go for the jugular. Lewis Vine rounds the keeper but sees his effort cleared off the line by a covering Buckland defender, and the away side also go close on several occasions.

Just when it looks as if they will have to wait for at least one more match to clinch the title, Matt Beer and Shane Gill combine to put Lynch in on the right, and the striker shows all his experience by scoring calmly with an angled drive that goes in off the far post. With literally seconds left, this triggers wild celebrations, which culminate shortly after when the final whistle puts the seal on their championship success.

There is no post-match trophy presentation, so after shaking hands and congratulating Roy and a couple of others, I head back to the car. It has been a close-run thing, but I am happy I have been there to see the Bucks do it. Yippee!

# Tuesday, April 26

I had originally decided not to attend a game this evening, but a window of opportunity has arisen whereby I can not only see a match but also do another new ground. This means another drive east along the A35 into Dorset before branching off for Wimborne, then heading a few miles north to watch Holt United's clash with Sturminster Newton.

This has similarities to 10 days ago in that the home side are hot favourites to take the points against their basement opponent. Newton defied the odds then and I am hoping for a repeat showing tonight – maybe I am a lucky charm for them!

It's a good run up and I arrive in plenty of time. There's not a great deal of parking available, but with all due respect it is hardly required. This venue is not the easiest to find, especially if you head for the village itself. The ground is actually a couple of miles away at Gaunts Common and is next to a single-track road. The car park is sited behind the goal, with a slatted wooden fence separating the two.

Across the other side is a flat-roofed building that houses the small clubhouse at one end and the dressing rooms at the other. At the far end of the fencing you enter the ground, a small concreted hut passing for a place where you part with £3. Alas, there is no programme, so I have to come back out and across to the ref's room so that I can get the team line-ups. Luckily, I have come prepared with a blank piece of paper – the saying preparing is preventing not applying tonight – and write them down.

On re-entering the ground I am asked to pay again but am let off by the secretary who, unlike the gateman, remembers me from the first time I came in a whole 10 minutes earlier. Talk about amnesia; it's not as if there is a massive attendance. While I am all for ideas to boost the funds of clubs like this, I am not going to pay double the rates.

Mind you, there was one occasion when I attended a Football League game and it turned out that *they* paid *me* to watch! What happened was that I handed over a tenner at the gate and, instead of giving me a fiver with my two pound notes, the turnstile attendant gave me another £10. I can honestly say I didn't notice the error until later, and I'm sure that if I had noted the oversight immediately I would have done the right thing, being the Mr Goody Two-Shoes that I was! However, it occurred nearly 30 years ago, so I can't swear to it.

I can say, though, that this place doesn't exactly have the wow factor as you come in. There is some standing cover directly to the right – an unusual structure with a flat wooded roof being held up by metal poles. At this end there is hardstanding that leads around to the dugouts on halfway. These form part of another covered area of a similar ilk, only being propped up by concrete blocks.

Beyond this it is open and grassy all the way around to the car parking end, with the opposite side composed of rough terrain and a tree line that divides you from the lane outside. Being open behind the far end and dugout sides makes for chilly conditions on a night like this – a fact I will be only too aware of as I have gone and brought along a lightweight jacket! A single metal rail surrounds the pitch, which looks a little on the bumpy side.

No lights, of course, so it is a 6.30 start time. We actually get under way at 6.40 for some strange reason – I told you it was a Dorset thing – and this Premier clash also takes its time to bed in. Both teams struggle to cope with the dry and anything-but-smooth surface, with Sam Purdy going close for the hosts and opposing striker Stuart Frear's effort producing a good save from Andy Knight.

Conditions are certainly making this an even contest, with neither side able to hold on to the ball for any length of time. A frantic finale to the half sees Ryan Murray shoot wide and Tom Willis head over, then virtually on the 45 mark Sam Stockley finds space on the right only to fire across goal and past the far post. Goalless at the break, and time for a cuppa.

During the half I have done my usual circuit of the pitch, passing what looked like a familiar face in doing so. I didn't say anything because he was of an average build, while the fella I was thinking it might have been was, shall we say, somewhat bigger. We meet up in the clubhouse, though, and having seen him face to face I realise it is indeed who I thought it was. Withdean – a bloke I haven't seen for ages and who has evidently gone on a diet.

Withdean is not his real name of course, just a nickname. It came about after a groundhop quiz night, when one of the questions concerned the name of the only league ground with an athletics track around it. He was on my team and we could not remember where it was. When we found out the answer, he (real name Martin – no, not him, another one) exclaimed that he lived in the Withdean area for a while, so the name stuck.

Last season he went to an obscene number of games that included all sorts – women's games, reserve, youth and obscure fixtures between teams I have never heard of in leagues I didn't know existed. Still, he lapped it up while taking a million photos in the process. His habit of buying a replica shirt from his Football League visits must have burned a sizeable hole in his wallet, while his car must be begging for mercy by now. It takes all sorts, though, and while I cannot claim to be one of his best mates, he's OK. It's nice to see him, anyway.

The sending off of Simon Edwards does not help Holt's cause as we resume hostilities. Frankly, the referee has no option but to give him a second yellow, which in fact could so easily have been a straight red. The visitors seem to gain encouragement from the ensuing quarter as their hosts feel frustrated at not being ahead at this point. This mood is hardly going to soften if they happen to concede, which is exactly what happens on 64 minutes when Wayne Moussalli receives the ball 30 yards from goal and strikes the ball low past the keeper – an effort that just sneaks in between him and his near post.

Stockley misses a sitter shortly after, so the fact that he is substituted within seconds can be seen as either punishment or mere coincidence. Holt then mount some serious pressure and are rewarded with an equaliser. Substitute Mike Barber makes a good run down the right and crosses from the byline to the far post, where fellow replacement Luke Stone is on hand to slide it in.

All-out attack is the name of the game now, making a winning goal seem inevitable. In stoppage time it arrives – but it's at the other end. Michael Budd gets the ball some 35 yards out and instinctively hits it towards goal, whereupon it flies into the top corner. With not enough time to respond, it gives Newton a shock win that keeps their hopes of avoiding relegation alive.

After saying my goodbyes to Withdean, I make my way home wondering if I should go and see Newton play on Saturday. They are at home and I have not been there, so maybe I should. Having seen them glean four unexpected points this month, I'm sure they will welcome me with open arms. OK, maybe not, although I do know that I am pleased to have come here tonight and not stayed at home.

# Wednesday, April 27

Watching football with an acquaintance of mine called Martin may have occurred by chance last night, but it is intentional this evening as I head for Taunton to meet up with the version I see on a regular basis. From here he will drive to our destination: Glastonbury, who have a Somerset County Premier game with Watchet.

Even though it doesn't make me lick my lips in anticipation, it will be nice to return to a venue that I have only visited once before – and that was several years ago. It doesn't take long to get there from Martin's place, which means that we arrive in good time at a ground easily found to the south-west of town, just off the bypass.

On the way there, I regale my good friend with my story about meeting up with Withdean – someone he also knows well – and he remarks on a similar encounter that saw him react in much the same way as I did. At least that makes me feel a little better about passing him by, as I did in the first half yesterday.

Perhaps this is the moment when I should reveal that I too have a footballing nickname, as Martin is one of the few who call me by that and not my real name. 'All right hedge' is said every time we meet up. It apparently stems from a match played at Buckland's old Homers Lane headquarters. On the far side of it was a dense line of shrubbery, where I was spotted on more than one occasion rummaging among the brambles in order to retrieve the ball. As with Withdean, the name appears to have stuck, and that's fine by me. After all, I could have a worse one.

Glastonbury is, of course, more renowned for its annual music festival than for anything the local football team have achieved, which is not a lot. Personally I have never been to the festival, but wish that I had in my younger days. What with the palaver of residing in tents and the certainty of bad weather during the event, it all adds up to a bit much for an old man like me!

U2, one of my favourite bands, have performed at Glastonbury, and it would have been great if I'd been there for that, although I enjoy listening to their older songs more. I did see them back in the mid-80s, when they were nowhere as big as they are now. Their songs had a rawness about them that no longer seems to exist, and I have to admit that Bono tends to get on my nerves at times now he has got somewhat political. The Edge is my favoured band member. Given my nickname, I guess this shouldn't surprise anyone, but it is sheer coincidence.

For the record (no pun intended, and anyway it's all CDs now) my favourite band of all time is The Beatles and, in contrast to U2, I view their later recordings as being better than those they started out doing. In my opinion, those were mainly produced to sell LPs and satisfy the teenage fans, whereas classics such as Sgt Pepper symbolise the creative talents they undoubtedly possessed. OK, so LSD allegedly played a substantial role in the making of that album, but it is still superb. Abbey Road's not bad either, although some may disagree.

Apparently, when I was little I used to run around the house singing Beatles songs, and I can still recall the lyrics from many of their hits. I have sung one or two of them at karaokes, but can definitely state that I am no budding Lennon or McCartney (or George Harrison, in my opinion the underrated one of the Fab Four).

I certainly couldn't sing any of the modern day stuff, and I am sure that if I tried to do a rap it would make me look like some sort of geriatric. And I was 25 years younger the last time I went to a live gig, where no canvas equipment or brollies were required. I think I'll leave the Glastonbury festival to the youngsters now.

Back in the present day, we find ourselves in the large parking area with ample time to spare. You enter to the left of a large building that holds the dressing rooms at that end and a good-sized clubhouse at the other. After passing through the entrance, you find a covered, tarmacked area to the front of this, with a plastic corrugated roof held by wooden uprights and joists. This is on halfway and is divided from the pitch by a small concrete wall. Along with the more orthodox covered standing area located directly around to the left – a rather old construction with two concreted levels – these are the only areas from where you can watch the game.

The remaining surrounds are open and grassy, with the elliptical shape providing ample evidence to the eye that greyhound races used to be staged here. There are old-fashioned lighting pylons all the way round, but only the three side ones have lamps on, and they don't work! There is also a distinct lack of any dugouts, with both teams having to do with open 'technical areas' on the far side. I am sure this ground is tidier than it used to be, but it is not exactly brilliant.

The visiting side are obviously not keen on a midweek jaunt to the Abbey Moor Stadium, as they turn up about 10 minutes before the scheduled start time. We kick-off 15 minutes late and see the hosts control the opening exchanges. Watchet are clearly not in the right frame of mind, and concede a sloppy goal on 20 minutes. Keeper Adam Bishop miscues an attempted clearance straight to Peter Boot, who squares it to fellow striker Alex Priddice for an easy tap-in. Ten minutes later scorer turns provider when Priddice finds Jason Loxton on the far post from the left, with his finely-struck effort zipping into the top right corner of the net. The only noteworthy effort by the away side falls to Aaron Deeks near the end of the half, but his shot is well saved.

Two things happen during the second half. One is the solitary goal scored by Boot, who latches on to a through ball down the left and beats Bishop with an angled drive; the other is an extremely rebellious move by Martin and myself. Despite not strictly being allowed to, we do a complete lap of the ground, even stopping at times to observe the action – what little there is. Given that neither of us is liable to chain ourselves to railings or engage in sit-down protests in the name of world peace, this is possibly about as anti-establishment as we will get, I suppose! There is a sparse attendance so I suspect the club are so grateful that we have paid to come in that we are never at risk of being thrown out.

When the final whistle blows, it brings to an end a lacklustre half of a game in which only the homesters have looked interested. Driving away, I think this: I have never been up to Glastonbury Tor, but will do some day; I have been to Glastonbury FC, but almost certainly never will again.

# Saturday, April 30

Today I make a decision I may live to regret. Instead of going to Sturminster Newton, I head in a south-westerly direction with Martin for the Peninsula Premier Division clash between St Austell and Torpoint. Unlike me, Martin has not been here before, and I feel the need to repay him by tagging along. He does not know the easy route to Poltair Park but I do, meaning I can use my navigational expertise as a perfect excuse to leave my car in the garage.

As it's a bank holiday weekend I think we might encounter a lot of traffic on our downward journey, but it isn't bad at all. We drive through the gate into the parking area beside the pitch with over an hour to spare.

It's a lovely sunny afternoon, unlike the last time I was here. I was driving, with Phil as a passenger, as we came down in good conditions for most of the journey. Five miles from our destination, though, it started to rain and it was heavy by the time we reached the ground. Despite my gloomy predictions (no change there!), the game against Hayle started, but the rain continued to lash down and it was abandoned at half-time.

We found out while in the clubhouse, which is where Martin and I will kill time for now. At least I am not at the wheel today, which means I can partake of a pint of the local ale – St Austell brewery is a stone's throw away, and it tastes good. Not as good as a pint of Sam's, of course – what is? – but refreshing on a day like today.

Martin goes and gets the team line-ups and before long we are outside again in time for the players to stand in line and do the respect handshakes. What a load of nonsense that is – just another silly PR stunt by the FA. Still, it's harmless and if it makes a difference in one or two matches then I guess it's worthwhile.

These two sides have scored almost 200 league goals between them during this campaign, so the game is never likely to be goalless. Right from the off they both go for it, and the only surprise is that it takes all of 14 minutes for a goal to be scored. It's a straightforward one too, as Lewis Edwards' corner on the left is headed in by Shane White at the far post to give Torpoint the lead. Inside two minutes the hosts level, Neil Slateford finishing off a jinking run on the right with an angled shot that creeps inside the far upright.

The home side should be in front by the break, but they contrive to squander a bundle of chances; Mike Body, the chief culprit, should have bagged a treble of his own. Visiting striker Josh Grant shows him how it should be done, bursting through the centre and coolly slotting under onrushing keeper Gary Penhaligon to give his side the lead.

My turn to buy the teas at half-time, these being acquired from a flat-roofed, rectangular building that also holds the officials' changing room. This is at the opposite end of the car-parking side and is set slightly back from the pitch. Bridging the two on halfway is a wooden stand, which is at a raised level and is accessed by a centrally located pair of staircases that meet in the middle. It has a sloping, corrugated metal roof and wooden bench seating within.

At ground level, the dugouts are to be found to the fore at each end, while the dressing rooms are underneath the stand. There is a flat, concreted area at the front of this structure, partitioned off by old-fashioned iron rails. At both ends of this venue we have grassy banks, with the far end now equipped with open hardstanding.

The opposite side, also uncovered, is not the place to be on a wet day as it gets somewhat boggy in places. A single horizontal rail surrounds the pitch, which has a slope from side to side and is quite good. There are no floodlights at present, but it will not be too long before this is rectified. The clubhouse is sited behind the stand and makes up part of a ground that has improved.

Any thoughts of things going quiet after the interval are soon scotched. Adam Carter poaches the visitors' third from a Lewis Edwards assist, and it's a strike that is quickly followed by Grant beating the offside trap on the left before rounding the keeper and slotting in. A spell of three goals in five minutes is completed when Carter does likewise on the right, with his third being grabbed in a similar manner on the left after 72 minutes. On all three occasions the St Austell back line are left just inside their own half appealing in vain for the flag to be raised.

They fail to learn from their mistakes during the remainder of the half and are only spared more punishment by wasteful finishing by Grant, who has been finding it too easy. He does get a hat-trick, though, as Carter unselfishly sets him up for a tap-in after finding himself unmarked on receiving the ball from the left. Penhaligon's fine save from Edwards denies Torpoint an eighth, and the hosts could have got a couple of their own in stoppage time, but it is fairly emphatic by the end.

If St Austell had taken their chances in the first half things might have turned out differently, but there we are. There is a good chance that they may score *and* concede 100 league goals in the season now, thanks to this scoreline. It has been highly entertaining stuff for us neutral observers: it was as open a game as you could possibly get.

The same cannot be said for a hop game here. The highlight came when the ball was kicked out of the ground at the end where the road runs behind. One hopper who has a fixation about touching the ball set off in hot pursuit, closely followed by others who, for some silly reason, were trying to prevent him from succeeding in his quest. I don't know who won that race, but I do know that my decision to come here with Martin has proved the correct one.

# Monday, May 2

The May Day bank holiday would not be complete without the Throgmorton Cup Final, and this year it is being staged at Newquay. Despite having attended the last 11 of these encounters, I am a tad reluctant to travel down, as the north-western resort is bound to be busy on the traffic front. Even the fixtures secretary (Phil) adding a morning game to the day's agenda could not persuade me to alter my way of thinking.

A phone call from Martin, telling me that he is driving down for this double helping, does change my plans for the day. So it is, then, as my day begins with him picking me up, and less than an hour and a half later we are parked up in the road outside the home of Godolphin Atlantic.

This morning they are entertaining their big brotherly neighbours in the form of Newquay, and if it is anything like last season's game – which the home side won 5-3 – it will be well worth watching. I also witnessed Godolphin win at Mount Wise by an identical score the year before, and wonder if a hat-trick is possible. Probably not.

This ground is about a mile to the north of the town centre, just off the main road. It has a clubhouse of sorts: the Godolphin Arms public house directly across from the turn into Godolphin Way. There is a narrow, rough track from here that brings you out at one corner of the ground.

Directly in front, and behind the goal, are two buildings. The first is a large construction that doubles up as hospitality area and refreshment facility. With grey walls, it has a coldness about its interior. The second holds the dressing rooms, with a more orthodox refreshment kiosk at the end. In front of this is some covered standing – a flat-roofed, wooded extension held up by timber posts. There is a gravelled surface under here, whereas the remaining sides of this venue at present are grassy.

The far side has a variation of concrete-blocked walls along its entire length – a boundary that divides the ground from private gardens. In fact, residential properties surround this venue, with dense shrubbery at the far end acting as another form of barrier. The pitch, which rarely suffers from postponements, is railed all around with the tiny exception of a gap at the near end behind the goal, with a shallow slope meaning that the height of the horizontal pole is a touch higher the further down you go.

Down at the far end of the near side, the boundary is at its closest to the playing area, progressively tapering to the extent that there is barely enough room to squeeze between barrier and prickly thorn bushes. The dugouts are of a solid, white-painted construction and face each other on halfway. There are no floodlights and the club are unlikely to get them given their surroundings. However, this does not detract from what is a cosy little ground in which to watch football.

Despite being the so-called smaller club of the two, it is the home side who are riding high in the league table, and mathematically they can still win it. Meanwhile, their opponents languish in mid-table obscurity, and this morning's match will be their manager's last in charge. His team certainly make the better start in this derby, with Luke Rigby's solo run and shot testing home keeper Shaun Semmens.

Sadly, this is as good as it gets for them, and they go behind midway through the half. Ollie Dart is the scorer, shooting low into the net from 15 yards after a left-sided cross is touched on to him. It's not until the 70th minute that the hosts confirm their superiority with a second. Mark Rose is left unmarked on the left, and he nets with an angled drive.

Newquay's misery is completed near the end when Josh Harris strikes home from the edge of the box – a goal that puts the icing on the cake as far as Godolphin are concerned. They surely seem to have the Indian sign over their cross-town rivals, and this has not been the best way for Jim Hilton to end his tenure.

One down, one to go. This involves a drive across town to our cup final hosts, and we get there in time to acquire one of the few parking spots available outside the ground. When I first drove up Clevedon Road and saw the spectator entrance at the top, I wondered if I had erred in locating this parking area, but when you get there the narrow access to your right becomes apparent. There is street parking but not a great deal of it, due to it being awash with cars parked there already.

This might be a concern for others this afternoon, but for us the only issue is how we are going to kill the next two hours. Doing the puzzles in the newspaper is a start. Martin, aka Mr Cleverclogs, manages to get the nine-letter word in a flash, while muggins here cannot see it for love nor money. I give up as we opt for a stroll down the hill into town to grab a bite to eat.

What has happened to good old-fashioned fish and chip shops? Here they are either closed or charging such amounts that would require me to remortgage my house. Plenty of pizzerias and kebab shops, of course. I don't know, maybe we are just looking in the wrong places. In the end we choose to purchase our grub at the ground, which at least helps towards club funds. Oh, and on the way back I finally suss that nine-letter word!

The double-turnstile entry to this venue may not be as grandiose as that at Penzance, but at least it gives a feeling of actually coming through from the outside, just as you get from stadiums at a higher level. Once in, you are on halfway with some covered standing to the right. This leads up to the refreshment kiosk in the corner and has a single row of bench seating at the back.

Go left and there is some uncovered terracing that is showing signs of old age, and shallows out around to behind the goal. Here it becomes a grassy bank and narrows around to the main feature of this ground, the wooded stand painted in the club's colours. This has wooden seating and a pitched roof, and the dugouts flank it.

The clubhouse building backs on to the other goal, with a narrow path in between that brings you to where the players enter the field of play from the dressing rooms located in the same building. Four floodlight poles are on each side of a ground that, thanks to its hilltop location, can feel a little exposed on a windy day.

Conditions, though, are good this afternoon. The same can be said for the prospects of the cup final too, as Plymouth Parkway take on St Blazey. Neither team has gone this far in the competition before, and to be honest I expect it to be a cagey opening (most finals tend to be, don't they?) but obviously no one has told the 22 players out there. The result is a crazy period that sees three goals scored in the first seven minutes!

First Danny Zalick turns his marker on the edge of the box to fire Blazey in front, only for Danny Brook to equalise at the second attempt after his initial shot is cleared off the line. Two minutes later, Andy Sargent's delivery from the left falls to Lee Doel, and the midfielder strikes the ball into the net.

Brook taps home Parkway's third after Sargent's effort has been saved by keeper Tom Blackler, and we then have to wait for all of 20 more minutes before someone else scores! Josh Higman gets it, lobbing Ben Elphick from the edge of the area.

Two minutes after the break it's all square as Chris Reski finds room on the right and strikes a low shot across the keeper and into the far corner. On 65 it's the turn of the green and blacks to go in front. Reski sets it up from the right and finds Dave Trott, who scores at the second attempt after his first effort is blocked on the line. Ten minutes later, Glynn Hobbs makes it 4-4 as he shows trickery on the left before firing past Blackler.

Although good chances are created by both teams, no more goals are forthcoming, which means extra time. After a barnstorming 90 minutes of action, I am sure nobody will grumble about seeing another 30. The one sour note has come during the second period, when words were exchanged between the Parkway dugout and so-called fans standing nearby, which got a little out of hand as verbals become physical. Thankfully, there are no Eric Cantona impersonators on the bench, but the game is held up for a while until order is restored.

In terms of goals, I have always come away from this ground with a good outcome. My first visit produced one of the best individual goals I have ever seen. Callington's second goal of the game, it was akin to Maradona's goal against England in the 86 World Cup (no, not the handball one, the other). While I may not have witnessed such wizardry today, I can safely say that my Mount Wise record has continued to blossom.

The same can be said about Parkway's chances of winning the cup before long, as goals either side of the turnaround in extra time put them in control. Chris

DIARY OF A SEASON

Wright coolly slots past the keeper from the left, then just 19 seconds after the brief interval Sargent turns and fires into the bottom right corner. It knocks the stuffing out of Blazey, and the Devon side are able to see out the remainder of the final.

And what a final it has been – one that will be remembered for a long time, and the only thing that has blown me away today was the football. Just think, I could have missed out on all the excitement. Thanks to Martin, I haven't.

# Tuesday, May 3

How on earth do you top the thrills of yesterday? Well, probably not by attending a meaningless league fixture, but that is on my radar this evening. My first thoughts have led me to the possibility of attending a Somerset County game at Winscombe, but in the end I opt for the short drive down to see the Royal Marines entertain Saltash United in a Peninsula Premier clash.

With the running costs of a car rocketing up by the minute, I suspect this will be the shape of things to come in my footballing life, with lengthy journeys being confined to new grounds or revisits that are of relevance from a personal, statistical point of view.

There are but a handful of grounds in this division that have no lights at present, with Endurance Park, sadly, being one of them. This means tackling rush-hour traffic on the way down, thus more than doubling my normal travelling time in order to get there in time to get the team line-ups and what have you. Sometimes this seemingly easy task can turn out to be harder than acquiring secret documents from MI5 but, as I know the secretary here, that will not be so this evening.

Ian Mulholland is a decent fella who finds it no bother to get the information across to a statistics freak like me when he probably has better things to do. I got to know him through my friendship with Phil – an outcome that strikes similar chords in other friendships on the Peninsula circuit – and he is another of those who are enthusiastic about what they are trying to do.

For the time being, that keenness is being reflected out on the field. This game is the penultimate fixture in the Marines' inaugural campaign in the Premier, having won the East Division by a landslide a year ago. In the process they scored over 100 goals and gobbled up a mega-sackful of points, but they have found life harder this time around. They did win the Charity Vase at the start of the season, though, and have just about held their own.

If I were a regular – and there are not many of them here – I would be satisfied with what is only their third year in the Peninsula. Mind you, they did not get it under way in style, with a 7-4 home loss to Bovey Tracey, a game I should have attended but chose not to. Instead I saw Bodmin win easily in an FA Cup tie at Elmore. This was a delightful result bearing in mind the home club's belief that the Peninsula would never work, instead choosing to be the only Devon-based Western First Division outfit.

I think the real reason was that they felt they would not fare as well in the new league – a fact ably demonstrated by the 4-0 loss to the Cornish side in which Elmore were lucky to get nil! Anyway, I made my first visit a fortnight after the Bovey game and still saw a lot of goals, all of them to the homesters. The Marines play a pleasing brand of football, so with tonight's visitors being a decent side, it makes for an intriguing contest.

Located between Exeter and Exmouth, this ground is simple to find and has open entry from the nearby lane. The person taking money is positioned next to the building in the near corner. This holds the refreshment and hospitality areas at the near end and the dressing rooms at the other. Hardstanding runs from here down the side of the pitch to a covered seated stand on halfway, with the dugouts flanking it.

These are certainly a lot smaller than the original versions erected three years ago. The club had a sponsorship tie-up with a company that supplies wooden sheds, meaning that the dugouts were precisely that – flippin' enormous and with enough space within to swing not just a cat but a brontosaurus. It also made for obstructed viewing from the blue plastic seating, which no longer applies.

Beyond this and around the rest of the perimeter is uncovered, soft standing behind a white plastic single rail held by sturdy posts of a similar ilk. The side opposite the stand is open and expansive, and you would get plenty of exercise in retrieving the ball, which would at least help to warm you up on a chilly day, as it is fairly exposed to the elements. However, this is an acceptable venue and one I would recommend visiting, especially when the club eventually get floodlights.

Both sides make a solid start once the game gets under way. The hosts win a debatable penalty after 18 minutes – one that some referees would not have awarded. Some might say justice is done when the resultant spot kick by Adam Fowler is saved, but I'm not so sure. However, there is no debate about Sam Hughes' blunder moments later, as it's a contender for miss of the season. The Ashes' frontman almost makes up for it on the stroke of half-time, but his effort is well saved by home custodian Craig Mulholland.

It's third time lucky on 63 when Hughes is at the far post to tuck away a Matt Cusack cross from the left. Both sides create further opportunities, but that single goal looks to be the winning one as we enter stoppage time. Then, from a drop-ball just inside the Marines' half, Marc Thorne punts it back towards the keeper, only for the ball to sail over him and into the net. Oh dear! Thankfully, order is restored as the away side allow Lewis Coombes to run through unchallenged and roll the ball in.

Seconds later the final whistle blows on a match that has at least given us a finale to remember. It has been, though, your typical end-of-season game.

# Wednesday, May 4

Decisions, decisions. I wonder how many on average we make per day? I guess it depends on who you are and what you do, but most of us have to undergo making decisions on several occasions once we are awake from our night-time slumbers.

When you think about it, decisions are not always significant, of course. Examples include whether you want tea or coffee with your breakfast, or what colour shirt you want to wear, etc. At the other end of the scale, though, are the big decisions that make their mark on your life and possibly other people's too. Having a loved one on a life-support machine and being asked for your permission to turn it off is one that, thankfully, I will never have to face.

Big or small, though, the fact remains that whenever there's a real, proper decision to be made, it always ends up being in *your* hands, and yours alone. You can take other people's advice on board, but at the end of the day it comes back to just you.

A shining example of this comes in my footballing world today as, not for the first time, I face the dilemma of choosing between one game and another. I have to decide on visiting Callington or Camelford, and as both games are significant it's a toss-up, as neither particularly stands out. In the end I opt for the shorter drive, mainly because Truro Reserves are the away club at Trefrew Park, whereas Perranporth provide first-eleven opposition at Callington.

It takes me about an hour to get to Marshfield Parc, as I negotiate the dual carriageway to Launceston then the never-ending 10-mile run south. I haven't been here for a while, but at least remember where the turn into the College is, unlike the time when I had to double back after passing it. Even when pulling into the car parking on the left there is no visible sign of a ground, which is a short uphill walk away. The club have no floodlights, which doesn't help, but rest assured you will not need a Sherpa guide or emergency supplies to get from your vehicle to the ground entrance.

My first visit here was the meat in the sandwich of a three-game groundhop day, although not a scheduled hop game. I attended the first one at Holsworthy and chose Callington instead of Launceston as I had already been to Pennygillam. A couple of hoppers, one of them from Chester, asked if they could come along as passengers, and I agreed to their request. We had a beer or two in a local hostelry prior to watching Liskeard stroll to an easy victory, then rejoined the others at Tavistock later. Further visits to this venue have not been so enjoyable on the social front, but have been all right.

Upon entry to this ground, you find yourself behind the goal on a flat but hardstanding area. On the right are the somewhat cramped changing rooms, while down in the corner to your left is a small refreshment kiosk attached to the hospitality room residing in what one could only define as a large Portakabin. Moving on down this side brings you immediately to a small covered standing enclosure then one of the dugouts, with the other directly opposite on halfway.

This and the far end are fairly narrow, non-hardstanding areas. The remaining side forms a grassy bank that provides good vistas, although the club have cut into it in order to erect a clubhouse, which they purchased from the cricket club – a financially welcome addition once up and running. The pitch, which is prone to waterlogging, has a single metal railed perimeter held up by white concrete posts. On a nice day this is a great place to watch football, with the views providing an excellent backdrop.

Callington are among three sides still bidding to become Peninsula West champions for the first time, and will have to beat the holders of this title tonight if they are to keep their hopes realistically alive. It certainly makes for a competitive match, and from kick-off the differing styles of play are plain to see.

Despite there being chances, it turns out to be a goalless first half, but it really shouldn't have been. This is due to a horrendous blooper by visiting midfielder Alec Penrose: a mix-up between keeper Tom Beman and his centre half presents him with an open goal, but somehow he puts it wide. If someone were to write a book on how not to score a goal this, along with Monsieur Hughes' effort last night, would definitely be in it!

At this stage I consider it more likely that £10 notes will start tumbling from the sky than that the home side will score, but four minutes after the break Chris Clarke's right cross is met at the far post by the head of Ryan Lucassi. One-nil to the hosts, then, as another of my expert predictions bites the dust! It is very much against the run of play, but once they're ahead Cally can and should wrap up the points.

In added time comes a critical passage of play. Ben Waters finds himself one-on-one with the visiting keeper but fluffs his big chance to seal the win. The ball is quickly transferred to the other end where a right-sided cross falls to Matt Luff, who flicks the ball past the onrushing keeper and into the net for a dramatic leveller, so late that there is barely enough time for the game to restart.

There is such a fine line between success and failure, and while this finale will not be recalled in the same way as Gordon Smith's miss in the '83 FA Cup Final, it is the defining blow to Callington's title hopes – the other teams have won tonight – but that's football. You win some, you lose some. Or draw.

# Thursday, May 5

With the exception of June and July, I have been to at least one new ground every month for over six years now. Yes, I know this so-called feat isn't exactly front-page headline material, nor a fancy chat-up line for the ladies, but it is one I would like to keep going for a little longer.

A combination of poor weather forecast for Saturday and my inbred impatience means I will be taking in an additional game this evening. Merley Cobham Sports are up against the newly crowned Dorset Premier champions Hamworthy Recreation in a fairly meaningless encounter. Pride, though, will be at stake as the two clubs are not that far apart, so I travel up the well-worn A35 path feeling that a reasonable game is on the cards.

Despite not having the best of journeys, I arrive about half an hour before kick-off. Once more, this is mainly due to rush-hour traffic, with the match being a 6.30 kick-off because there are no floodlights at Merley Park. It is located just to the south of Wimborne and can be found without too much difficulty. A mere stone's throw from the main road, you enter through a gate and drive down a narrow tarmacked road that runs alongside the pitch to your right.

Quite why there is a series of narrow road humps along here is a mystery, for it is only about 100 yards in length and I cannot see it being an attraction for the local speed freaks! There is a similar thing on the lane leading up to Cullompton's ground, which is even more baffling as, unlike here, the road has many potholes. Anything more than 10 mph along there and it's bump, bang, bump, hit head on car roof!

Anyway, having tackled the obstacle course you go around and park behind where the facilities are. As Merley's name suggests, more than just football is staged here, with the alternatives appearing to be housed at the far end. This includes a bar and social area, which must pass as the clubhouse as there is no refreshment kiosk to speak of.

The first building you encounter on approach is a flat-roofed structure that holds the dressing rooms, while the pitch has a single metal-railed perimeter all round with the exception of the changing room end, where the larger building does the job. There is a small covered standing enclosure on halfway next to the road leading which, like the dugouts on either side of this, are made of concrete and painted white. The opposite side and far end are open, expansive areas that form part of this recreational facility. It's all pretty basic stuff but nonetheless OK.

There is no programme issued here, so it's just as well I have come prepared. By accessing the league's website you are able to print off a list of available players for each club that goes with the fixture you want to attend. As a result, I am able to look at the team sheets and simply mark the number next to the player name – easy and handy for someone like me.

For some reason, the home side are only able to name one substitute and the number three shirt has gone missing. Apart from that, everything appears to be hunky-dory, but upon leaving the ref's room I espy the two managers having a chat. Now I'm not one for eavesdropping, but I cannot help but hear remarks that get my negative vibes going even before a ball is kicked.

The remark 'it's really bad out there' refers to the bone-hard surface, while the talk of 'taking it easy' doesn't help. They are really pally as they shake hands, although of course they could be good mates as well as rivals for all I know. With hindsight, though, it's an exchange I wish I'd never seen or heard.

Five minutes later than scheduled – Greenwich Mean Time obviously means nothing in this county – the game gets under way. James Pinder goes close for the home side and colleague Marin Warren does likewise, forcing a decent save from Kevin Leonard. Hamworthy appear to be a threat going forward themselves, as a team with over 100 league goals should, but fail to register a shot on target in a goalless first half.

On resumption, Warren is through on goal for Merley but blasts over, while the visitors continue to show little interest in scoring. By now my mind is awash with the belief that it's a bit too friendly out there. Aren't derby games supposed to be a least a tad feisty?

Then something occurs on 70 minutes that I have never seen before and hope never to witness again: a slick move by the away side tees up Mike Notley inside the six-yard box with an open goal and an easy tap-in. The fact that he somehow scoops it well over is bad enough – an embarrassing moment that has been seen at much bigger venues than this – but the reaction by the player and his teammates is laughable! The next few minutes see a brace of straightforward chances spurned amid more mirth among the Rec side.

It's all getting a bit too much – if I didn't know better I'd say they are missing deliberately – and with 10 minutes plus added time to go I do something I don't ascribe to – I leave.

About a quarter of an hour after driving away, I have the awful realisation that I could have made a mistake. Sod's Law tells me it is almost inevitable that a goal will come in my absence, so when I get home I telephone the club to find out the final score. It's funny how the mind works, because after they inform me of the goalless scoreline, my first thought is 'thank goodness I didn't miss a goal' followed quickly by 'well, there was never going to be one even if they had carried on for another 90 minutes or more'.

If I'd known what was going to happen I wouldn't have gone near this game with a bargepole. Come to think of it, you could tape another bargepole to it and still say the same. It's not just the disappointment of seeing my second 0-0 of the season, but the way it has come about.

The annoying thing is that it could have been a decent match, but there we are. These things happen, and it's my fault for being over-eager in my bid to tick off a new ground for May. It's not the end of the world, but I should have stayed at home tonight.

# Saturday, May 7

So much for the forecast of rain today. Not for the first time, the Met Office has got it wrong and, like many, I wonder how they are able to continually do so despite having all that fancy equipment. Once I watched the forecast for the next day on three separate occasions, and it changed every time!

And what about those times when you put the forecast on BBC then turn over to ITV, and find differing predictions of what is to come? I thought the two channels vied for ratings over soaps, not the bloomin' weather! 'You'll get a much better forecast if you watch us' seems to be the way of it. Surely both sides get the same information, even if it is wrong at times. Accuracy would be nice too, but I guess I am asking for too much there.

The good news is that I am now able to travel east and not worry about making a wasted trip. This means another jaunt along the Honiton-to-Dorchester road, then the short drop down to Weymouth. My destination is the College grounds to the north of the town centre, as Dorset Premier outfit Chickerell United play their home games there. I have not been to this ground before, and realise that my doing it only reinforces my 'look back in annoyance' feeling about Thursday. Both clubs today also have nothing to play for but pride, so I could be asking for trouble. In a rare moment of optimism, though, I sense that lightning will not strike twice in three days.

Despite being delayed by a traffic jam near Bridport, I still arrive at Chickerell's Cranford Avenue headquarters with over an hour to spare. There is a large car park with meters at regular intervals, but after enquiring I find there is no need to pay today. The ground is at the far end of this vast area, with the dressing rooms being passed as you drive in off the road. Thus it is a lengthy stroll across tarmacked ground from these facilities to the pitch, an arrangement not often seen at footballing venues, and I plonk my vehicle smack bang in the middle of the two.

With time to kill, I make the short walk to the seafront for a stroll along the prom, prom, prom. There is no brass band playing tiddly-om-pom-pom, but on a sunny day like today it's bracing. By the time I get back to the ground there is just enough time for me to pick up the team line-ups from the referee and walk down to the pitch alongside the participants in this afternoon's contest.

A high wire fence separates the pitch from the parking area, with the entrance in the left corner. A small booth doubles up as a refreshment kiosk and a place where you hand over the £3 admission fee. There is no programme, which I was half expecting, and I make my way along a pathway to a small covered standing enclosure on halfway.

This is the only hardstanding, with the remaining sides being grassy. The far end has another pitch behind the goal, thus providing another opportunity for getting plenty of exercise in retrieving the ball, while the playing area used for this game is totally surrounded by a single metallic rail and is in really good condition given the time of year. Overall, while it's not liable to be in the running for any awards, this ground is acceptable.

Westland Sports, who have travelled down from Yeovil this afternoon, make a good start to the game. The third-placed outfit are unable to find an opening goal though, as solid defending keeps them at bay. Skipper Terry Oldrid is leading by example, giving his colleagues the confidence to push forward a little more.

Just past the half-hour mark, Liam Beades goes perilously close to putting Chickerell ahead, but moments later he combines with Ben Skelton, the latter being put in on the left. I am virtually behind that goal as his angled shot flicks the far post before going in – a goal that gives the hosts a well-deserved lead at the break.

You would have thought, given the distance between changing rooms and pitch, that both teams would have stayed where they were. The fact that they all choose to go must have resulted in the shortest half-time team talks in history. With an interval time of not much more than 10 minutes, including the long amble to and from the changing rooms, there clearly isn't time to plan any fancy tactical alterations. Or maybe there is.

I am obviously not privy to those details, but whatever has been uttered in the Westland changing room seems to ignite their players, as seven minutes into the second period they level the scores; centre-forward Jack Williams receives the ball on the right and crosses for Matt Day to head in from close range. The hosts react by hitting the woodwork twice, the second time after keeper Tom Hinder tips Jon Welch's piledriver brilliantly on to the crossbar.

A great opportunity for the visiting side to snatch the points presents itself, but an open goal is missed. It's not unlike what happened on Thursday, but this time no cackling can be heard from the culprit or his teammates. I know that the game shouldn't be taken too seriously at this level, but there is a limit, surely, and, from my point of view, travelling all that way to witness what occurred then was somewhat vexing. As you can tell, I'm still smarting about events two days ago, but you really had to have been there in the flesh to understand what I am talking about.

Anyway, an honourable draw looks on the cards until Richard Lindegaard's stoppage time free kick on the left touchline sees Aaron Mead get ahead of the keeper's attempt to punch clear and head in the winner. It's tough on Chickerell, who have belied their league position by doing really well in what has been a very good Dorset Premier encounter.

Despite being meaningless, it has been competitive and highly enjoyable, and during my drive home afterwards I am feeling as if I have almost exorcised the Merley demons. Almost.

# Sunday, May 8

We're on the march, we're Hedge's army, we're all going to Wembley … OK, I'm actually driving there, and I and my one passenger could hardly be defined as an army, but Martin and I are heading to the capital for this afternoon's FA Vase final between holders Whitley Bay and Coalville.

As former winners in this competition, my companion's club are entitled to complimentary tickets in the Club Wembley enclosure on the halfway line. He acquires a pair of these and gets across to Ilminster, where I pick him up. After a journey devoid of hold-ups, we get there ridiculously early – and then Martin realises we have no car-parking pass.

Having made a similar trip to last year's final, we knew one was offered, so I have to wait at the entrance while my passenger makes the long walk to get what's needed. Thankfully, he is successful, as I don't fancy selling my car in order to pay for parking, nor take on the enormous trudge on foot from a faraway street.

There was a time when you could park about a mile away from Wembley, but that has long gone thanks to residents-only restrictions. This is annoying, and past experience tells me that those areas were not exactly choc-a-bloc with vehicles. Alas, the local council has taken it upon itself to ban stadium users from parking their cars for free within about three miles, so that's that. I used to park near a hospital, and once got myself back on to the motorway within half an hour of walking out of the stadium. Not bad considering I parked for free, and certainly impossible to achieve now.

Back in the present, we go off to grab a bite to eat. Twelve months ago we made the mistake of thinking there would be a complimentary buffet – there always had been one in previous years – only to find we had to pay an extortionate amount of cash for a mere plate of chips. Martin yielded to temptation, but my taste buds had to settle for the consumption of a sausage roll that I just happened to have with me. The fact that I was carrying this savoury was thanks to Phil, who warned me about the chances of there not being any free grub. His astute mind was fully aware of Wembley's money-grabbing deeds and, having seen it with my own eyes in the past, I really should have known this too. Mind you, I did think there would be tea and coffee available at the very least, but no.

The more things change, the more they stay the same as the saying goes, and this is an apt appraisal of this place. The ground may be completely different but the attitudes within remain as they have always been. At least they have not stopped issuing a free programme for this game, which is something, although it won't surprise me if you have to pay for it in future. Printed team sheets are given out as well, so it's not all bad.

Our seats are confined within the walkways the players take when going up to receive their medals. They are padded and offer good views of the pitch. To be fair, the same can be said for just about every seat in this arena now, unlike the old one, but this depends on whether you like to watch from a great height or not.

Two years ago my freebie ticket was up in the gods on halfway, one that ought to have come with a telescope so that I could see what was going on below. I suffer from a touch of vertigo and, thankfully, was able to transfer to a place about two dozen rows further down.

It has to be said this is a fantastic venue now, and the arch is a feature I have grown to like. However, upon approach I cannot help but imagine a large hand coming out of the sky and trying to pick the ground up as if it were a massive shopping basket!

On a more serious note, I have to admit that I don't miss the twin towers, whereas at one time I was all for the idea of incorporating them into the new structure. And I cannot ever imagine that I will reminisce fondly about the smelly, antiquated and run-down features, which have been replaced by a brighter and tidier version. Shame it took so long to build it and, as ever, Joe Public is – literally – paying the price for the vast overspend on the project.

I went to the 'old' Wembley about 50 times in all. My first visit was for the 1981 League Cup final, which saw Liverpool score a goal near the end of extra time that should not have been given. How Clive Thomas could give it remains a mystery to me, but even he was aware of the fact that you can only have one goalkeeper, so Terry McDermott's save was punished by the cool head of Ray Stewart, who gave West Ham a replay (no penalty shoot-outs then, thank goodness).

Before that game I popped across to buy a ticket for an England friendly against Spain about 10 days later. You could purchase tickets like that back then, and I have watched our national side on about two dozen occasions. The last of those was the Euro '96 semi famed for Gareth Southgate's penalty miss and Gazza almost scoring in extra time, but does anyone also recall Darren Anderton hitting the post from close range as well? I am in no doubt that we would have gone on to win the trophy against the Czechs but, of course, we will never know.

I witnessed the three group games, with the Holland match being a stand-out, but missed the goalless Spain contest. The other memory that springs to mind is the San Marino match, not because of David Platt's penalty miss that denied him a nap hand, or because of the disgraceful booing of John Barnes. No, it was the pre-match generosity of a couple of Middlesbrough fans.

It all started, as usual, with a Wembley classic: the non-opening of the cheaper areas of the stadium. As a consequence, I was £2 short of the entry fee payable at the gate (as I've said, things were different back then). Naturally, my feeble attempt to get in was rebutted, but these lads coughed up the money I needed. It was a great gesture and one I've never forgotten. Thanks, boys.

Today will also see parts of the stadium closed off to spectators, but this time it is understandable. This ground holds around 90,000 and will, at best, be 15 per cent full this afternoon.

There appear to be slightly fewer followers from the North East, but it is they who are cheering when the first goal arrives in the 27th minute. Paul Chow took just 21 seconds to open his account in the Wroxham final last year, but here it takes him a little longer as he gets on the end of a right-sided cross from Paul Robinson. Coalville's front two look threatening but are being shackled well by a workmanlike back four, and the outcome is a one-goal lead for the holders at the break.

Matt Moore has already thudded the base of the upright with a blistering effort for the Leicestershire outfit, and 12 minutes into the second period he loses his marker, ghosts into the six-yard box and meets Cameron Stuart's whipped-in ball from the left touchline with a downward header. He then hits the post for a second time, and from there the ball is transferred down the other end; Damon Robson, from the right, crosses for Lee Kerr to flick his header in at the near post.

Now behind, the Midlanders push players forward and get their reward with 11 minutes left; Adam Goodby gets his head on to a great cross by Anthony Carney at the far post to level the scores once more. Whitley Bay are under the cosh, and only two fine saves from keeper Terry Burke deny their opponent a third goal. Instead, it's the Northern League outfit who snatch the winner on 85 when, after Kerr's free-kick has been touched on to the bar, Chow follows up to knock it over the line.

The final whistle brings a terrific final to an end, with the result making it three Vase wins in a row for Whitley. Unlike their opposition from last year, Coalville have played well but have been outwitted by more experienced players.

After watching the presentations, we make a good getaway from the car park. I need to refuel at a nearby Tesco station, where I sit in a queue as there are several others with the same idea as me. I, of course, pick the wrong pump and have to wait patiently while the person in front takes for ever to perform the complex task of putting fuel into his car. Perhaps it's just me, but I always think of this task as straightforward. Not to others apparently; they look upon it in the same way as I would regard explaining Einstein's Theory of Relativity. Still, it's only a minor inconvenience that can happen on any day and it isn't the end of the world.

Three and a half hours later I am opening the front door of my house to a welcome only a dog can give, and over a cup of tea I reflect on what, for me, has been a super Sunday.

# Tuesday, May 10

On the way back from London on Sunday, Martin and I talked about going to two or three Welsh League games before the season's end. Before bidding farewell, he came up with the idea of one for this evening: Cambrian & Clydach's encounter with Barry Town.

This will be another instance of my travelling companion revisiting a venue I have yet to see a game at, so I cannot help but wonder if he is doing it as much for me as for himself. He knows how much I enjoy doing new grounds, so that may well be the case. All I know is that it's a win-win situation for me, especially tonight as Martin is driving. Our trips to Easington and St Austell at least proved that it is not all one-way traffic, and I sacrificed a visit to Sturminster Newton in order to help my friend do the latter, so I am reciprocating to an extent.

Our recent travels to the land of leeks have taken us from the sublime to the ridiculous. Goytre saw us arrive too early, while Ton Pentre saw us get there just in time. Thankfully, this jaunt couldn't have been more perfect, as a traffic-free run sees us reach our destination about 30 minutes before kick-off. The last time we were in this part of the world it was dark, so you could not see the scenic landscape that presents itself on the latter part of the drive here. Also, unlike then, we find our way straight to our intended destination.

Initially Martin parks on an incline, but as we make our way to the ground he spies a closer spot and goes back to move his vehicle. I'm not sure I would have done the same, but that extra minute or two may be significant on our way back to the M4. By that I mean that, if we are on the road that bit earlier, we could be ahead of a slow lorry instead of behind it. On a long journey home a hold-up can make it feel longer, even though it's probably only adding seconds, and I admit that when I am behind the wheel I can get irked at times when stuck behind someone, especially when I glance across and see I am being overtaken by a snail! My chauffeur this evening does not have such impatience, or at least doesn't show it, but clearly we both want to get back home ASAP.

This Welsh Division one venue is located in the Clydach valley. Martin has told me what a marvellous backdrop there is here, and boy, is he right. It is fantastic, and the ground is respectable enough too. It is enclosed by a high wire fence on three sides, while on the remaining side a fence is not necessary as there is a steep slope.

That side has a flat-roofed structure on halfway with steel girders that obstruct views of the action from its three rows of plastic seating. There is a small concrete wall at the front of this stand, while the dugouts sit either side. A blue metallic rail surrounds the pitch elsewhere, with a hardstanding path running all the way round. Floodlighting is provided from four poles, each with a pair of lamps.

You enter at the near end, where an old shipping container holding a refreshment kiosk sits to the left, while the dressing rooms are based in a building just outside, near where you go in. This results in my paying to get in then going straight back out to get the line-ups, although with a small crowd in attendance this does not require the gateman to test his memory powers too much. Or maybe I have got one of those faces that is unforgettable!

A visiting defender seems to suffer a touch of amnesia in the opening minute of this contest, as a through ball down the middle catches him unawares. Mike Jones is alert enough to beat the keeper to the ball, nudging it past him to the left. It seems to take forever to cross the line but it gives the home side, who are going for the title, an ideal start.

They control the remainder of the half. Huw Bowtell hits a post but is on hand to head in a cross from the right in the 37th minute. Two minutes later, Cambrian go three up as Jones gets his second of the night, taking a touch and firing into the bottom right corner from the edge of the penalty box.

Barry, who have not had any chance of note, concede a fourth midway through the second period. It comes when Bowtell bursts through the middle, chipping the keeper then following up to head over the line. A fine save denies him a hat-trick while his fellow two-goal striker rattles the upright and has two headers cleared off the line.

In stoppage time, the away side finally conjure up a chance to score what would have been a scant consolation goal – an opportunity that should have been taken – and are well beaten by the end. The playing surface is understandably showing signs of wear and tear, which has not helped at times, but it's no excuse; after all, it has been the same for both teams.

Our run back to the motorway is swift, although whether my friend's car being moved 300 yards closer to the ground has made this possible I do not know. In the end, it takes longer to get back anyway, as a motorway closure means we have to circumnavigate Newport to the south, but it does not take anything away from what has been a gratifying night out.

I can see why Martin wanted to return to that place, but in all probability I will not. There are times when, despite enjoying a visit, I feel no need to go back. This is one of those instances.

# Thursday, May 12

I quite like the drive over the second Severn crossing. The way it gradually makes its way up to the middle section – the suspended part with H-shaped piers that support the cables – and then descends in a similar manner is a pleasurable experience, albeit a darned expensive one. Tonight I will be undertaking that run behind the wheel as, for the second time in three days, Martin and I will be attending a Welsh Division One fixture.

This time the journey isn't as long and our destination is not in a picturesque area, as Cwmbran is our port of call. To be fair, this town, located just to the north of Newport, is in a reasonable enough setting; just not as good as the one of two days ago.

There are no floodlights at the ground so it's a case of swings and roundabouts – the shorter drive being offset by the earlier kick-off – and we arrive in good time for the advertised seven o'clock start. This is thanks to some astute thinking from my passenger, who has brought the exact money in order for us to pass through the toll more quickly than on Tuesday. On that occasion we had to queue as my payment required change from the manned booths, and took much longer. So, after a straightforward run, we are parked up in the designated area that lies next to the Cwmbran athletics arena.

This is where I saw my first Welsh League game – a Premier clash with Aberystwyth – and it is sad to see that Cwmbran have dropped down the divisions like a stone since then. Anyway, it is now coming up to 6.30 and Martin gets it into his head that we are in the wrong place. He thinks it's further down the road and, unbelievably, I take his word and drive out again.

As I proceed further on down I glance right and see a game that is about to start. It is not long before it becomes obvious that we were in the correct place to begin with, so we speed back to find that not only has the game started earlier but also that we have missed a goal in the first soddin' minute. Aargh! This is definitely a time when my lack of assertiveness has come to the fore, as every instinctive bone in my body told me we were in the right spot. Martin apologises of course, but I am hacked off as I stand at the top of a grass bank behind the goal.

I get chatting to a guy standing nearby and he gives me a warts-and-all description of the goal – a 25-yarder from the right into the top corner – and, with my photographic memory, I can picture it being scored in a manner that make me feel I *have* seen it. For the record, Owen Llewellyn put Cwmbran Celtic in front with that strike.

At least I am there to see tonight's visitors, Caerau (Ely), level the scores. This comes from a set piece, as Jordan Cotterill's corner from the left is headed in at the near post by Tyrell Webbe. It stays that way until the break, although Jon Down spurns two good opportunities for the home side.

By this time I have made my way down to the far end, where the clubhouse and dressing rooms are located in the far corner. With no money being taken it is a freebie, but I do not have a programme as they have all been sold. At this point, Martin, just as he did at Tipton, somehow manages to get hold of one for me. That, accompanied by a refusal to take cash for it, is a gesture typical of the man. He then introduces me to someone he has just met although, unbeknown to him, the introduction is not needed as it's Terry, my mate from Dorchester.

His pre-match tale is not unlike ours in that he missed the start, except that in his case it was due to a hold-up at the toll. He presumed he was witnessing the kick-off upon arrival, only to be informed it was the restart from the goal that he, too, missed. It is hardly comforting to know that he is in the same boat as us, although by then I have become more rational in my thinking about it all.

Celtic Park, understandably, does not get anywhere near the standards of its Glasgow namesake. The pitch perimeter has an open hardstanding path all around, while the railing is singular and held by concrete posts painted alternately in yellow and blue. There is a small covered standing area on halfway that is set well back from the pitch, with trees and shrubs forming the outer perimeter of the ground down this side.

The clubhouse end is open as such, which can also be said for the car park end and remaining side, the main difference being the unpainted metal spiked fence boundary that, while functional, does the ground no favours. Facility-wise it trails in the wake of its bigger neighbour, but I think it is the better of the two.

Eight minutes into the resumption of this league clash, Llewellyn scores his second to restore the hosts' lead. A good passage of play sees the ball reach him in space on the left, and he takes advantage by netting with an angled drive from 10 yards. Back come the away side, who trigger a rapid-fire burst of goals by equalizing through Cottrill. Celtic appeal in vain for handball as Tim Oguyinni plays the ball through for the scorer to slot into the corner of the net.

The homesters go ahead for the third time when a centre from the left is mishit across the six-yard line, ricocheting off Rakesh Patel's shin before going over the line. Going into added time it looks as if that moment of daftness will guide Celtic to victory, but not so as the keeper fumbles Cottrill's free kick at the far post, where Oguyinni is Johnny-on-the-spot to poke in. Moments later the final whistle blows on what has been an entertaining contest, and one that the hosts are unlucky not to have won.

At least the point guarantees their survival in this division, so it's not all bad. I guess the same can be said for my visit here; missing a goal was a pain in the neck, but what followed has been nothing of the sort.

After saying auf Wiedersehen to Terry (who probably speaks German as badly as me), we head back to the car. Martin says sorry again, but in my mind that episode seems years ago now. This is reinforced by a text from Phil telling me of the Devon Premier Cup Final result – a scrappy one-goal win for Liverton. So my decision to do the new ground instead has proved a good one in the end.

OK, so my rules mean a second trip to this venue is a must, but it is one I will not mind making anyway, just as long as I see it from beginning to end on that occasion, whenever that may be. Possibly never, as I do not regard it as a priority. It might come around in the long-term future, but my more immediate thoughts turn to a seasonal landmark …

# Friday, May 13

… and that is to occur just over 24 hours later. Yes, the Somerset Senior Cup Final is my 100th game of the season, which will make it the 11th season in a row that I have reached the three-figure mark. No celebratory parties will be held by yours truly though, as I am only too aware that my tally of games pales into insignificance compared with other people's.

For starters, Martin has done more games, while Phil has galloped off into the distance – he'll have done over 150 – and I'm sure others will have done even more than that. My figure may be respectable enough, but it's not going to win me any groundhopper of the year awards – not that there are any to my knowledge – and it is merely a small note of personal satisfaction.

For the fourth time this week I am travelling with Martin, as the final is being staged at Street. His place is about two-thirds of the way there, but I leave my vehicle outside his place and travel the remaining miles in his car.

This is a brave decision on my part, not because of my worries about his driving but for the fact that it is Friday the 13th. Ugh! I don't normally like to be out and about on this day, and I will undertake this journey full of trepidation. Not only that, but my abhorrence of the number 13 is such that I will do just about anything to avoid it.

Some examples, such as a seat with that number, are clearly evident, but my obsession goes much further. Here is an example: I went into the petrol station at Sainsbury's with my Nectar card and picked up a receipt that gave me my points balance. The sum of the four figures added up to thirteen, so I had to make a food purchase in order to change that. The most frustrating time for me comes when I have no option but to grin and bear it, like when I buy a ticket and it comes back as seat 139. Yes, I know it is silly and there is a name for it – "Triskaidekaphobia" – but I reckon at the end of the day I'm just stark raving bonkers!

Despite my wariness, we arrive at the Tannery Ground in good time. Fellow Somerset County Premier outfits Nailsea United and Watchet are the finalists, so a close match is in store. You enter the venue on about halfway and find yourself under cover with a seated stand to one side and terracing on the other. Another much older seated area, on a slightly raised plane, sits directly opposite its brother.

Elsewhere there is an open hardstanding path behind a rail interspersed with advertising hoardings. The near end is open, with a small fence separating the ground from another pitch behind, while the far end is narrow and tree-lined. A wider expanse is to be found in between this and the cover near where you come in, with the clubhouse and dressing rooms lying to the rear. As a rule these can only be accessed from just outside the spectator gateway, with the players entering the field of play nearby.

When I first came here there were no lights, but now each of the four poles along each side has two horizontal struts that hold the lamps – an unusual feature that makes them look a little like telegraph poles. This ground is all right, and is much better than it used to be.

Once the game gets under way it's Watchet who make the early running. They should go ahead in the third minute, but Chris Sully blazes over the bar from close range. They find it hard to break down their opposition's defence, though, and find the Nailsea keeper in good form when they do. A disappointing and goalless half concludes when Aaron Deeks' fine half-volley brings about another good stop from Luke Davies.

A crowd of over 300 sees the referee award United a penalty in the 50th minute, but the handball offence is not punished as Ryan King blasts over the bar. Ten minutes later Watchet are given a chance of their own to net from 12 yards, but Deeks does likewise in his attempt to smash it into the top corner. It's not often you see both sides miss spot kicks in rapid succession, but I've seen it twice in just over a month now.

The similarities to that match at Dartford continue when a third penalty is given and, just as at Grassbanks, this one is tucked away. John Harris is the hero of the hour, coolly dispatching the ball into the top left corner of the net. The net result – no pun intended – is not only that Nailsea are one down in the scoreline, but one man down on the field thanks to the sending off of James Taylor, who had hauled down Tayler Maddocks as he burst into the box.

The men in green and white proceed to dominate the next 20 minutes but cannot find a second and clinching goal. Deeks is the main culprit, missing two gilt-edged opportunities, but a couple of his colleagues are also found guilty in this respect as they look for the glory instead of setting up a teammate for a much easier chance to score. They pay for this in stoppage time when substitute Harry Hope swings in a cross from the left for James Lee to meet on the volley and force extra time.

Having grabbed themselves that lifeline, it is the reds who look stronger now, but they are caught napping when Paul Raymond receives the ball on the right edge of the box, his left-footed strike deflecting off a defender and looping over keeper Adam Bishop and in. It seems to knock the stuffing out of Nailsea, and Watchet are able to see out the remaining time without any real cause for concern.

There is no doubt in my mind that the best team have won a match that undoubtedly improved after a poor opening. I was fearing the worst after those missed pens, but my fears have proved to be unfounded. Combined with an incident-free journey home, it puts the Friday the 13th jinx to bed – at least until next time!

# Tuesday, May 17

My non-attendance of a game on Saturday is something I'll have to get accustomed to in the next couple of months, but at present those habits seem to lie in my routes to football grounds. Yet again my destination is dragon country, and once more it is via Taunton. Martin is the designated driver as we head across to Newport, where the YMCA side entertain Cwmaman Institute in a Welsh Second Division encounter.

Mendalgief Road is not that difficult to locate, being less than a mile from the southern ring road. The unmissable landmark here is the transporter bridge, which you pass just before turning off that road and which is visible from the venue itself. On our way in we also travel past Newport County's Spytty Park home, which I have only been to once.

That was for a Southern League game for which I made the journey up on the Tiverton supporters' bus. Because it is one of those self-loathed athletics arenas, I vowed it would be my first and last visit there. I did go to Somerton Park twice, which was not the most salubrious of places but at least was a proper ground. It was a fair old hike from the railway station too, made all the more frustrating by the fact that the stadium was sited right next to the rail line on the way in. A walk to Newport's present ground would take for ever and is one I wouldn't wish to undertake; and I won't. Ever.

We arrive just after 6pm at a venue that has no lights. Actually, make that nearer five past, as my driver suffers a bout of Cwmbrancelticitis. Just like then, we drive into the parking area and out again, then down the road only to return to our original place. We missed the start at Cwmbran, but not tonight as we park next to the YMCA building and pass through the entrance sited beyond the right side of it.

Once inside, you go left to find the small refreshment area that forms part of this structure, with the dressing rooms further on. All of those facilities are placed behind the goal where there is little room to spare, with a path leading down, then along the near side. This paved line also lies directly ahead as you come in, where it is open with a shrubbed backdrop. The far end is the same but grassy, and this leads around to the cantilevered cover on halfway that has four terraced steps inside.

The concrete block dugouts flank this, while a solid path leads from here back towards the main complex. You have to make a slight detour near the corner flag, where there is a combination of a tarmacked area with some wire fencing. If nothing else this is an oddity, as is the looming spectre of a large electricity pylon in the far corner. The wires are probably too high to reach with a hoof of the ball although it wouldn't surprise me if someone has unintentionally had a go.

I wonder what would happen if that spherical bag of air did hit the lines – not a lot, I suspect. My longing to find out equates to my questioning how earthworms mate! In other words, I'll not lose any sleep if I never find out. One thing is for sure: I would not be shocked if I did!

Cwmaman need a point from this contest to clinch the runners-up spot in this division, and take a step forward in their quest after just four minutes; Antony Waters receiving the ball outside the area and striking it low into the right corner. It is not long before they double their advantage, with Ian Traylor slotting in from 15 yards after his dribble in from the left touchline.

The hosts respond well, going close on two occasions before pulling one back on 39. A fine solo run down the flank by a full back sets up Alex Jenkins, whose 20-yard strike takes a hefty deflection before nestling in the bottom left corner of the net. The scorer goes close again just before the break, to which the players go with the match on a knife-edge.

I go berserk with my money in the refreshment area again, splashing out on a plate of chips to go with my cuppa – well, they did smell nice – and Martin has some as well. I assume his reasons are not akin to mine, as he chooses to smother his chips with curry sauce; and when I say smother I mean a ruddy camouflage. If you have seen the scene in the film Cobra in which Brigitte Nielsen squirts almost a whole bottle of tomato sauce on her chips, you'll have some sort of idea. I guess most of us have our eccentric ways in this respect, mine possibly being the consumption of Branston Pickle sandwiches. Yummy!

So to the second half, and Newport's continuing quest for an equaliser. I think they have it, only for the official to disallow the goal for a foul on a defender. I think it's the correct decision this time, but how often do you hear the whistle go for a foul on a defender that no one else has seen or, looking at it another way, how often does the ref blow for a penalty as a consequence of an attacking player being fouled?

The man in black could spot an offensive misdemeanour from a hot-air balloon hundreds of feet above the ground, but is oblivious when the opposite occurs. I estimate the ratio to be over 1,000 to one in favour of defenders, and cannot understand why this should be so. Last Friday's second penalty award *did* come as a result of a defensive foul from a corner, so it has come to pass. What followed was the simultaneous fainting of all standing spectators due to shock ... OK, maybe not, but it caught everyone by surprise. Surely, though, a foul is a foul no matter who commits it, and if an official can see it one way then he can see it the other way too.

Anyway, the perceived wrongdoing of our referee this evening seems to affect the home side, and near the end they concede a third goal. Traylor starts the move by putting Jarrod Price in goal from the right, and the striker rounds the keeper before sliding it in. The last action of the game sees Cwmaman almost score a fourth, only for an excellent stop to prevent them putting the icing on the cake.

When the whistle blows for time it brings to an end a strong, competitive match between two in-form sides. If YMCA hadn't wasted 10 to 15 minutes in grumbling about their self-induced sense of injustice they might have got something out of the game, but there we are. I feel the three officials have done well this evening – a description that epitomises our visit as a whole. Martin chose it, and he chose well.

# Thursday, May 19

Having borne witness to the Somerset Senior Cup Final last week, I decide to pair it up with the League's version this evening. This is helped along by the small matter of Martin also going, which enables me to scrutinise his driving capabilities once again on the road up to Portishead, where Backwell and Shirehampton will lock horns this evening.

He passes the examination – not that there was one as such – in that we reach our destination in the same manner as my past attempts to get there. Like me, he takes the shorter route that sees us come off at Clevedon and travel up via a series of villages. This takes longer but means we do not have to double back from the next junction.

The downside comes when driving along the Bristol Road, as the sign indicating the ground entrance can't be seen from the direction from which we are coming. As a result, we go past it before having to turn back for what is now a left turn into the car park. This is my fourth visit and on every occasion I have done the same damn thing, but at least I have the consolation now of knowing I am not the only one.

We still arrive in good time, unlike my first time here. Holiday traffic made me miss kick-off, although missing that sign didn't help; neither did my mistake in plonking my car in the first parking bay, as I didn't realise you had to drive in a bit more to a bigger area next to the venue itself. If I had performed these tasks correctly, I would not have missed the game's only goal that day – one that was scored just seconds before I entered.

It wasn't the greatest of matches, and I returned later that season for another Western First Division encounter. That one was not exactly a thrill-a-minute clash either, although I did at least see all of it, along with both of the goals scored. The erection of lights saw me make a midweek trek up here with Phil, with the end result being the same on a cold night when the outbreak of a decent game was about as probable as a spaceship landing on the centre circle, with a little green man getting out and asking for directions to the nearest petrol station.

Yes, I think it's safe to say that this ground has been an entertainment-free zone on my visits, and I can only hope that tonight can break that sequence. With both finalists playing in a league that is one step down from the host club, I am confident this will occur.

The ground entrance is at the far end of the second car park, with the old-fashioned clubhouse being passed by to the right on the way in from the main road. This probably explains why I parked erroneously first time around, although my panicking at being late did not help. I find this state of mind results in logic being thrown out of the window, but that's possibly a self-induced phobia.

What I do know is that, upon entry through the elaborate turnstile, I find no programme has been issued. Martin enquires as to why this should be, to be told that it has nothing to do with the club. Apparently it is the Somerset FA's fault, although a representative of this association says this is not so. Having paid so much to get in, I would have expected some effort to be put in to print something for what is, after all, a county cup final, but there we are. Of course, I was not prepared for this eventuality, so end up scribbling down the line-ups on a scrap of paper found in the depths of my inside coat pocket.

You come in to this venue on halfway, with a small covered standing enclosure directly to your left. Beyond is a series of old, green-painted Portakabins that hold the dressing rooms at the far end, with a refreshment kiosk located on approach to the first of these. A hardstanding path runs along the entire length, parallel with a high wire fence to the right upon entry. This boundary continues behind the goal at this end.

The remaining sides are grassy, with the addition of a seated stand at the midway point on the opposite side. Views from here are slightly obstructed by the middle one of the three floodlight poles located on each side, and I cannot understand why the hardstanding has not been extended towards these seats.

The pitch, not that good at the best of times, is railed all around, with the dugouts flanking the stand in such a way that they do not really hinder sightlines. Shrubbery provides a backdrop along here and the far end of a ground that, to be frank, is one of those that is better seen during daylight hours.

Once the game gets under way it is Backwell who make the running (they are actually called Ashton & Backwell now, but still play at the same Playing Fields home. As far as I'm concerned they are the same team as they were in the Western League). Lee Webb forces a good stop from the keeper and it is only poor finishing that stops them from leading at the end of a goalless half.

Shirehampton create nothing whatsoever as they continue to be stifled by opponents who, while controlling things, carry on from where they left off at the break. In one passage of play they hit the woodwork and have a brace of shots cleared off the line, all of which shows ominous signs. Lo and behold, with extra time looming, a rare foray into the box by Shires midfielder George Brimson sees him fall under a challenge and the referee gives a penalty, albeit from some distance. Jack Barnes drills the spot kick into the left corner with his right boot, leaving Backwell with little time to recover.

Talk about a smash and grab cup final triumph; this has been a shining example of that. It completes a league and cup double for the Bristol outfit, who have won tonight with that solitary chance. Backwell, though, have only themselves to blame for spurning their opportunities in what has been a disappointing final all round.

I am loth to state that that is because of where it has been played – a mere coincidence, methinks – but I do not envisage my returning here any time soon. When I'm here I seem to send some unintended telepathic message to the players, telling them to play the crummiest football imaginable, as I'm sure they have had good matches here at some point.

A more realistic solution lies in this equation: Hedge + Portishead = Game to avoid. I wish I'd applied that theory tonight and do not want to sign my season off in this manner although, unlike the last two Thursdays, I have seen a full 90 minutes. On we go, then.

# Tuesday, May 24

Here we go again. Another drive up to Taunton to link up with Martin, then on from there in his car towards what are becoming familiar surroundings. Under different circumstances I might have asked to lodge at my friend's flat, what with me spending so much time in his company, but I suspect that I would be a pain in the derriere to live with.

Besides, I'm happy where I am. Perhaps, though, we should get together and learn how to speak Welsh some time. It might come in handy, especially tonight as our umpteenth crossing of the Severn takes us on into valley territory. Our destination this time is Abertillery, who are up against Croesyceiliog in a Division Two encounter.

This venue has no floodlights, so we have to negotiate rush-hour traffic on our way out of Taunton. This takes a while, but we appear to be doing well after a successful passing of the toll queues. However, as the journey progresses to Pontypool and beyond, things are getting tight as far as making it on time are concerned.

With 10 minutes in hand, Martin finds an astute means of reaching the outskirts of the village, where we pick up the recommended route to the ground. Now, bearing in mind our Bryntirion and Ton Pentre experiences, this is by no means a guarantee of reaching our goal.

To begin with all goes well, but it's too good to last. We ascend a street and have to go right at the end, only to find no ground. Martin drives on for a bit until it's obvious we are lost. Five minutes of faffing around eventually takes us back, where we stumble around for a bit. Why is there never anyone around when you need some bleedin' directions?

In desperation – bearing in mind we are over five minutes late now – I tell Mart to turn right at the top of the ascent instead of at the end as we were told, and this proves to be the correct call. It seems I have my uses too, although my stress levels have gone through the roof during these last 15 minutes. My poor old driving companion is feeling it too as we both pick up the action in a rather peed-off mood.

Twelve days ago we missed a goal as well as the start, but it's still 0-0 upon our arrival this time. Cwmantygroes is an open ground, so no gate money is taken, or at least no one is present to do the job. Martin is a much calmer customer than yours truly, so he takes on the job of finding a couple of programmes. Apart from the necessity of purchasing one, as it is a new ground for both of us, it will give us the opportunity to make a contribution towards funds. However, he returns empty-handed as the small number of printed issues have all gone. Oh dear! Then Martin informs me that two copies will be sent to his address at a later date, which is terrific. I don't know how he does it, but it's a forte of his that has certainly come in handy tonight.

It may well be a swine to locate, but once here you will marvel at this ground's setting. I would describe it as a three-quarter bowl with a steep incline of trees down one side that, at a distance, arc around the car parking end. The opposite side is similar, only with trees at the top of tall grass banking. We entered through a gap in the shrubbery at one corner; open hardstanding runs down this side.

Across the pitch on halfway is a covered standing area with five shallow steps within. This is a rather old structure, which has the dressing rooms positioned directly behind, forming part of a building that hosts the clubhouse. It is quite small inside but has a viewing balcony to the fore. Elsewhere, it is open and grassed, with the pitch totally enclosed by a single metal rail. It's definitely worth a visit.

I have never seen either of these sides before, but with lots of blue in evidence it doesn't need a genius to work out who the home side are. Needing points to stave off relegation, they miss an open goal just after our late arrival. By half-time, however, they do lead thanks to a free kick thundered into the top right corner from 35 yards out.

At the break Martin manages to get the team line-ups, which I was planning to do later, and this brings a surprise. The team in blue are in fact the away side as they brought the wrong kit, meaning the hosts are in their away strip. This confusion means that, as expected, it is the promotion-seeking visitors who lead, with Jody Jenkins being the game's goalscorer.

During this interval I bump into someone I have met before on my travels. Like me, he is visiting here for the first time. His story of how he has got here makes ours seem like an absolute cakewalk, as it took him over an hour to find the ground, mainly because he did not have Martin's awareness of a shorter run into the village.

It just goes to show how tricky the ground is to find, and I cannot help but picture in my mind some poor, demented soul going round in circles trying to reach it. I picture him on his hands and knees pleading for help after days of fruitless searching, then giving up as he sees it as akin to solving Rubik's cube blindfolded.

Oh, how the imagination can run amok at times; that is what finding grounds like this one can do to you.

Less than a minute into the second period, the high-flying visitors grab a second goal; Callum Miles making a penetrating run down the left before slotting in between keeper and near post. Just past the hour, the home side are given a possible lifeline when a foul in the box gives them a penalty. Mister Melville has not read the script, though, as his spot kick is saved by the goalie to his right. Mike Dewar is booked for protesting too vehemently and minutes later sees red for doing likewise after a foul.

Now one man down, the away side spend the rest of the match relying on counter-attacks. They go close on a couple of occasions but run out comfy winners in the end – a result that gives them a good chance of nicking the third promotion spot.

It has not been the greatest of games and it has been one that, thanks to our late arrival, has really put my 90-minutes-seen rule to the test. My missing a goal at Cwmbran, along with its more convenient location, do make for a possible revisit. Still, if I do return to this venue I will at least be able to find it!

# Saturday, May 28

And now the end is near, and so I face the final curtain … of my season. This was due to come down via a low-key cup final at Topsham, but plans change at the last minute. Well, why should I go to the East Devon final down the road when I can make a rare trip into Welshland, as I have not been there for all of four days? Perhaps I should have rented an apartment over there for a month, as it would have saved me all that travelling.

Mind you, it's mostly been in Martin's vehicle so, as he is keen, I pick him up on the way to Welsh Division Two outfit Cwmaman Institute. They clinched runners-up spot with that win at Newport YMCA, but the game is relevant for their opposition this afternoon. AFC Porth are vying with Croesyceiliog for third place, and need at least a draw to achieve this. What with it being a derby fixture as well as a new ground for the both of us, it makes for an intriguing clash.

As it is a bank holiday weekend, I allow extra time for our journey, which pays off as a snarl-up on the approach to the tolls causes quite a delay. Apart from an absolutely necessary rest break, the remainder of the drive is all right as we replicate the route taken to Aberaman in February. We pass this ground and travel a mere handful of miles before reaching the village.

The now fabled direction planner makes our route seem unbelievably complex, but it is actually quite easy to find the ground. Basically, you drive into the centre, then go right and find it to the left on the other side of Cwmaman. We arrive with half an hour to spare, and elect to park in the puddle-ridden area just beyond the pitch instead of out in the road.

Well, I thought Cambrian was set in great surroundings but, amazingly, this is even better. With rolling hills all around in the background, this is how I would envisage your typical Welsh valley league venue. Instinct has told me to bring my camera along for the ride, and I'm pleased that I have.

It has to be said, though, that the ground itself is fairly basic, with a single metal rail all round the pitch perimeter and no hardstanding. There is a small, two-stepped covered standing enclosure near halfway on the opposite side, which does have a tiny bit of firm standing to the fore, with the dugouts flanking this area.

Entry to this venue takes you immediately around and past a small, white-painted building that holds the dressing rooms and has a small refreshment hatch at the front. The venue is partially fenced off, with open terrain at the far end and shrubbery behind the covered enclosure. If you regard facilities as important this ground is not for you, but I would recommend it for sure.

The opening exchanges of the encounter see both sides go close before the hosts open the scoring. Lee Williams and Carl Jenkins combine on the right, with the former crossing to the far post for Ian Traylor to meet with a downward header that goes in off the right post. Seven minutes later, the lead is doubled as Shaun Chappell's long-range strike takes a slight deflection before going in off the left upright this time.

Porth hit back just before the interval with a penalty, thanks to a foul on Craig Davies by Jack Howe. There may have been contact, but the visiting player certainly makes a meal of it. He has no trouble in getting up and dusting himself off before firing his spot kick straight down the middle.

So when is a dive not a dive? Not here, methinks, with the defender sticking out a leg for the Porth player to go over as his momentum took him goalwards. However, there are numerous instances when a player does go over without being touched, which I define as cheating. Yes, cheating. There is no other word for it, and I am fed up with it, to be honest. All this talk about eradicating it is just that: talk. Isn't it about time we clamped down on diving? I suggest we ban offenders for a certain number of games, which will affect clubs and fans but simply has to be done.

I also have a bone of contention over the definition of 'contact' in these scenarios. For me, there are cases when a player deliberately goes out of his way to be knocked over by an outstretched leg, going down for what the official rightly sees as a penalty offence. Players go to ground far too easily these days – a fact that has not gone unnoticed by some of my non-football loving friends, who say the game has gone soft.

I don't believe that, and wouldn't want to go back to the 70s, when **GBH** on the field got you, at worst, a booking. It has to be said, though, that we have gone too far the other way – a trait that applies not only to simulation but also to such things as so-called fouls on the keeper.

Here we have gone from zero protection (witness the 1957 FA Cup Final, when Peter McParland clobbered Ray Wood well after he had collected the ball – it was deemed a 'fair shoulder charge' by the commentator! Or the following year, when Harry Gregg was bundled into the net by Nat Lofthouse; goal given) to about a trillion per cent protection, making goalkeepers almost as much a protected species as the white tiger.

Maybe I am an idealist, but all of these shenanigans do make the referee's job much harder. The oft-trotted out excuse that it is all part of the game does not wash with me either, but there we are. Our money-oriented game, along with its win-at-all-costs ethos, has produced such casualties I'm afraid, and there's no going back now. Shame.

Eight minutes into the second half, the away side complete their comeback as a cross from the right is flicked on at the near post for Stuart Brock to bundle over the line. He goes close again moments later as the game develops into an open affair. Both sides have their chances to win it, but a thrilling finale fails to yield a fifth goal.

Shortly after the final whistle, news comes through that Croesyceiliog have also drawn, meaning Porth will join the hosts in celebrating promotion. I have to say that I have been more impressed with the showing of the visiting club today than I was with Tuesday's, although it would be unfair to judge their respective merits on one game.

What I can say is that I am happy to have finished my campaign on a positive note, for you cannot ask for any more than to end with an enjoyable contest played in a fantastic location. May has indeed been a merry month as, thanks to the late ending of the Welsh League, I have been able to finish off in style with a glut of new grounds.

It's been quite a season for me, and a one-off I suspect, but through it all I stood tall, and did it m-y-y-y w-a-a-y-y-y! La, la, la, laaaa, la, la, la, laaa …

ADRIAN WICKS

# Afterword

## Sunday, September 18

A new season has, so far, seen me attend my usual variety of matches. Yesterday saw me at Woodstock's Hellenic fixture with Clanfield, a game played on their own ground at New Road. In the summer they severed their arrangement with North Leigh while at the same time relegating themselves into the Western Division. I assume finances held the upper hand in the making of this decision but, whether so or not, I believe it was a good thing.

It's certainly easy to see why they cannot stage higher-level football, as the ground is pretty basic. Apart from having no lights there is no cover or hardstanding, unless you count the area in front of a low, flat-roofed building on halfway that holds the clubhouse. I quite like the ground for what it is, but they'll need a whole raft of improvements to make it up to Premier standard; you don't need to be an expert to see that.

I'm not revelling in their lower status now, and I wish them all the best. Just to prove my point, I will refer to the news that Roman Glass and Winterbourne – who have no lights – are entering into a ground-share scheme at Almondsbury's Gloucs HQ base. This is being done to prevent these clubs from being demoted, so I am sticking to my utterings from 12 months ago in this respect. Sorry.

Bickleigh pulled out of the Peninsula League at the last minute, citing player shortages that may have seen them unable to fulfil fixtures. They are now in one of the lower divisions of the Devon & Exeter, effectively replacing their reserve side. I, along with others, thought they may have been able to bluff their way through the campaign before reassessing, but you have to respect their decision.

Dawlish Town dropped out of the Western League due to financial difficulties, and I suspect they will not be the last side to do this in the near future. Times are hard, especially in non-league circles, and everyone has to make cuts.

What I find amazing, especially when you consider our size, is that we have over 100 full-time clubs in this country, which is more than others, and I cannot help but think that, at some time soon, some of these will have to go part-time in order to balance the books a bit more. Of course, no one wants their club to fall into this category, but I fear it is inevitable.

Positive news came from Sidmouth's application to join the Peninsula. I went there two weeks ago for their game against Okehampton and saw visible improvements. A green-coloured hardstanding path now runs along one side, with a railed perimeter that resides at one end as well. Permission has been granted for a covered stand, which was one of the stipulations. With hindsight, I would not have come here back in January, but at the same time I would not have met Terry. Obviously he was not there which, naturally, could also be said for the

Prince of Wales!

They are not the only new members of Phil's league, with Cornish outfits Helston and St Dennis joining the West Division. I did both of those in August, and they are quite good. I have to be honest and say that Kellaway Parc is not as wondrous as I was led to believe, but Boscawen is a tidy set-up with a scenic backdrop. No doubt I will make a second visit to one or both of these in time.

I have never gone a whole season without a goalless draw, a fact that will remain for yet another year. I felt that payback was due to Martin, so I gave him a lift to Vospers Oak Villa for their game against Callington. There should have been a goal for the home side, but their greedy forward decided he wanted to get the final touch on a shot from an offside position; if he had let it go it would have counted.

Never mind, although if that turns out to be my only 0-0 this season I will not be as philosophical about it. My hatred of goal-free matches stems back to the mid-80s, when I made a bet with someone over who could see the fewest that year; I won, but in the long term I have lost out big-style.

I almost allow these things to dictate my day-to-day existence which, I know, is crazy. I have no family and, to all intents and purposes, am married to the game.

Bill Shankly's quote about football being more important than life or death may have sounded excessive, but it could so easily be attributed to me. Addicted is a term defined as 'devoted or wholly given over to', and it sums me up perfectly.

ADRIAN WICKS

# Match summary

1. Tadley Calleva 2, Amesbury 0
2. Slimbridge 2, Highworth 1
3. Andover New St 1, Fleet Spurs 7
4. Willand 2, Merthyr 0
5. Stockwood Green 3, Castle Cary 1
6. Langford R 4, Cutters Friday 1
7. Chesterfield 4, Hereford 0
8. Clevedon Utd 1, Easton-in-Gordano 1
9. Cheddar 4, Taunton Blackbrook 0
10. Tavistock 1, Taunton 2
11. Sherborne 3, Hamworthy U 0
12. Newton Spurs 1, Galmpton 1
13. Watchet 4, Winscombe 1
14. Bitton 3, Wells 3
15. Bodmin 1, Poole 4
16. Kidlington 1, Woodstock 2
17. Bedfont T 2, Soham 1
18. Cullompton 2, Royal Marines 4
19. Bishops Lydeard 2, Cheddar 1
20. Studley 2, Malvern 0
21. Budleigh 3, Axminster 2
22. Binfield 3, Hillingdon 2
23. Dawlish 1, Barnstaple 1
24. Wantage 3, Oxford Nomads 1
25. Hatherleigh 0, Axminster 4
26. Merthyr 1, Almondsbury UWE 0
27. Ilminster 1, Minehead 0
28. Saltash 2, Launceston 0
29. Ardley 4, Fairford 2
30. Tipton 2, Sheffield FC 0
31. Bicester 0, Headington 2
32. Cadbury Heath 6, Bradford T 1
33. Shirehampton 2, Watchet 2
34. Wellington 1, Taunton 4
35. Pegasus 0, Ardley 4
36. Finchampstead 0, Penn & Tylers 2
37. Welton 1, Bristol Manor Farm 3
38. Totton & Eling 2, Brading 4
39. Beer Alb 2, Plymstock 5
40. Perranwell 1, Penryn 2 aet

| | |
|---|---|
| 41. | Exeter City 5, Sheff Wed 1 |
| 42. | Hayle 3, Perranporth 1 |
| 43. | Witheridge 1, Buckland 8 |
| 44. | Plymstock 4, Holsworthy 1 |
| 45. | Exeter Civils 2, Exmouth 2 |
| 46. | St Blazey 1, Bemerton Heath 2 |
| 47. | Westfields 1, Billingham Synth 2 aet |
| 48. | Tiverton 3, Royal Marines 0 |
| 49. | Flackwell H 2, Shrivenham 0 |
| 50. | Sidmouth 1, Liverton 2 aet |
| 51. | Bryntirion 3, Cardiff Corinths 0 |
| 52. | Fleetwood 2, Forest Green 0 |
| 53. | Dorchester 1, Chelmsford 1 |
| 54. | Aberaman 0, Pontardawe 7 |
| 55. | Thame 0, Wantage 0 |
| 56. | Taunton 0, Chippenham 2 |
| 57. | Liskeard 1, Plym Parkway 2 |
| 58. | Wincanton 2, Hamworthy Rec 7 |
| 59. | Ton Pentre 2, AFC Porth 1 |
| 60. | Morecambe 0, Oxford U 3 |
| 61. | AFC Totton 5, Gosport 2 |
| 62. | Plym Parkway 3, Saltash 0 |
| 63. | Ottery 0, Liverton 5 |
| 64. | Dartmouth 0, Bodmin 4 |
| 65. | Goytre U 0, Afan Lido 3 |
| 66. | Easington Sp 3, Lydney 1 |
| 67. | Almondsbury UWE 1, Hengrove 1 |
| 68. | Holyport 1, Woodley T 2 |
| 69. | Biggleswade T 6, Northwood 2 |
| 70. | Bickleigh 0, Liverton 2 at Exmouth |
| 71. | Westbury 0, Merthyr 2 |
| 72. | Axminster 1, Stoke Gabriel 2 |
| 73. | Exmouth Amateurs 4, Heavitree 1 |
| 74. | Crediton 2, Budleigh 2 |
| 75. | Daventry T 2, Leighton 0 |
| 76. | Braintree 1, Dorchester 1 |
| 77. | Sturminster Marshall 1, Hamworthy Rec 0 |
| 78. | Dartford 3, Woking 2 |
| 79. | Liverton 4, Newton Spurs 1 |
| 80. | Seaton 3, Clyst Valley 3 |
| 81. | Buckland 4, Launceston 3 |
| 82. | Hamworthy Rec 1, Sturminster Newton 1 |
| 83. | Poole Boro 1, Parley Sports 1 |

| | |
|---|---|
| **84.** | Bovey Tracey 1, Buckland 4 |
| **85.** | Bickleigh 1, Appledore 1 |
| **86.** | Alfreton 4, Redditch 0 |
| **87.** | Elburton 1, Buckland 2 |
| **88.** | Holt 1, Sturminster Newton 2 |
| **89.** | Glastonbury 3, Watchet 0 |
| **90.** | St Austell 1, Torpoint 7 |
| **91.** | Godolphin 3, Newquay 0 |
| **92.** | Plym Parkway 6, St Blazey 4 aet at Newquay |
| **93.** | Royal Marines 1, Saltash 2 |
| **94.** | Callington 1, Perranporth 1 |
| **95.** | Merley Cobham 0, Hamworthy Rec 0 |
| **96.** | Chickerell 1, Westland Sports 2 |
| **97.** | Coalville 2, Whitley Bay 3 at Wembley |
| **98.** | Cambrian & Clydach 4, Barry T 0 |
| **99.** | Cwmbran Celtic 3, Caerau (Ely) 3 |
| **100.** | Nailsea U 1, Watchet 2 aet at Street |
| **101.** | Newport YMCA 1, Cwmaman Inst 3 |
| **102.** | Backwell 0, Shirehampton 1 at Portishead |
| **103.** | Abertillery 0, Croesyceiliog 2 |
| **104.** | Cwmaman Inst 2, AFC Porth 2 |

# Seasonal statistics

**Games:** 104
**Goals:** 392 (home 188, away 183, neutral 21) average 3.77
**Home wins:** 43
**Away wins:** 37
**Draws:** 19 including 2 goalless
**Neutral wins:** 5
**Highest score:** 8 (Buckland)
**Highest aggregate:** 10 (Parkway 6, Blazey 4)
**Most number of times team seen:** 4 (Buckland, Ham Rec, Liverton, Watchet)
**Number of 'new' grounds visited:** 55
**Best game seen:** Bitton 3, Wells 3
**Worst game:** Merley Cobham – enough said!

**NB:** the FA Vase Final at Wembley was my 100th 'neutral' game of all time!

# Acknowledgements

I would like to thank Martin for being a good travelling companion.
I have at times made what appear to be less than favourable comments about things such as his driving, but they should be taken lightly. I have enjoyed our trips together and hope for more of the same in years to come.
Good friends are hard to come by, and he is one.

Thanks too go to the publisher, who deems my work worthy of printing.

All statistical and relevant notes such as ground details are strictly personal and have not necessitated any reference to other publications.

www.ingramcontent.com/pod-product-compliance
Lightning Source LLC
Chambersburg PA
CBHW032115090426
42743CB00007B/359